BUSINESS PROGRAMMING IN C
FOR DOS-BASED SYSTEMS

A.C. MILLSPAUGH
Mt. San Antonio Community College

The Dryden Press
Fort Worth   Philadelphia   San Diego   New York   Orlando   Austin   San Antonio
Toronto   Montreal   London   Sydney   Tokyo

Senior Editor:	**Richard J. Bonacci**
Editorial Assistant	**Lisa Toftemark Rittby**
Project Editor:	**Sheila M. Spahn**
Assistant Project Editor:	**Matt Ball**
Designer:	**Burl Sloan**
Production Manager:	**Marilyn Williams**

3 4 5 6 7 8 9 0   0 9 8 7 6 5 4 3 2

Printed in the United States of America

Cover Photo: Copyright © The Stock Market/Peter A. Simon, 1991.

Library of Congress Catalog Card Number: 92-073139

Microsoft and QuickC are registered trademarks of Microsoft Corporation.
Turbo C, Turbo C++, and Borland C++ are registered trademarks of Borland International, Inc.

ISBN: 0-15-500139-6

The Dryden Press Series in Information System

Arthur Andersen & Co./Flaatten, McCubbrey, O'Riordan, and Burgess
Foundations of Business Systems
Second Edition

Arthur Andersen & Co./Boynton and Shank
Foundations of Business Systems: Projects and Cases

Anderson
Structured Programming Using Turbo Pascal: A Brief Introduction
Second Edition

Bradley
Introduction to Data Base Management in Business
Second Edition

Brown and McKeown
Structured Prgramming with Microsoft BASIC

Carney
Advanced Structured BASIC for the IBM PC

Coburn
Advanced Structured COBOL

Coburn
Beginning Structured COBOL

Dean and Effinger
Common-Sense BASIC: Structured Programming with Microsoft QuickBASIC

Electronic Learning Facilitators, Inc.
The DOS Book

Electronic Learning Facilitators, Inc.
The Lotus 1-2-3 Book

Electronic Learning Facilitators, Inc.
Stepping Through Excel 4.0 for Windows

Electronic Learning Facilitators, Inc.
Stepping Through Harvard Graphics for Windows

Electronic Learning Facilitators, Inc.
Stepping Through Windows 3.1

Electronic Learning Facilitators, Inc.
Stepping Through Word for Windows

Electronic Learning Facilitators, Inc.
Working Smarter with DOS 5.0

Electronic Learning Facilitators, Inc.
Working with WordPerfect 5.0

Electronic Learning Facilitators, Inc.
Working with WordPerfect 5.1

Ellis and Lodi
Structured Prgramming Using True BASIC

Federico
WordPerfect 5.1 Primer

Goldstein Software, Inc.
Joe Spreadsheet, Macintosh Version

Goldstein Software, Inc.
Joe Spreadsheet, Statistical

Harrington
Making Database Management Work

Harrington
Microsoft Works: A Window to Computing

Harrington
Relational Datatbase Management for Microcomputers: Design and Implementation

Laudon and Laudon
Business Information Systems: A Problem-Solving Approach
Second Edition

Laudon, Laudon, and Weill
The Integrated Solution

Lawlor
Computer Information Systems
Second Edition

Lawlor
Introducing BASIC: A Structured Approach

Liebowitz
The Dynamics of Decision Support Systems and Expert Systems

McKeown
Living with Computers
Fourth Edition

McKeown
Living with Computers with BASIC
Fourth Edition

McKeown
Working with Computers

McKeown
Working with Computers with Software Tutorials

McKeown and Leitch
Managing with Computers

Martin and Burstein
Computer Systems Fundamentals

Martin and Parker
Mastering Today's Software with DOS WordPerfect 5.0/5.1, Lotus 1-2-3, dBASE III PLUS (or dBASE IV)

Martin and Parker
Mastering Today's Software with DOS WordPerfect 5.0/5.1, Lotus 1-2-3, dBASE III PLUS (or dBASE IV) and BASIC

Mason
Using IBM Microcomputers in Business: Decision Making with Lotus 1-2-3 and dBASE III Plus (or dBASE IV)

Millspaugh
Business Programming for DOS-BASED SYSTEMS

O'Brien
The Nature of Computers

O'Brien
The Nature of Computers with Tutorials

Parker
A Beginner's Guide to BASIC

Parker
Computers and Their Applications
Third Edition

Parker
Computers and Their Applications with Productivity Software Tools
Third Edition

Parker
Microcomputers: Concepts and Applications

Parker
Productivity Software Guide
Fourth Edition

Parker
Understanding Computers and Information Processing: Today and Tomorrow
Fourth Edition

Parker
Understanding Computers and Information Processing: Today and Tomorrow with BASIC
Fourth Edition

Robertson and Robertson
Microcomputer Applications and Programming: A Complete Computer Course with DOS WordPerfect 5.1, Lotus 1-2-3, dBASE III PLUS (or dBASE IV) and BASIC

Robetson and Robertson
Using Microcomputer Applications (A series of Computer Lab Manuals)

Roche
Telecommunications and Business Strategy

Swafford and Haff
dBASE III PLUS

The HBJ College Outline Series

Kreitzberg
Introduction to BASIC

Kreitzberg
Introduction to Fortran

Pierson
Introduction to Business Information Systems

Veklerov and Pekelny
Computer Language C

Preface

Over the past few years, C increasingly became the programming language of choice in business and industry. Once restricted to the scientific and technical world, the potential of C is now realized for the programming of business applications. It is for that market this textbook was written.

The enrollment in C courses consistently increases with a large number of professional programmers from industry entering the classroom and joining traditional students to learn this relatively new language. Knowledge of C translates more and more into career opportunities. The motivation level among students of all backgrounds seems extremely high and the dropout rate low. Because of the necessary prerequisites, the strong individual backgrounds, and the high level of interest brought by the students to the course, the success rate is high for the class as a whole. The course can be taught at a more advanced level if the students have had adequate exposure to the logic of programming.

Approach

This book is aimed at an introductory course in C taught in programs of business and information systems. The example programs and exercises are designed primarily around business applications differentiating this text from the bulk of C textbooks on the market. Other factors that make this text distinctive are the early coverage of string handling and the emphasis placed on screen design and report generation, which are important elements of business programming.

The text emphasizes
- keyboard and file input
- screen and printer output
- arithmetic, relational, and conditional operators

- arrays
- pointers and their relation in C to arrays
- C data structures

Graphics, linked lists, and object-oriented programming are also introduced.

Because this book focuses on the needs of business students, the applications are directed primarily toward accounting, marketing, and finance. Most other existing C books tend to concentrate on the wealth of operators in C without exposing the students to real-world applications. By contrast, the sequence of topics in this text quickly enables the students to reach a point where they can produce an actual printed report that has both an attractive and effective screen design and layout. Other applications use a menu design, encouraging user-friendly programming.

Prerequisites

Students are required to have some programming background in a procedural language before attempting the course in C. In the past, those students with prior knowledge of programming in COBOL, BASIC, dBASE, Pascal, FORTRAN, or an assembler language were successful with this text's approach. The technical level of the text makes learning easier than with most texts on the market.

Features

This book stresses **structured programming** using a top-down approach. The program planning techniques include **hierarchy charts** and the book contains many examples of **fully developed programs** that give students an opportunity to see the language in a useful and meaningful way. All complete programs are indicated by an icon throughout the text and are available on disk to adopters.

The text follows a **building-block style** so that students will continue to use early concepts in future programs. Through this approach, students should be able to see the advantages of **structured design** and the trend toward creating "objects." This style makes the book continuously useful while assisting the student in adapting to new versions of C, particularly those incorporating **object-oriented programming,** as their language proficiency develops.

Although at first glance C code can appear difficult to comprehend, it is actually a simple language. I have attempted in this text to show the elegance and simplicity of C. It is important for an instructor to understand the material and to communicate that understanding. It is equally important for authors to facilitate that task for the instructors, even in qualitative areas such as **programming style.** In my own class, the students tell me that I make the material easy to follow. I have attempted to translate my students' helpful feedback into a text that will be easy for others to teach and learn from.

The text encourages students to write user-friendly programs with well-designed **data entry screens** and allows them to understand the potential of their programming skills and apply those skills toward meaningful applications. Although graphics are not standard to C, the text covers **presentation graphics,** such as bar charts and pie charts, for business applications using the Borland International C++ and Microsoft C compilers. In addition to programming design, the text discusses potential logic problems and the pitfalls of precedence of operators.

Chapter Pedagogy

The pedagogy of the text is designed to reinforce the concepts being taught. Each chapter contains

- chapter objectives
- an overview
- examples
- hierarchy charts
- sample code
- self-testing questions
- a summary of material
- review questions, and
- exercises for assignments

The **glossary** is provided both in the margin, for easy reference, and in compiled form for the entire text. Each glossary term is boldfaced in the text complete with a corresponding marginal definition.

Each programming skill or major function of C is reinforced by an **example.** The examples include a problem statement, analysis, charting, coding, and an integration of chapter topics into **applications.** Each topic discussion ends with **a self-test along with answers** to help students evaluate their understanding of the material.

At the end of each chapter is a **summary** of the major concepts and the **key terms** covered in the chapter, followed by a list of short-essay or coding **review questions.** A variety of **exercises** with varying levels of difficulty enables students to apply the concepts covered in the corresponding chapter.

The **Hayley Office Supplies case** provides a continuing exercise that carries a common theme throughout the chapters. At the end of each chapter, an exercise based on the topic covered in the chapter is applied to the company. Although the applications weave throughout the various divisions of the company, they all relate to the same industry.

The **appendices** include a summary of standard functions in the various header files, a list of reserved words, a table of the precedence of operators, and information about Microsoft and Borland International editors. They serve as a ready reference for more efficient review.

Supplements

Business Programming in C for DOS-based Systems is supported with a detailed **Instructor's Manual** which contains teaching notes, answers to review questions, solutions to exercises, and solutions to the Hayley Office Supplies case study. There is also a selection of true/false and multiple-choice questions that can be used in creating tests.

An **Instructor's Disk** packaged with the Instructor's Manual contains the program code for all complete examples in the text and the solutions to the exercises.

Instructors are free, upon adoption, to use files from the Instructor's Disk to create a **Student Disk** for distribution to their class.

C and C++ Compilers

The C language has undergone several changes since its initial introduction to DOS-based microcomputer systems. The C standard established by the American National Standards Institute (ANSI) serves as the foundation of all **standard** compilers and allows for a uniformity of programming code and portability among the various Microsoft and Borland International products. The programming examples presented in this text and provided on the Instructor's Disk strictly adhere to the ANSI standard, where applicable, and can therefore be run on the earlier compilers such as Microsoft C and Borland's Turbo C as well as on the most current QuickC or C++ environments. Presentation graphics and object-oriented programming are not governed by the standard but are illustrated with examples from specific compilers that support these extensions.

Acknowledgments

I would like to thank the wonderful people at HBJ/Dryden Press. Book writing is a team project with many stages between idea and publication. My sincere thanks to the many people who played critical roles in the book's development: Richard J. Bonacci, senior editor; Lisa Toftemark Rittby, editorial assistant; Sheila M. Spahn, project editor; Matt Ball, assistant project editor; Marilyn Williams, production manager; Burl Sloan, designer; and Kevin Cottingim, marketing manager, who have all worked many hours since the inception of this project.

In developing this text, I depended on the many useful suggestions and helpful advice of the reviewers who evaluated the manuscript at various stages. I would like to thank them for their advice and continuous encouragement. This text would not be possible without them.

Eric P. Bloom, Bentley College

Glenn F. Boswell, San Antonio College

Charles F. Bowman, CFB Systems, Inc.

Jan W. Buzydlowski, Community College of Philadelphia

David Cheslow, Texas A & M University

Richard W. Corner, The University of Findlay

Jan de Lassen, Brigham Young University

Barbara Gentry, Parkland College

Richard Hatch, San Diego State University

Greg M. Perry, Tulsa Junior College

Joan K. Pierson, James Madison University

Robert S. Roberts, New Mexico State University

To my students and those of the reviewers who class-tested the preliminary version of this text, I extend a special thank you for their patience and numerous useful suggestions for improving the teaching effectiveness of this text.

And lastly, a very special thanks to my husband Andy, my daughter Tricia, and my son Eric for their patience and understanding as I sat month after month in front of the computer.

Contents

CHAPTER ONE

An Introduction To C

CHAPTER OBJECTIVES   2
CHAPTER OVERVIEW   3

The History of C   4
    Advantages of C   4
        Portability   4
        A Large Selection of Operators   4
        Structured Design   4
        Flexibility   4
    Disadvantages of C   5
        Cryptic Appearance   5
        Misused Pointer Access   5
        Operation Confusion   5

Running a C Program   5
    Editors, Compilers, and Linkers   5
    Steps to Programming   7

The Main ( ) Function   8
Printing   9
    Screen Output   10
    Advancing to a New Line   10
    Sending Output to the Printer   12
    Skipping Blank Lines   13

Documentation   14
Dividing a Program Into Parts   15
    Creating Functions   15
    Calling the Function We Create   16
    Hierarchy Charts   17

Programming Style   17
Programming/Debugging Hint   18
Key Terms   19
Chapter Summary   19
Review Questions   20
Exercises   20
Hayley Office Supplies   21

CHAPTER TWO

Data Types, Variables, and Entering Data

CHAPTER OBJECTIVES   22
CHAPTER OVERVIEW   23

Data Items and Data Types   24
    Constants and Literals   24
    Preprocessor DEFINED Symbolic Constants   26
        ANSI codes for Clearing the Screen and Cursor Location   26
    Variables   28
        Declaring a Variable   28
        Global and Local Variables   29
        Initializing Variables   30
        Assigning Values to a Variable   32
        Assigning a Value to Multiple Variables   32
        Printing Variables   34
        Entering Data   43

Example Program   48
    Programming Style   50
    Programming/Debugging Hint   50

Key Terms   52
Chapter Summary   52
Review Questions   52
Exercises   52
Hayley Office Supplies   54

CHAPTER THREE

Iteration—Creating a Loop

CHAPTER OBJECTIVES   56
CHAPTER OVERVIEW   57

Making Comparisons Using Relational Operators   58
    Comparing Numeric Data   58
    Comparing Character Data   58
    Implied Conditions—True or False   60
    The Logical Operators   61
    Precedence of And and Or in Compound Conditions   61
    String Comparisons   62
        Comparing Strings and Ignoring the Case   63
        Finding the Length of a String   63
        Combining String Fields—Concatenation   64

Loops   66
    The While Loop   66
    Infinite Loops   67
        Priming Input   68
        Flushing the Buffer for Strings in a Loop   69
        Placing the Input Function Inside the Condition Expression   69
    Do *Loop*   70
    for *Loop*   72
        Multiple Initialization, Condition, or Action   74
    Nested Loops   75

A First Look at Calculations   77
A Report Program   77
Sample Program   78
    Alternative Solution   82

Programming/Debugging Tip   85
    Pausing the Screen   85

Key Terms   86
Chapter Summary   86
Review Questions   87
Exercises   88
Hayley Office Supplies   91

CHAPTER FOUR

Processing Data: Calculations and Decisions

CHAPTER OBJECTIVES   92
CHAPTER OVERVIEW   93

Arithmetic Operators   94
 Binary Operators   94
  Precedence of Operators   94
  Modulus   96
 Unary Operators   96
  Increment Operators   97
  Decrement Operators   97
  Prefix versus Postfix   97
  Another Look at Precedence   98
 Assignment Operators   99
  Placing the Assignment Operators in a Loop   100
  Precedence   101
  Mixing Data Types in Calculations   102
  The sizeof *Operator   103*
  Exponentiation   103
 Decisions—The If Statement   104
  Nested If *Statement   108*
  Compound Conditions   109
  Conditional Operator   110
  Highest/Lowest Logic Using the If   *116*
 Precedence of Assignment, Logical, and Relational Operators   118
 Programming Style   121

Key Terms   123
Chapter Summary   123
Review Questions   124
Exercises   124
Hayley Office Supplies   129

CHAPTER FIVE

Creating Menu Programs Using the Switch Statement

CHAPTER OBJECTIVES   130
CHAPTER OVERVIEW   131

The Switch Statement   132
 Break   132

More than One Alternative for a Case   133
 Example Program   136
Using the switch *for a Range of Values   137*

Menu Programs   139
 Structure of a Menu Program   140
 Sample Program   140
 Using Letters or Numbers for Menu Options   145
 Menu Hints   147

Multiple Level Menus   148
 Running Executable Files or DOS Commands from the Menu   153

Programming/Debugging Hint   154
 Reverse Video   154
 Using Screen Colors in a Program   155
 Boldface and Italics   156
 Printers   156

Key Terms   156
Chapter Summary   156
Review Questions   157
Exercises   157
Hayley Office Supplies   159

CHAPTER SIX

More Details About Functions and Variables

CHAPTER OBJECTIVES   160
CHAPTER OVERVIEW   161

 Storage Types   162
  Auto   162
  Static   162
  Register   163
  Extern   163
  Storage Types for Functions   164

 Visibility of Variables   165
 Function Call by Value   167
  Passing Values to a Function   168
 Returning a Value from a Function   172
  Using the Return Value from a Function   173
 Data Types for Functions   174
 Cohension and Coupling   181
 Programming/Debugging Hint   182

Lvalues versus Rvalues 182
Key Terms 183
Chapter Summary 183
Review Questions 184
Exercises 184
Hayley Office Supplies 187

CHAPTER SEVEN

Arrays: Single and Multidimensional

CHAPTER OBJECTIVES 188
CHAPTER OVERVIEW 189

Single Dimension Arrays 190
    Declaring an Array 190
    Initializing an Array 190
    Initializing an Array of Unspecified Size 191
    Partially Filled Array 191
    Subscripts 191

For Loops and Arrays 192
    Using a for Loop on Partially Filled Arrays 194

Multidimensional Arrays 198
    Initializing Multidimensional Arrays 198
    Accessing a Two-Level Array with Nested Loops 199

Accessing Data in an Array 205
    Searching an Array 205
        Serial Search 206
        Binary Search 209
    Soring Data in an Array 213
        An Exchange Sort 213
        Using the qsort ( ) Function 215
        The compare function in qsort ( ) and besearch ( ) 216

Programming/Debugging Tip 218
Key Terms 218
Chapter Summary 218
Review Questions 219
Exercises 220
Hayley Office Supplies 224

CHAPTER EIGHT

Aggregate Data Types: Structures and Unions

CHAPTER OBJECTIVES   226
CHAPTER OVERVIEW   227

Aggregate Data Types   228
    Structures   228
        Structure Tag   229
        Structure Variables   229
        Size of a Structure   229
        Referring to a Field within a Structure   230
        Structures within Structures   231
        Arrays of Structures   231
        Entering Data into a Structure Array   232
        Placement of Array Brackets   233
        Naming Tags and Variables the Same   233
        Replacing Multidimensional Arrays with an Array of
            Structures   234
    Unions   235
        Size of a Union   236
        Structures and Unions   236
    Enum   237
        Assigning Values to the Constant Names   238
    Typedef   240
        Assigning typedef to an Array   241
Date and Time Functions   242
    The time ( ) Function   243
    Converting time ( ) Seconds to tm Structure   243
    The asctime ( ) Function   243
    An Easier Way   243
    Putting the Date in a Title   244
    Performing Date Arithmetic   244
    Summary of Date Functions   245
Key Terms   251
Chapter Summary   251
Review Questions   251
Exercises   252
Hayley Office Supplies   254

CHAPTER NINE

Pointers

CHAPTER OBJECTIVES   256
CHAPTER OVERVIEW   257

Pointer Variables   258
   Pointer Operators   259
   Declaring a Pointer   259
   Assigning a Pointer to the Address of a Variable   260
   Combining Declaration and Assignment of Pointers   260
   A Pointer Contains Memory Address   261

Summary of Pointer Characteristics   263
Pointers to Pointers and Levels of Indirections   264
Pointer Calculations   266
Pointers and Arrays   270
   Accessing a Single-Dimension Array with Pointers   272
   Accessing a String using Pinters   273
   Multidimensional Arrays and Pointers   274
      Pointers to Points and Multidimensional Arrays   274
   Incrementing the Pointers   275
   Summary of Relationships   276
   Accessing a Multidimensional Array with Pointers   276
   Accessing a Multidimensional Array as a Single Array   276
   Pointers as Function Arguments   278
      Function Call by Reference to a Local Variable Address   278
      Passing an Array to a Function   279

Pointers and Structures   284
   Programming/Debugging Hint   286
   Data Validation   286
      Inputting One Character at a Time   286
      Default Values   288
      Converting String to Numeric Types   288

Key Terms   293
Chapter Summary   293
Review Questions   294
Exercises   294
Hayley Office Supplies   297

CHAPTER TEN

File Input/Output with Structures

CHAPTER OBJECTIVES   298
CHAPTER OVERVIEW   299

Data Files   300
   Opening a File   300
      Declaring a Stream Name   300
      The fopen ( ) Function   300
      Testing if the File Exists   302
   Writing to the File   303
   Closing a File   304
   Example Creating a File   304
   Reading Data from a Disk File   307
   Testing for the End of the File   307

Sequential vs. Random File Access   310
   Using Structures in Data Files   310
   Random File Access   310
   the fwrite ( ) Function   311
      Writing an Array of Structures   311
      Creating a File   311
   Reading a File   314
      Advantage of Reading Multiple Records at a Time   314
      Example Using fread ( )   314
   The fseek ( ) Function   316

Updating a Random File   317
   Adding Records to the File   320
   Deleting or Editing a Record   322
   Delete   322
      Flagging a Record for Delete   322
   Editing Records   326
   Listing Records from the File   329
      Printing to the Screen   329
      Printing to the Printer   329
   Replacing Deleted Record Positions During Add   333
   Using a Delete Code   333

Programming/Debugging Tip   333
   Hash Addressing   333
   Hashing Algorithm   334

Using fscanf ( ) with String Arrays   335
Key Terms   337
Chapter Summary   338
Review Questions   338

Exercises   *339*
Hayley Office Supplies   *341*

CHAPTER ELEVEN

Creating Multipage Reports with Subtotals

CHAPTER OBJECTIVES   *342*
CHAPTER OVERVIEW   *342*

Multipage Reports   344
   Multipage Output   344
   Placement of the Line Counter Decision   345
   Changes to the heading ( ) Function   345
   Form Feed   345
      Summary of Steps for Multipage Output   *346*

Control Breaks   351
   The Subtotal Function   353

Multilevel Control Breaks   358
Key Terms   363
Chapter Summary   363
Exercises   363
Hayley Office Supplies   364

CHAPTER TWELVE

Linked Lists

CHAPTER OBJECTIVES   *366*
CHAPTER OVERVIEW   *367*

Allocating Memory   368
   calloc ( )   368
   malloc ( )   369
   realloc ( )   369
   free ( )   370

Linked Lists   373
   Coding a Linked List   375
   Adding an Element to a Linked List   375
   Deleting an Element from a Linked List   382
   Printing Data from a Linked List   384
   Complete Link List Example   390

Key Terms   399
Chapter Summary   399
Review Questions   399
Exercises   399·
Hayley Office Supplies   400

CHAPTER THIRTEEN

Using Graphics in C

CHAPTER OBJECTIVES   402
CHAPTER OVERVIEW   403

The Graphic Library   404
Clearing the Screen and Positioning the Cursor   404
    Microsoft   404
    Borland   405

Setting Text Colors   406
    Colors in Borland   408
    textcolor ( ) and textbackground ( )   408

Setting Type Fonts   409
    Microsoft   409
    Borland Fonts   410

Text Screen vs. Graphics Screens   412
Microsoft Graphics   412
    Setting Video Mode   412
    Setting Graphics Colors   414
    Painting a Pixel   414
    Drawing a Line with _lineto ( ) _moveto ( )   417
    Drawing a Rectangle with _rectangle ( )   418
    Drawing a Circle with _ellipse ( )   418
    Drawing a Partial Circles with _pie ( ) and _arc ( )   420
    Filling is an Odd Shape or the Background   421
    Setting up Windows   423

Borland Graphics   424
    Initializing a Graphics Mode   424
    Setting Graphics Colors   426
    Drawing a Pixel   426
    Drawing a Line Using the putpixel ( )   427
    Drawing a Line with line ( )   427
    Drawing a Rectangle   428
    Drawing a Circle   428
    circle ( )   428

arc ( )   429
ellipse ( )   430
pieslice ( )   430
Setting Fill Colors and Fill Styles   431
window ( )   433
setviewport ( )   433

Uses of Graphics in Business Programming   435
Creating a Bar Chart   435
Creating a Pie Chart   439
Using Graphics Functions for a Light Bar Menu   442

Programming/Debugging Tip   451
Working with Various Graphics Modes   451
Setting a Program List   451

Key Terms   452
Chapter Summary   452
Review Questions   452
Exercises   452
Hayley Office Supplies   453

CHAPTER FOURTEEN

A Look at C++ and Object-Oriented Programming

CHAPTER OBJECTIVES   454
CHAPTER OVERVIEW   455

Object-Oriented Programming   456
Characteristics of an Oop Language   456
Characteristics of C++   456
Comments   457
A First Program in C++   457
Security of Data and Functions   458
Creating an Object   459
The Declaration of the Object   459
Definition of the Object Functions   460
Accessing the Object   461
Declaring Variables as Needed   462
Overloading   462
Functions   462
Operators   463
Constructors and Destructors   463

Container Libraries   463
Categories of Classes   464

Utility and Helper Classes   *464*
BIDS   *464*

Key Terms   *465*
Chapter Summary   *466*
Review Questions   *466*
Exercises   *466*
Hayley Office Supplies   *467*

Appendix A - ANSI C Reserved Words   *468*

Appendix B - Common Library Functions   *469*

Appendix C - Precedence of Operators   *470*

Appendix D - Using the Editors   *471*
The Edit Environments   *471*
Parts of the Editing Screen   *471*
Entering a Program   *471*
Compiling and Running a Program   *472*
Debugging Tools   *473*

Glossary of Terms   *474*

BUSINESS PROGRAMMING IN C
FOR DOS-BASED SYSTEMS

CHAPTER

CHAPTER OBJECTIVES

By the end of this chapter, you should be able to:

■ Understand the history, advantages, and disadvantages of the C language.

■ Cite the steps for writing a program.

■ Grasp the purpose of the main( ) function.

■ Write a program that will output constant/literal data to the screen or to the printer.

■ Know the importance of documentation, indentations, and blanklines for readability of code.

An Introduction to C

CHAPTER OVERVIEW

*This first chapter will introduce programming in C with a short
program. An important aspect of this program will be to demonstrate the use of punctuation in C. Functions for producing output to the screen or to the printer will be used. In addition, a
discussion of style and the importance of documentation and
spacing to produce code that is easier to read and to debug will
be presented.*

```
void main( )
{
   printf("Welcome to Programming in C");
}
```

⑨ ❶ ❷ ❸ ❹ ❺ ❻ ❼ ❽ ⑨ ❶ ❷ ❸ ❹ ❺

The C language was originally developed by Dennis Ritchie of Bell Labs. It is based on two languages that did not contain data types: B created by Ken Thompson and BCPL written by Martin Richards.

C is general purpose programming language and has gained in popularity in recent years. The majority of the UNIX operating system was written in C, as well as many of the programs that run under that operating system. C compilers are currently available on a number of operating systems, including DOS. As the use of the language has grown, the American National Standards Institute (ANSI) has developed a standard for the language. Standard C code should be hardware independent, therefore, it should run on any compiler without requiring changes to any of the code.

Advantages of C

There are four major advantages of C; they include (1) portability, (2) power (due to a large selection of operators), (3) structured design capability, and (4) language flexibility.

Portability   The popularity of C is due to its power and flexibility despite the small size of the language. There are only 32 reserved words in the C language. Most of the programming done in the language uses a variety of functions that are stored in header files and libraries. The function names remain the same from one machine to another. This is because the machine dependent code is written inside the standard library functions. The contents of these library functions may change from system to system, but the calls to the functions used by the programmer remain the same.

A Large Selection of Operators   Despite the small number of reserved words, C has a large number of operators that often make the code look cryptic. These operators are easy to learn and soon you will be able to read this cryptic looking code.

Structured Design   Even though the code punctuation and symbols may appear strange in the beginning, the function design of C provides an ideal environment for well-structured programming. The language is designed with a main( ) function that then calls any necessary functions. In addition to the functions available in the standard libraries, it is easy and appropriate for the programmer to create any needed functions.

Flexibility   C's ability to manipulate data and memory locations allows programs to be written at almost an assembly level . With the large number of operators and library functions, it can also function as a powerful high-level language. These two approaches to programming in C make it a very versatile language.

Disadvantages of C

Some difficulties also arise from the language's compact style. The code may become difficult to read, or may contain difficult to find logic errors due to misuse of operators which do not generate syntax errors.

Cryptic Appearance   Because of the ability to write very compact code with embedded logic, C can be very difficult to read. It is very important in C to write well-documented programs and to use white space as needed to improve the readability.

Misused Pointer Access   Since this language allows the programmer to manipulate data at the bit level and to access data and functions by their memory address, some difficult-to-find bugs may be introduced. With the use of pointers, one of the powerful features of C that allows the programmer to access the address of an item, it is possible to inadvertently access anywhere in RAM. With a poorly defined pointer, the programmer might accidentally access the storage area of the program or even the operating system. Such errors in logic may be very difficult to locate.

Operator Confusion   Another common error for beginning C programs results from the large number of operators. It is very important to be familiar with and to refer to the precedence tables of the operators. Operators may be used anywhere, regardless of context. The assignment operator (=) could inadvertantly be used when equality (==) is intended. In addition, the same symbol is sometimes used for different operators depending upon the context.

RUNNING A C PROGRAM

This text has been designed for those who already have a knowledge of programming. The logic structures and flow control statements that are available in most procedural languages are similar in the C world.

C programs are created with an editor and then processed by a compiler. The programs in this text have been compiled with Microsoft QuickC™ and with Borland Turbo C++™. There may be some differences, depending on the compiler, although the text adheres primarily to the ANSI standard. (An exception is the chapter on graphics.) Some constants will be defined that will work only in a DOS environment with ANSI.SYS.

Editors, Compilers, and Linkers

In order to code and run a program in C it is necessary to have a text editor, a compiler, and a linker (see Figure 1-1).

FIGURE 1-1
Creating Executable Code

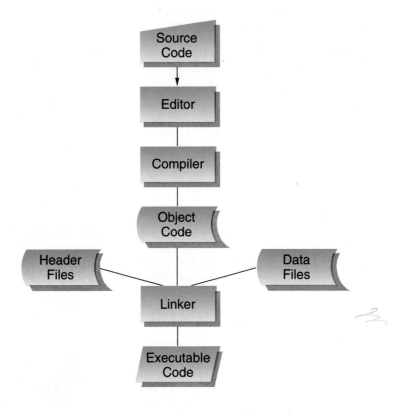

The text editor may be a part of your C environment or it may be an independent editor. Both Borland and Microsoft provide a text editor as a part of their C packages. The **text editor** is used to enter the program into the machine and should provide the ability to edit easily your programming code (**source code**). These edit features usually include cut and paste, and searching operations. Such capabilities will help speed up the development time of your program. Details about the Microsoft and Borland editors are found in Appendix D.

A **compiler** translates your source code into **object code.** As the compiler attempts to perform this translation it will be able to locate any syntax errors. Syntax errors consist of punctuation or spelling that cannot be translated by the compiler. The level of this error checking can usually be set as part of the environment.

After the program is compiled the **linker** will be accessed to combine all necessary object files and data files to create an executable program. This step is done automatically for the programmer in both Microsoft QuickC and the Borland environments.

The text editor, the compiling process, and the linking process are all a part of the total environment provided by the Borland C++ and Microsoft QuickC programming packages.

text editor   Used for entering the source code for a program; usually allows for editing features such as search and replace, cut and copy.
source code   Programming instructions written in a programming language prior to compilation.
compiler   A program that translates a programmer's source code into object code.
object code   The compiled version of the program that will be linked into the executable code.
linker   A program that combines object files and data files to create executable code.

Steps to Programming

In solving programming problems, we need to approach them in an organized manner. Designing programs can be broken down into four steps: (1) analyze, (2) chart, (3) code, and (4) debug.

1. _Analyze._ To **analyze** a program means to understand the problem and to break it down into parts. If you do not understand how to solve a problem, it would be impossible to give the computer instructions to solve that problem. In understanding the problem, it is a good idea to state the problem in terms of the output, the input, and the processing.

    The output is listed first, because we must know what we are trying to produce in order to determine how to produce it. The results that are produced will be coming from input or from processing. When we know what the output is to be, it will be easier to list the required input and processing needs.

    analyze To break down a problem into parts.

2. _Chart._ Just as a builder needs the designs in the form of a blueprint, the programmer should have the program design in a pictorial form (**chart**) or pseudocode. For our examples, we will use the hierarchy or organization chart. This type of chart gives a breakdown of the parts of the program which we consider as functions.

    chart A diagram of the user-defined functions in a program and the relationship between the functions.

    Let's consider an example of a chart to break down the task of painting a wall (see Figure 1-2). Each of the parts could probably be broken down into further parts. Set up will include surface preparation and getting out tools and paint. Performing the task is the actual painting including the wall and trim work. The job will not be finished until the cleanup is complete.

3. _Code._ The **coding** step requires that the program plan be translated into a computer language, which in our case means writing the program in C.

    code To write a program in a computer language; refers to source code.

    It is wise to write the code out before sitting down in front of the computer. It is sometimes tempting to just jump in and start from the coding stage. However, the time spent in planning will result in a much shorter time spent during the debugging phase. This will be truer as the programs become more complex.

4. _Debug._ To **debug** means to eliminate the errors. Two types of errors may occur in a program: syntax and logic errors. The syntax errors, as

    debug To eliminate errors in a program.

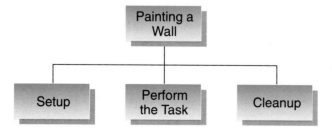

FIGURE 1-2
Hierarchy Chart for
Painting a Wall

previously mentioned, are typically caused by punctuation or spelling errors and will be found by the compiler. What is really happening with a syntax error is that the compiler cannot understand a part of the code and is therefore unable to translate the code to machine language.

If the code compiles without any errors but the results are not what was expected then the culprit is a logic error. In C, this can frequently be caused by a misunderstanding of the hierarchy of the operators. To find a logic error, it is up to the programmer to walk through the code and "play computer" to determine what each line of code is instructing the computer to do. Remember, the computer will only do what it is told to do.

THE MAIN( ) FUNCTION

main( ) function   A required function in C that contains the beginning and ending statements for the execution of the program.

All C programs contain a **main( ) function**. This function controls the entire program. The program will always begin and should end execution in the main( ) function.

```
void main( )
{
          program statement(s)
}
```

The instructions in this main( ) function are enclosed in braces{ }. Other programmer-created functions will also be enclosed in braces. The **braces** are used to mark the beginning and the end of a series of statements called a block. The main( ) function is an example of a block.

braces { }   Used to enclose a block of code.

The set of parentheses following the word main( ) are used to enclose any informational items that need to be sent to the function. In our first example, we will not be sending any information to main( ) so the parentheses will be empty. Any items that are enclosed inside of these parentheses are called **arguments**. All function names will be followed by the parentheses whether they accept arguments or not.

argument   A value being received by a function; enclosed in parentheses in the function header.

The word *void* before main( ) indicates that this function will not return any values. The use of a return type such as void is required by the ANSI standard. Many compilers will not generate an error but will cause a warning if the return type is not used. This warning can be suppressed by setting the compiler error settings under OPTIONS. It is best to include the word void to document that there is no return value from this function.

Let's take a look at a short C program.

```
void main( )
{
    printf("This is a C program");
}
```

Notice that:

1. The word main( ) is followed by ( ) parentheses. The names of all functions are followed by parentheses.
2. The braces{ } enclose the statements or instructions.
3. The statement ends with a semicolon.

This program example accesses another function called printf( ). This is the library function used for formatted printing. Notice that the item to be printed is enclosed in parentheses. The item(s) to be printed are the arguments to be sent to the printf( ) function.

The printf( ) function is stored as part of the standard C library. This particular function is accessible to many C programs as part of the normal compile without having to include the header file. Some systems may require extra code to be accessed from one of the standard libraries.

Self-Test

1. What function is required in all C programs?
2. What is the purposes of the braces { } in C?
3. Is printf( ) a reserved word in C?

Answers

1. All C programs must have a main( ) function.
2. The braces { } in C are used to enclose a group of statements called a block. In the earlier example the braces were used to enclose all of the statements which compromised the contents of the main( ) function.
3. No. The printf( ) in C is a function which has been stored in the standard library. It is not really a reserved word but rather a function that could be examined by listing the source code in the standard input output library.

PRINTING

Let's start the use of C by creating output. The most common destinations for output are to the screen and to the printer. We will deal with files later.

C uses functions to produce output rather than reserved words, demonstrating the ability to remain hardware and operating system independent. The two output functions that we will discuss are the printf( ) and the fprintf( ). The difference between the two is that the printf( ) produces output on the standard output device (which is usually the screen) while the fprintf( ) allows you to specify the output device.

The format of the printf( ) function is:

```
printf([format,] items to be printed);
```

The items to be printed may be variables or constants. Note that the word format is enclosed in square brackets [ ]. The brackets are used to indicate that this part of the `printf( )` function is optional. We will look at formatted output in the next chapter.

For now let's look at the `printf( )` in an example that prints a constant. The words to be printed will be enclosed inside of double quotation marks.

```
void main( )
{
printf("This is my first C program");
}
```

This program will print exactly what is inside the quotes, printing it all on one line. The following will produce exactly the same output:

```
void main( )
{
    printf("This ");
    printf("is ");
    printf("my ");
    printf("first ");
    printf("C ");
    printf("program");
}
```

Each function call to `printf( )` will print what is inside the quotes and it will print on the same line because no instruction is given to advance the line.

Advancing to a New Line

The \n can be used inside of quotes to tell the output device to go to a new line. This will assure that the next item to print will not print on the same line. The \n (newline character) can be used anywhere in the quote. To leave a blank line, use one newline symbol to exit the current line and a second one to skip a line.

```
printf("1\n2\n3\n");
```

will print as

```
1
2
3
```

Remember, when no newline symbol was included, the second `printf( )` continued on the same output line as the previous `printf( )`.

Watch what the output will be for the following program.

```
void main( )
{
    printf("Happy ");
    printf("Birthday!!\n");
}
```

Output

```
Happy Birthday!!
```

The newline symbol or character is at the end of the second line, so that if there were any more `printf( )` calls, they would be on a new line. In this case, both words printed out on the same line because there was no newline character inside the quotes on the first call to `printf( )` or before the word "Birthday" in the second call to `printf( )` function.

If we wished to print three letters on three separate lines, we could do it with a single `printf( )` or with multiple printf( )s.

```
printf("A\nB\nC\n");
```

is the same as

```
printf("A\n");
printf("B\n");
printf("C\n");
```

The newline character is our first example of an escape sequence. We will describe more of these in the future.

Self-Test

1. Write a printf( ) function call that will print

   ```
   This is fun!!!!
   ```

2. Write a single printf( ) that will print your name on the first line and the date on the second line.
3. What is wrong with each of the following:

   ```
   a. print("Programming in C");
   b. printf(I know what's wrong with this);
   ```

```
c. printf("OOPs, another wrong one);
d. printf("Maybe this one is correct")
e. printf("print and then go to a newline"\n);
```

Answers

```
1. printf("This is fun!!!!");
2. printf("your name here \n then the date");
3. a. The function name is printf( ).
   b. The information to be printed should be in
      quotes.
   c. The closing quotes are missing.
   d. There is no semicolon at the end of the
      statement.
   e. The \n newline character must be inside of
      the quotation marks.
```

Sending Output to the Printer

Sending output to the printer is most easily accomplished using the `fprintf( )` function. This function is a part of the header file called stdio.h. It will be necessary to tell the compiler to access this file from the library by using an `include` statement. An `include` is an example of what is called a preprocessor directive. This directive must come before the `main( )` function.

Preprocessor directives begin with a # sign and do not have a semicolon at the end. The lack of a semicolon is due to the fact that these are not really C statements but rather instructions that will be executed prior to compilation of your program. These directives cause some action to be taken prior to your program; hence, the name "preprocessor."

With an include directive, the appropriate file containing the library function definitions will be included in your object code. You will not see the actual lines of code unless you list the source code of the header file. However, as the program compiles, the line count of the header files will appear as the header files are included into your object code.

As we send output to the printer we will need a function called `fprintf( )` that is part of the standard input output header file. The required preprocessor directive that will be used in the following programs using `printf( )` is:

```
#include <stdio.h>
```

The # sign before the word include must be the first character on the line. One or more spaces may be used after the # and before the first letter of the directive.

Notice that the punctuation used are the symbols < >. These symbols around the header file name indicate that the file may be found in the normal disk directory for header files. You may use any path name for header files if you enclose the path and filename inside of quotes such as

```
#include "a:stdio.h"
#include "c:\cprog\my.h"
```

The format for the `fprintf( )` function is

```
fprintf(stream, [format,] items to be printed);
```

The parameters inside of the parentheses for the fprintf( ) are almost identical to the `printf( )`. Formatting is optional but the device is required. You may specify any defined output stream. In ANSI C, an output stream has been defined for the printer. This name is **stdprn**. The `fprintf( )` function could also send the output to the screen by using **stdout** as the output stream.

stdprn   Stream name referring to the printer; used with output functions.
stdout   Stream name referring to the monitor; used with output functions.

```
#include <stdio.h>

void main( )
{
  fprintf(stdprn, "This will go to the printer\n");
}
```

Of course, multiple `fprintf( )` can be used to produce several lines of output or to continue the first line depending on the use of the new line escape sequence.

Note, however, that some printers require a carriage return as well as a new line sequence. If your printer just goes down one line but keeps the same position across the line where it left off on the previous line, you will need to use `\n\r` to go to the beginning of a new line. The `\r` is the escape sequence for a carriage return.

Skipping Blank Lines

To skip a blank line on either a printf( ) or an fprintf( ) it is necessary to use two newline symbols as in "\n\n". This would also occur if one `printf( )` ends with a newline and the next `printf( )` begins with a newline. The effect is the same as having put both of the newline symbols together.

If we want to print the title and column heading for a report, we would probably print the title on one line, skip a line, and then print the column headings. This would be easiest to accomplish with a series of fprintf( )s.

```
fprintf(stdprn,"              Alpha Company\n");
fprintf(stdprn,"             Inventory Report\n\n");
fprintf(stdprn," Product      Quantity     Unit\n");
fprintf(stdprn," Description   on hand      Cost\n");
```

would print as:

```
                              Alpha Company
                            Inventory Report
          Product              Quantity      Unit
          Description          on hand       Cost
```

DOCUMENTATION

Good programs will contain comments as necessary to make the code easier to interpret. It is important not only for other programmers who will need to understand the logic to make modifications to your code but also for yourself. You may have discovered in your past programming experience that if you go back to make changes to a program that you've written a while back, it may be hard to follow quickly some of the steps in the code.

A comment can be included in C by bracketing all information that you don't want the compiler to translate with slashes and asterisks.

```
/* this is a comment line and may go anywhere */
```

A dangerous fact about the C method of commenting is that it can be opened anywhere and will continue through until the closing symbols. You may turn several lines of code into a remark. This may be handy when debugging but will be frustrating if actual instructions are commented out by accident.

It is a good practice to have each comment line contain its own set of /* */, to be certain that each comment is closed. If there is no closing on a comment line, the comment will continue until a closing */ is found. An exception to this may be at the beginning of a program where you may have several lines of comments describing the program and would like to make it one comment.

```
void main( )
{
        /*    this program will print on one line */
        printf("Have ");
        printf("a ");
        printf("nice ");
        printf("day!!!");
}
```

Self-Test

What output will the following statements produce and to what output stream?

```
1. fprintf(stdprn, "X\nY\nZ Corporation");
2. fprintf(stdprn, "XYZ Corporation\n\n");
3. fprintf(stdout, "Client name: ");
4. fprintf(stdprn, "\n Name");
5. fprintf(stdout,"\nName");
```

Answers

1. ```
   X
   Y
   Z Corporation
   ```

   (Would be sent to the printer.)

2. ```
   XYZ Corporation
   ```

   (Would be sent to the printer, followed by two blank lines.)

3. ```
   Client Name:
   ```

   (to the screen)

4. ```
   Name
   ```

   (Printer, skips a line and then a space because of the space after the \n).

5. ```
   Name
   ```

   (Screen, no space before the word "Name".)

DIVIDING A PROGRAM INTO PARTS

In addition to the ability to call C functions that are stored in a library, it is possible to create functions. A **function** is a group of related statements. The functions we create can also receive arguments and/or return a value. Passing arguments and returning values will be covered in Chapter 6.

function A block of named code that may be called from within the code; values may be passed to a function and a single value returned; default data type is int for the returned value.

A program is divided into functions according to the role or purpose that the statements are intended to serve. At this point, we have discussed sending output to the printer and to the screen. For a program that will perform both of these jobs, we could place each task in a separate function.

Creating Functions

To create a function we must give it a name and then follow it with parentheses and any arguments inside of the parentheses. For now, we will not pass any arguments but we must still use the ( )
   ```

```
void print_to_screen( )
void print_to_printer( )
```

The function must be declared before any function calling it, specifying what the return value will be. In some cases, we may wish to return a value from the function we create. If there are no return values, use the return type of void just as we have been doing before `main( )`.

Below the function name will be a set of braces {} enclosing all of the statements that are a part of the function.

```
void print_to_screen( )
{
        fprintf(stdout,"Name:      ABC Incorporated\n");
        fprintf(stdout,"Date:         September 5\n");
}
```

Calling the Function We Create

When the function is to be executed, it can be called by referencing the function name. The function name will be followed by a semicolon because the call is a statement. The function may be called as many times as necessary.

```
print_to_screen( );
```

In the example below, `main( )` will call the following two functions: `print_to_screen( )` and `print_to_printer( )`. Typically, we will put `main( )` first followed by the other functions.

```
/*  A program separating code into two functions   */

#include <stdio.h>

void print_to_screen( );
void print_to_printer( );
void main()
{
     print_to_screen();    /* calls the screen print function */
     print_to_printer();   /* calls the hard copy print function */
}

/* Following is the actual function and the enclosed statements that */
/* get executed when the functions are called from main( )     */
```

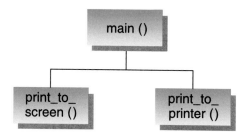

FIGURE 1-3
Hierarchy Chart 1-1. c

```
void print_to_screen()
{
  fprintf(stdout,"Demonstrating that what prints to the screen\n");
  fprintf(stdout,"will not always be the same as what goes to\n");
  fprintf(stdout,"the printer\n");
}
void print_to_printer( )
{
        fprintf(stdprn,"                        ABC Incorporated\n\n\r");
        fprintf(stdprn,"                        1115 Main Street\r");
}
```

Hierarchy Charts

This breakdown of the program into parts could be depicted with a hierarchy chart. A hierarchy chart is similar to a business organization chart used to show how the company is organized or broken down into parts.

The two functions can be represented in a hierarchy chart with a rectangular box for each. Two boxes representing print_to_screen( ) and print_to_printer( ), will branch off of the top box which represents the main( ) (see Figure 1-3).

PROGRAMMING STYLE

The indentations and blank lines that are placed in a C program do not affect execution of the program. The use of both indentations and blank lines is for readability of the program listing.

```
#include <stdio.h>

void main( )
{
  fprintf(stdprn, "This will go to the printer\n");
}
```

In the program that we discussed earlier you will notice certain things about the spacing. The preprocessor directive is usually placed first in the program. Following the #include is a blank line. We will use a blank line at the end of all preprocessor directives to separate them from the actual C code.

The `main( )` is placed on a line by itself, we will place the function name on a separate line. The braces that indicate the beginning and end of the `main( )` function are aligned. Later, we will use more sets of braces so it will become very important that each opening brace is aligned vertically with its closing brace.

The statement(s) inside of the braces should be indented a space or two to make it easier to spot the braces at a quick glance. Some people prefer to indent by an entire tab stop. Notice that in the next program all of the statements in the `main( )` function have been indented and aligned with each other.

```
void main( )
{
    /*     this program will print on one line */
    printf("Have ");
    printf("a ");
    printf("nice ");
    printf("day!!!");
}
```

There will be further discussion of programming style as more statements are introduced, so we will continue to deal with this topic as we progress through the language.

PROGRAMMING/DEBUGGING HINT

Use the fact that `fprintf( )` can output to the screen and to the printer to your advantage. When you are testing a program, you may wish all of the output to go to the screen so that you can see it before you actually send it to the printer.

Write your program with `fprintf( )` using stdout. After you are satisfied with the way the output looks, you can do a search and replace (usually available in the editor) to change `stdout` to `stdprn`. The program will then send the output to the printer.

If you need to have both printer and screen output, you can do a copy in the editor to duplicate your `fprint( )` line, and then have one function call to `stdout` and one to `stdprn`.

```
#include <stdio.h>

void main( )
```

```
{
        /*           to the screen              */
        fprintf(stdout,  "Name:        Anita Mills\n\n");
        fprintf(stdout,  "Phone:       555-1111");

        /*           to the printer             */
        fprintf(stdprn,  "Name:        Anita Mills\n\n");
        fprintf(stdprn,  "Phone:       555-1111");
}
```

These statements could be typed in once and then copied. Be sure to change the output stream or you will have two copies of the output on the same device.

KEY TERMS

analyze	compiler	object code
argument	debug	source code
braces{ }	function	stdout
chart	linker	stdprn
code	main( ) function	text editor

CHAPTER SUMMARY

C is a portable language that is used in many environments. The language is very flexible and is often considered the closest to assembly level language of all higher level languages. The use of standard functions stored in libraries allows the hardware-dependent information to be removed from the programmers' realm and implemented as a part of the language functions.

All C programs contain a main function that may be located anywhere within the program but must exist. Other functions will be called or created as needed.

Two functions providing formatted output are the `printf( )` and the `fprintf( )` functions. The `printf( )` outputs to the screen only, which is considered the standard output device. The `fprintf( )` allows the output stream to be specified.

Programs may be divided by the programmer into functions that s specific purpose.

1. Why is the `#include` required when using an `fprintf( )`?
2. How would the example that prints "Have a nice day!!!" be modified so that each word prints on a different line?
3. Modify the example so that only one `printf( )` is required to print the phrase "Have a nice day!!!"
4. What is the significance of the `main( )` function?
5. Explain the use of the following punctuation marks:
   a. { }
   b. ( )
   c. ;
   d. */
6. Is it necessary to place each statement or instruction on a separate line? If not, why bother doing it?
7. What is a comment?
8. Why has C become such a popular language in such a short time?
9. Some people feel that C is a low-level language like assembler and others consider it a high-level language. Discuss what is meant by each of these views.
10. What is the relationship between a text editor, a compiler, and a linkage editor?

EXERCISES

1. Create a student survey printout. Print information on the screen and the printer about yourself. The output will contain name, phone number, major, previous programming background, and a reason for taking this class. Each item will be on a separate line. Include the appropriate information about the program as comments at the beginning of the program, and before each function definition.
2. Write a program that will produce the following form on the screen.

```
                        Ace Designs        Date:
Customer Name:
Customer Address:
Customer Phone:
```

3. Write a program that will print out 5 features of the C language to the screen and to the printer. Include a title and your name at the top of the list. Leave a blank line before the list and after the title. Print each feature on a separate line.
4. Create a program to print a list of names and phone numbers to the printer. Include a title and column headings at the top of the list. Leave a blank line between the title and column headings and another between the headings and the first name and number. Double space the lines that contain the names and the numbers.

5. Write a program that will print a memo on the printer indicating that hours will be extended to 8 a.m. to 6 p.m. effective July 1. The memo should include a heading with the current date and topic, change of hours, and a from line containing your name. Leave a blank line between each of the heading lines, and double space before the body of the memo.

6. Write a program that will print out a cover sheet for your assignments. The sheet will be sent to the printer and will contain your name, course title, time, and days that the class meets. Draw some sort of border around the information and center it on an $8^{1}/_{2}$ by 11 sheet of paper.

7. Write a program to write out a short-term and long-term plan of your goals: educational, career, and personal.

HAYLEY OFFICE SUPPLIES

Write a program that will print a letterhead for Hayley Office Supplies. The letterhead should be centered at the top of the page and will include the Company Name, Address, and phone number.

Sample Output

Hayley Office Supplies
1111 Main Street
Chino, California 91710
(714) 555-1111

CHAPTER

Data Types, Variables, and Entering Data

CHAPTER OVERVIEW

This chapter will build on the print functions covered in the previous chapter by introducing the use of variables and the associated format specifiers. Data entry functions will also be introduced to create interactive programs. The concentration will be on designing user interfaces with well-laid-out screens and printed reports. Tools for design and planning will be introduced. These include a screen layout form, and a printer spacing chart for output design, and a hierarchy chart for planning top down program structure.

variable   Value may change
during execution of the program;
an identifier is used in association
with a memory location.
constant   A value that does not
change during execution of the
program.
data type   The type of
information that can be stored in a
variable such as *int* or *float*.

Data items may be variable or constant. As with other languages, data that is **variable** may be changed during the execution of the program while **constant** data remains the same every time the program is executed.

The way that data is handled is determined by its **data type.** The types of data in C are integer, long integer, short integer, signed integer, unsigned integer, floating point, double precision, and character. These may be modified as long integer, short integer, signed integer, or unsigned integer.

The different types of data require different amounts of memory for storage. This varies from 1 byte for a character to 8 bytes for a double precision number. The amount of storage required may vary from one machine or compiler to another. The following sizes are for our compilers:

char	1 byte	character data
int	2 bytes	integer data
short	3 bytes	short integer
long	4 bytes	long integer
unsigned	2 bytes	unsigned integer
signed	2 bytes	signed integer
float	4 bytes	floating point numeric
double	8 bytes	double precision float

Constants and Literals

Constants will not change values during the execution of the program. Constants may be either numeric or alphanumeric.

Numeric constants may be an integer such as 5 or a floating point values that contain a decimal such as 5.05. These numbers could be used in a calculation, assigned to a variable, or used in a print function.

A character constant contains only one character and is enclosed in single quotes such as `'c'`. Character constants may be a single letter, a digit, a symbol, or they may be escape sequences. **Escape sequences** are typically used to represent white space, such as a tab or newline, or to represent unprintable characters such as the bell; and are preceded by a backslash \, such as the new line escape sequence \n from last chapter. The backslash can also be used in C to allow certain special characters to be used in a print string that might otherwise be interpreted differently. For example, if we want to print a quote we cannot place the quotation marks inside the print quotes because the compiler would interpret the quote as an opening or closing of what was to be printed. However, we can actually print the quotation marks if we precede them with a \. This means that the escape sequence \" used inside a `printf( )` quote will cause quotation marks to be printed.

escape sequence   Value
beginning with backslash usually
used to control peripheral devices.

Common escape sequences include the following:

\a	bell (the a comes from "alert")
\b	backspace
\f	formfeed
\n	new line
\r	carriage return
\t	tab
\0	null character
\'	single quotes
\"	double quotes
\\	backslash
\%	percent

Some printers require a carriage return at the end of each line. The tab can be used for spacing out the print line and aligning the columns of text.

A **string literal** is a constant containing multiple characters and is enclosed in double quotes, such as "This is my first C program." String literals can be used in situations other than printing.

Examples of constants and literals include the following:

Integer	5
Float	.05
Character	'c'
Character	'\n'
String	"literal"

string literal A constant value enclosed in quotes that is stored as an array of characters.

Self-Test

1. What is the difference between a character constant and a string literal?
2. Are the following constants numeric, character, or invalid?
   a. 5
   b. .05
   c. 5%
   d. '5'
3. To test the tab stops on your system, type in the following program and execute it.

```
#define CLS printf("\033[2J")

void main( )
{
    CLS;
    printf("\t\tHelp!!!!\n\n");
    printf("1234567890123456789");
}
```

Answers

1. A character constant contains only one character or an escape sequence and is enclosed in single quotes, while a string literal may contain multiple characters and is enclosed inside of double quotes.

2. a. numeric, integer
   b. numeric, floating point
   c. invalid—cannot have the % unless the two characters are inside of double quotes making them a string constant.
   d. character

Preprocessor DEFINED Symbolic Constants

In the last chapter, the concept of #include was introduced. Another example of a preprocessor directive is the definition of a constant. A preprocessor defined constant is called a manifest constant or a **symbolic constant**. If the value contains a statement or expression it is called a **macro.**

These constants are defined by using the directive #define followed by the **identifier** and the assigned value. An identifier is a name created by the programmer and used to distinguish an individual variable, symbolic constant, or function.

```
#define PI 3.14
```

The symbolic constant causes the assigned value to be substituted for the constant name throughout the program before compilation. This means that once the object code has been created, the name PI will never appear, only the value 3.14.

The advantage of a symbolic constant is that the code can be made more meaningful by using the constant name in the source code. It is also easier to change the value in one location in the source code if it should become necessary; when compiled, all occurrences of the symbolic constant will be changed to the new value. This gives the advantage of using a word (the symbolic constant) in the program code while the value is assigned only once at the beginning of the program. However, after the value has been replaced, it is impossible to change the value of a symbolic constant during execution of the program.

It is a convention for C programmers to use uppercase for symbolic constants while variables will normally be lower or mixed case.

ANSI codes for Clearing the Screen and Cursor Location   To clear the screen in C we can assign the ANSI escape code* for clearscreen to a symbolic constant. For this to work in a program you must have ANSI.SYS installed as part of your CONFIG.SYS. (The Config.Sys file must contain a line that declares: device = ansi.sys.)

symbolic constant An identifier specified in a preprocessor definition for which a value will be replaced prior to compilation.
macro Statement defined at preprocessor time that will be substituted directly into the code before compilation.
identifier A name given to a variable or a function.

---

*The escape sequences are established by ANSI (American National Standards Institute) and should not be confused with the standard for C, which was set by a different ANSI committee.

```
#define CLS printf("\033[2J")
```

This macro could now be used in a C program and the compiler would replace the macro with the expression. Notice that the expression can be anything, including a call to a function, such as the call to the `printf( )` in this example.

Another example is the ANSI code for locating the cursor on the screen. Although we are defining LOCATE as a macro there are still two items that will change each time the LOCATE is used in a program, the row and column of the cursor. This definition is:

```
#define LOCATE(r,c) printf("\033[%d;%dH",r,c)
```

To use this macro, we substitute the desired row and column number for the r and the c. The statement in the program might be

```
LOCATE(10,15);
```

Just before compilation, the LOCATE will be replaced with the `printf( )` while the 10 will be substituted for r and the 15 for c.

These symbolic constants and macros are defined prior to their use in a function and outside all functions. They may be defined between functions anywhere in the program but will only be visible to the program from the point at which they were defined. *Note:* The graphical C functions for clearing the screen and for positioning text are not standard ANSI C code. They are covered, though, in Chapter 13 on Graphics.

Self-Test

1. Define a preprocessor constant called TAX_RATE with a value of .065.
2. Create a constant called MESSAGE1 that will print Please try again.

Answers

1. `#define TAX_RATE .065`

   notice that there is no = sign and no semicolon.

2. `#define MESSAGE1 printf("Please try again")`
   once again there is no semicolon on the #define but when using this macro(constant), it will be necessary to use a semicolon at that point. The statement would become
   MESSAGE1;

Variables

A data item most frequently needs to be variable allowing the value of the data item to change during execution of the program or from one run of the program to the next. Variables may be one of several data types but are differentiated when they are declared. The programmer makes up names for the variables, called identifiers, but the names do not necessarily tell the type of data unless the programmer uses a variable name, which denotes the contents.

Rules for identifiers used in naming variables:

1. Up to 31 characters. (Some systems only recognize the first eight characters.)
2. May contain letters, numbers, and underscores.
3. No embedded spaces.
4. May begin with a letter or underscore.
5. C is case sensitive so it matters if you use upper- or lowercase.
6. No reserved words.

The type of data that the variable can hold will be specified when the variable is declared. C requires that all variables be declared before they are used (not true with C++). Variables may be declared before the main( ) or at the beginning of any block.

Declaring a Variable   To declare a variable the data type is followed by the variable name.

```
float amount;
int quantity;
```

declaration A statement that specifies an identifier to be used as a variable name and associates it with a data type.

The variable **declarations** are followed by a semicolon. Remember, all C statements and declarations will end with a ;.

The possible values for data types is not set by the ANSI standard but depends on the compiler implementation. The following data types are used to declare the variables to the given ranges on the PC.

char	-128 to 127 (ASCII characters)
int	-32,768 to 32,767
short	-32,768 to 32,767
long	-2,147,483,648 to 2,147,483,647
unsigned	0 to 65,535
signed	-32,768 to 32,767
float	7 digit precision
double	15 digit precision

There are additional data types available as extensions to standard ANSI C on most compilers.

String Variables

Strings are not really a separate type of variable. They are really an array of characters. To specify the maximum number of elements in an array, follow the variable name by the (number) in square brackets. To declare a field called name that will be 20 long, the declaration would be:

```
char name[20];
```

This field will actually hold only 19 characters. A character array should always be terminated with a null character. In the case of the string literal the machine supplies the null automatically. With a string variable it may be automatic in most cases but you must allow enough space in the array for it.

Declaring Multiple Variables of the Same Type

When multiple variables of the same type are declared, they may be declared with a single statement. Each of the variable names will be separated by a comma.

```
float amount, totalamount;
char letter, name[20];
```

Global and Local Variables   Where a variable is declared determines where the variable may be used. Variables that are declared outside of a function, usually before the main( ) function, are called **global** or external variables. Global variables may be used in any function after the point where they are declared, and any function may change the value of the variable. This is referred to as the **scope** or visibility of the variable. A global variable is visible to all functions after the line in which it is declared. The initial value of a global numeric variable is set to 0.

Variables that are declared inside a block are visible only to that block and can be changed only by statements in the block that. These variables are said to be **local** or internal. Local variables must be declared prior to the first program statement or instruction within the function or **block.** A block is a series of declarations and statements that are enclosed inside of curly braces. Local variables are not initialized.

global variable A variable that is visible to all functions after the point where the variable is declared.

scope Visibility of a variable or function.

local variable Only visible to the block in which the variable is declared.

block A unit of code enclosed within braces {}.

Example

```
int number;
float amount;

void main( )
{
  .
  .
}
```

Note that both of these variables have been declared prior to the `main( )` function. Therefore, both of these variables are global.

Self-Test

1. Declare an integer variable called number_days.
2. Are the following variable names valid? If not, why not?
   a. sale.amount
   b. %ofsales
   c. main( )
   d. valuable
3. In the following code, are the variables local or global?
```
main( )
{
    int i, index;
         . . .
}
```
4. Declare a variable that will hold a character address that may be up to 30 characters long.

Answers

1. int number_days;
2. a. invalid, cannot contain a period.
   b. invalid, the % sign is not a valid character.
   c. invalid, main( ) is reserved.
   d. valid.
3. The variables are both local because they are defined inside of the function.
4. char address [31];

Initializing Variables
Variables can be given a beginning value when they are declared.

```
int number = 0;
```

This statement would create the integer variable called `number` and assign the value of 0 to the variable at the same time.

Initializing String Variables

String variables can also be initialized when they are declared. Technically, the initialization assigns a character to each position of the array.

```
char word[6] = {'H','e','l','l','o','\Ø'};
```

Fortunately, we do not need to assign each position individually. The following declaration and initialization works exactly the same.

```
char word[6] = "Hello";
```

Remember to put the string literal in double quotes and allow for the trailing null character.

If a string variable is initialized when it is declared, it is not necessary to specify the size of the array. The proper amount of storage will be allocated according to the size of the assigned literal plus a null character.

```
char word[] = "Hello";
```

Multiple Variables Being Declared

When multiple variables are declared with the same statement, the initial value applies only to the one to which it is assigned.

```
float amount, totalamount = 100.0;
```

The value of 100.0 is stored in the variable called totalamount. The value of amount depends on whether it is global (defaults to 0.0) or local (undefined).

```
float amount = 0.0, totalamount = 0.0;
```

This statement will cause two variables to be declared and both will be initialized to 0.0.

Self-Test

What, if anything, is wrong with the following?

```
1. int number = 5.0;
2. int number
3. char letter = "c";
4. char letter[5] = "abcde";
5. char code = '\n';
```

Answers

1. The value 5.0 is not an integer.
2. The semicolon is missing.
3. A character constant is enclosed in single quotes.
4. There is no room left for the null character to terminate the string. The size should be 6.
5. Nothing.

Assigning Values to a Variable   Variables may also be assigned values after they have been declared. As in the previous declaration and initialization, the symbol that will be used for assignment is = (with the exception of string data). Let's repeat the earlier example, initializing the variable number as it is declared and assigning a value to amount separate from the declaration.

```
int number = 0;
float amount;

void main( )
{
 amount = 0.0;
 .
 .
 .

}
```

One note to make in this example is that the type of data that is assigned to a variable should match the data type of the field. The integer was initialized with the value 0 while the floating point variable was assigned the value 0.0.

Assigning a Value to Multiple Variables   It is possible to assign the same value to several variables in C at the same time. The assignment is performed from the right to the left.

```
int x,y,z;
x=y=z=1;
```

The assignment statement will assign a 1 to z, then the value of z is assigned to y, and finally the value of y is assigned to x. The significance of the sequence of the assignments may not seem important at this time, but will become very significant as more operators are introduced.

Self-Test

1. Declare a variable called total_pay as type float and initialize the variable to 0.
2. Assign a value of 0 to the field totamount.
3. Declare the variables malecount and femalecount as integer and initalize them to a beginning value of 0.
4. Set the values of two integer variables, total_possible and total_correct to 100, assume the fields have already been declared.

Answers

1. float total_pay = 0.0;
2. totamount = 0;

3. int malecount = 0, femalecount = 0;
4. total_possible = total_correct = 100;
   OR
   total_possible = 100;
   total_correct = 100;

Assigning Values to a String Variable

Strings cannot use the assignment operators because they are not really a data type but rather an array of type char. The strings must be assigned values through the use of a string function called `strcpy( )`. The string functions require the inclusion of the `string.h` file.

The string copy can be used to copy the contents of one string variable to another or it may be used to assign a string constant to a string variable. Remember that string constants are placed inside of double quotes.

The format of the `strcpy( )` function is:

```
strcpy(string1, string2)
```

where the value of string2 will be placed into string1. String2 may be a variable or a constant but string1 must be a variable in order to provide a memory address for the copied string to be stored.

```
strcpy(message,"Press Enter");
```

will place the string "Press Enter" into the variable called message.

```
strcpy(current_name,name);
```

places the value that is in the variable called `name` into the field called `current_name`.

```
strcpy(name,"quit");
```

This statement moves the string quit to the string called name.

The null character is automatically placed at the end of the string name. If there was a value in name before the `strcpy( )` it will be replaced when the function is executed. Notice that the movement is from string 2 to string 1. String 1 must be large enough to contain string 1 plus a terminating null character.

Moving a Portion of a String

The `strncpy( )` allows the number of characters to be moved from string 2 to string 1 to be specified. The format is

```
strncpy(string1, string2, number of characters)
```

A terminating null character is not added when the number of characters is less than the size of string2.

Assuming `name` contains the value "Mary Lou":

```
strncpy(account,name,3);
```

The first 3 characters of the variable `name` will be moved to the variable `account`.

Self-Test

1. Assign the string "Press any key to Continue" to the variable message1.
2. What is wrong with the following?

```
char salutation[10];
. . . . . . . . .
strcpy("Hello",salutation);
```

3. Would it be possible to use the statement

```
address = "123 Main Street";
```

4. What will happen in the following?

```
char abbrev[4], month[10];
. . . . . . . .
strncpy(abbrev,month,3);
```

Answers

1. strcpy(message1,"Press any key to Continue");
2. The first item inside of the parentheses for the strcpy( ) function must be a variable because it is the location where the second item will be copied to.
3. A string cannot use a numeric assignment symbol, the value must be copied into the variable using the strcpy( ).
4. The first three characters from the month string variable would be moved to the abbrev string field.

Printing Variables   Because variables are of different types, they should be treated differently when they are printed. Each type is actually stored differently, thereby requiring different handling.

To control the display of a variable in the `printf( )` function it is necessary to use a **format specifier** to tell C how the data is to be treated. The following `printf( )` function call illustrates this specifier.

format specifier A string that determines how the values of variables will appear when being displayed or printed.

```
printf("The amount is %f",amount);
```

The % symbol indicates that a specifier is to follow. The f tells the compiler that the data should be treated as a floating point. If you use the wrong specifier, you will usually get the wrong output. An error message is not generated. The `printf( )` will simply attempt to print according to the specifier that was used. Sometimes, we can use this to our advantage. With a character variable, we may want to print the character itself or use an integer specifier to get the equivalent ASCII code.

The following is the list of specifiers for the data types we are using:

%d or %i   int
%li   long integer
%f   float or double
%c   character
%s   string

It is also possible to use a specifier to print out an integer value in hexadecimal or octal notation.

Using the specifiers unaltered will print out the field contents right justified. The right justification rule holds true for numeric fields as well as for the string and character fields. Floating point fields will print with a default of six decimal positions.

```
printf("To print the integer 10 use %d",10);
```
constant

The constant 10 after the print string will replace the specifier %d inside of the string. This would print as

```
To print the integer 10 use 10
```

Another example:

```
float abcde = 45.23;
```

then

```
printf("%f",abcde);
```

will print as

```
45.230000
```
6

Notice that the print format string may contain words and specifiers. The values to be substituted into the specifiers are placed after the print string. Although the first example placed the constant 10 into a specifier, we would not normally do this. The constant 10 could have been placed inside of the print string because it will not change. In the second example, however, `abcde` is a variable where the value may change, so a specifier is used in the print string to indicate how and where to print the value of the variable.

Multiple variables may be printed with a single `printf( )` function call. The variables will be listed in the same sequence as their matching specifiers.

```
float num1 = 0.0, num2 = 1.0;
printf("num1 = %f\nnum2 = %f",num1,num2)
```

will produce

```
num1 = 0.000000
num2 = 1.000000
```

Notice that the first variable in the list replaced the first specifier and the second variable replaced the second specifier. The number of specifiers must match in number, type, and sequence to get the correct results.

Formatting Data

The size or format for the data to be printed may also be specified. A number inserted between the % and numeric specifier will determine the minimum width of the field for output. For example, `%4f` would create a float field at least four characters wide. The number of decimal positions (precision) may be specified as in `%4.2f` which means 4 wide and 2 positions after the decimal. The decimal portion will be rounded if necessary.

If we wish to have a number in the format `###.##`, we would specify the format as `%6.2f`. Notice that all of the characters count towards determining the width of the field, including the decimal point.

Format	Specifier
##.#	%4.1f
###.###	%7.3f
#.#	%3.1f

Example

2 - 1 . C

```
void main( )
{
   int intnumber = 1;
   float floatnumber = 1.0;
   char letter = 'C';
```

```
    printf("Print the integer %d, %3d\n", intnumber, intnumber );
    printf("Print the float %f, %4.2f\n",floatnumber,floatnumber);
    printf("Print the character %c, %d\n",letter,letter);
}
```

Output

```
Print the integer 1,     1
Print the float 1.000000, 1.00
Print the character C, 67
```

The integer prints first without any extra spaces on the %d. With %3d, a column 3 characters wide is printed with the 1 right justified and the remaining positions to the left—filled with spaces.

The floating point number prints with the default of six decimal positions when the format is %f, but it only prints 2 decimal positions when given the specifier %4.2f. *NOTE:* In C, the decimal portions may be rounded, but no significant digits will be lost.

The %c specifier printed out the letter C while the %d printed the ASCII code which is 67. Notice that a comma placed inside of the printf( ) string actually prints out. \n was used on each printf( ) string to cause the output for each printf( ) to appear on a newline.

```
void main( )
{
        float floatnum =1.26;
        printf("%5.1f",floatnum);
}
```

This example will cause the number to be rounded to 1 decimal place. The output will have 2 blank spaces before the 1 because of the column width, which is specified as 5 with 1 decimal position. The output is

```
  1.3
```

A Specifier that is Too Small

When the specifier in a numeric field is too small for the actual value that the field holds, no significant digits will be truncated. Although it would be better to have the specifier the correct size, a field that is too small will not cause erroneous output. In the following example, the float field specifier is too small but the answer remains the same as it did previously.

Example

```
void main( )
{
  int intnumber = 1;
  float floatnumber = 1.0;
  char letter = 'C';

  printf("Print the integer %d, %3d\n", intnumber, intnumber );
  printf("Print the float %f, %3.2f\n",floatnumber,floatnumber);
  printf("Print the character %c, %d\n",letter,letter);
}
```

Output

```
Print the integer 1,    1
Print the float 1.000000, 1.00
Print the character C, 67
```

Controlling Column Width

To control the width of a column of data we can make the minimum width large enough to allow for spaces between columns. Rather than just using %d for our integer field we might use %10d to print the number and extra spaces. The number will be right justified within that field. Therefore, if the number 12 is printed using the format %10d, the column will contain eight spaces followed by the two digits 12, for example:

```
printf(" %10d %10d %15.2f\n", integer1, integer2,float1);
```

Every time this function is called, the first integer will be right justified 11 spaces from the left edge (10 plus the space before the %). The second number will be right justified another 11 spaces to the right. The final float will print over another 16 spaces, with the decimal always in the same column. If we were to print several lines, they would all align.

```
  5   15     123.45
122    3       7.00
```

Formatting String Fields

The minimum width may also be specified for string fields. The number after the decimal determines the number of characters from the string that will be printed. A specifier of %15.10s indicates that the column width for the field will be 15 wide, but only 10 characters from the string are to be printed. Any other characters in the string will be truncated from the right side.

%10s   a string field minimum 10 characters wide

%10.5s   the print field is 10 characters wide but only 5 characters
          print

With the specifier %10s, the width of the string will be a minimum of 10 characters. If the string is shorter, the extra positions will be padded with spaces. If the string is longer, the entire string will be printed. This will not work well when we are trying to align a column of information unless the string never exceeds the minimum column width that is specified.

Using the %10.5s, the column width will never vary because only 5 characters will print. This method would allow a guaranteed number of spaces between columns but it may cause some of the string data to be truncated.

The alignment of string output is the same as with the numeric fields. The data will be right justified. A minus sign can be used with any field to change to left justification.

%-10s   minimum width of 10 characters, left justified

%-20.10s   field width 20, 10 characters printed, data is left justified

Example

```
#define CLS printf("\033[2J")

int number = 0;
float amount;

void main( )
{
   amount = 0.0;

  CLS;
  printf("%15.2f   %5d",amount,number);
}
```

Output

```
           0.00         0
Scale
12345678901234567890123456789 0
```

The 0.00 ends at column 15 because of the 15 after the %. There are two decimal places as requested.

Because the printf( ) has 2 spaces before the %5d, 0 is printed 7 columns over. Every space inside of the quotes on a printf( ) will be printed in addition to those spaces requested with the specifier.

The format for printing out variables using the `fprintf( )` is the same as it is for the `printf( )`. The only difference is the need to specify the output stream.

Screen Layout Forms and Printer Spacing Charts

Two forms are available to aid in determining column widths and placement of information on the screen or on a printed report. The screen is 24 lines by 80 characters in text mode. For 8½" wide paper, an 80 character width works well also.

To design our output for the screen or for the printer, it will be easier to know how many spaces to leave if we visualize the spaces in relation to the size of the screen or the page. The screen layout form (see Figure 2-1) can be used to place the titles and headings in the desired columns and align the spaces for the data to be printed below the headings (see Figure 2-2).

There are printer spacing charts that will allow for up to 132 or more characters across the page. If we are printing our report in portrait (normal) rather than in landscape (sideways) mode, the printer spacing chart will be more than we need (see Figure 2-3 on page 42).

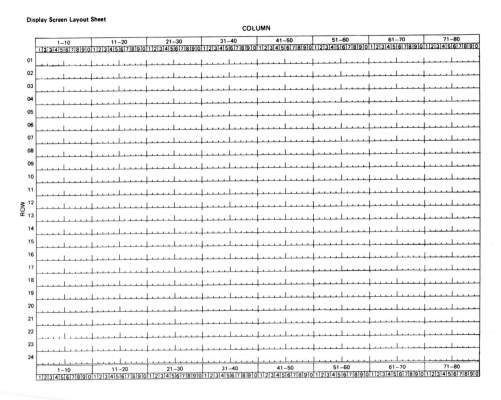

FIGURE 2-1
Display Screen Layout

Display Screen Layout Sheet

FIGURE 2-2
Example Screen Layout

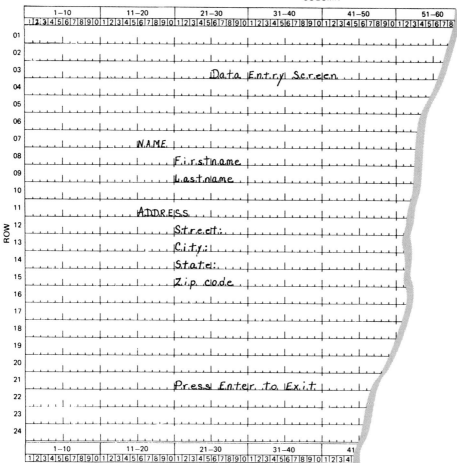

Self-Test

What output will the following produce given:

```
int number = 7;
float amount = 2.25;
char letter = 'c',name[15] = "Jack Spratt";
```

1. printf("%-15s%10.2f",name,amount);
2. printf("%15s %10.3f\n",name,amount);
3. printf("%-10.5s %4i",name,number);
4. printf("\n\t%c\n",letter);
5. fprintf(stdprn,"\n%-25s %10.2f %10i",name,amount,number);
6. fprintf(stdprn,"\n%-25s %10.2f %10i",number,name,amount);

FIGURE 2-3
Sample Print Chart

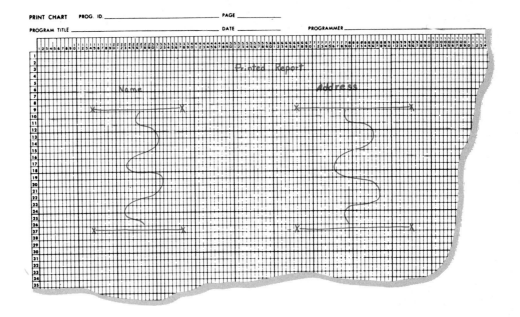

Answers

1. The name is left justified in 15 spaces—amount right justified.

```
Jack Spratt     2.25
```

2. The name is right justified in 15 spaces and the amount is right justified in 10 spaces.

```
Jack Spratt     2.250
```

3. Only five characters will be printed from the string and they will be left justified. The number will be right justified over four spaces.

```
Jack      7
```

4. On a new line, one tab will be printed and then the character C

```
      C
```

5. The name will be left justified and then followed by spaces for a total column width of 25 characters. The amount will be printed in the rightmost four positions of a column 10 wide. The number will be printed in the rightmost position of a column 10 wide.

6. Strange stuff—the format specifiers are not in the proper order for the data, so C will attempt to print accordingly.

Entering Data   Two functions used to obtain data into variables are `scanf( )` and `gets( )`.

scanf( )

The `scanf( )` function requires the use of a specifier to indicate the way in which the data is to be handled. The specifier will indicate the type of data that is being entered but will not be formatted because the specifier does not have control over the format of the data being stored but only over the type—integer, float, or character.

```
scanf("conversion specifier",variable address);
```

The conversion specifiers will be the same as the ones used for the `printf( )` function. To tell the computer to put the data at the address of the variable, the & symbol will precede the variable name. This is true for all types of variables with the exception of string data. The reason strings are different will become clear later.

```
int number = 0;
float amount;

void main( )
{
   scanf("%f",&amount);
   printf("%15.2f    %5d",amount,number);
}
```

Notice that the size is not required in the input format string (`scanf( )`) but merely the type of data, which in this case is float. On the output line (`printf( )`) both the size and the type of field was specified for the two fields, because the print format is being indicated.

The data entry into the variable specified by a `scanf( )` call function will be terminated when the user presses an enter or any white space. After a blank, `scanf( )` does not store any more information into the variable but execution of the program will not continue until the enter key is pressed. Since the characters after a blank are not stored in the variable, `scanf( )` will not work well for entering in information, such as a name. When entering a blank space between the first name and the last name, `scanf( )` will accept the data as two items rather than one. A blank space is considered to be a "white space." To eliminate this problem, it is possible to use a different function for the input of string data or to enclose the input data in quotes.

gets( )

Another alternative for obtaining strings is the gets( ) function. `gets ( )` does not require a specifier because the function is written to handle only string data. The syntax for the `gets ( )` is

```
gets(string variable)
```

The `gets ( )` function will terminate input when the enter key is pressed. The string can include blank spaces because the input is not terminated by space.

Prompts

Calls to `scanf ( )` or `gets ( )` are usually preceded by a `printf ( )` statement to **prompt** the user for specific data input. It is not possible to include a prompt or question as part of the `scanf ( )` or `gets ( )` function. The printing of a question or prompt is a separate instruction from the input of a response.

Example 1

```
char name[20];
. . . .
printf("Enter your name");
gets(name);
```

Example 2

```
float acctnum;
. . . . . . .
printf("Account Number:   ");
scanf("%f",&acctnum);
```

These examples could be improved by controlling the position of the cursor. This can be accomplished by the preprocessor defined constants referred to earlier for clearing the screen and positioning the cursor.

Combining the gets( ) and scanf( ) functions

If you need to place a `gets ( )` after a `scanf ( )` function, you will find that the program does not pause to get the data for the string variable specified in the `gets ( )` function. This is caused because the buffer already has data in it.

To correct the situation, you must clear the buffer. This can be done with the ANSI standard function `fflush ( )`.

```
fflush(stream);
```

In our case, we need to clear the input (keyboard) buffer. The input stream for the keyboard is stdin. Therefore, the statement preceding the `gets( )` function will be an `fflush(stdin)`.

```
fflush(stdin);
gets(name);
```

When the same variable has data repeatedly put into it by the program, it is necessary to use `fflush( )`. This will occur frequently when we use loops.

Sample Problem: Write a program that will clear the screen and ask the user to enter their name and social security number. The information will then be output to the printer.

This will require us to have two variables: one for the name and one for the social security number. Since neither of these is to be used in calculations they will not be numeric. Both will contain multiple characters so we will make them both character arrays. It is up to the programmer to select names for the variables we will call them name and social_sec_number.

To clear the screen we define the ANSI escape code as a preprocessor directive. In addition we will define a second ANSI escape code as a macro to locate the cursor on the screen.

Because we are using `fprintf( )` it will be necessary to include the `stdio.h` file.

```
Programmed by:
Date:
Purpose:   Enter SSN and name from
           screen and print info on
           printer
#include <stdio.h>
#define CLS printf("\033[2J")
#define LOCATE(r,c) printf("\033[%d;%dH",r,c)

char name[20],social_sec_number[12];
/* remember the extra space for the null*/

void main( )
{
CLS;
   LOCATE (10,20);
   printf("Please enter your name:    ");
   gets(name);
   LOCATE (12,20);
```

```
      printf("Social Security Number     ");
      gets(social_sec_number);
      fprintf(stdprn,"Name: %s\n",name);
      fprintf(stdprn,"SSN:  %s",social_sec_number);
}
```

A Better Input Screen

When writing programs, it is important to consider the needs and preferences of the user. A good program will be used much more often than a poor one. This consideration is also important in the design of screens.

Most people are familiar with completing a form of one type or another. It would then be more familiar to the user to design the screen to appear like a blank form. It is disconcerting to answer one question, press enter, and then have another question appear. Therefore, it would be preferable to print all of the questions on the screen prior to asking for the inputs.

By using the command to locate the cursor, we can print a nice "form" on the screen and then relocate the cursor behind each of these questions to allow the user to "answer" (scanf( ) or gets( )) each question (see Figure 2-4).

```
/*              set up the screen "form"        */
CLS;
LOCATE(10,20);
```

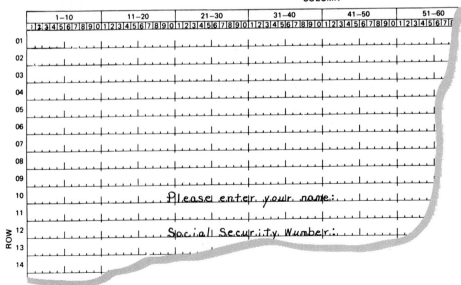

FIGURE 2-4
Input Screen Layout

```
printf("Please enter your name:   ");
LOCATE(12,20);
printf("Social Security Number:   ");

/*                    input the information          */
LOCATE(10,50);
gets(name);
LOCATE(12,50);
gets(social_sec_number);
```

Screen Output

```
Please enter your name:          _
Social Security Number:
```

The cursor is positioned after the first question, but the user can see what both questions are before responding to any prompts.

Other Screen Design Concerns

Other factors to keep in mind when designing screen layouts:

1. Do not scroll. People are accustomed to the concept of turning the page, not to having one line disappear and another print at the bottom. To accomplish this, do not locate the cursor below row 23.
2. Give the user sufficient time to respond. Let the user have control over time. The input functions will do this, waiting patiently for a response.
3. Use on-screen instructions to reduce the demands on the user's short-term memory.
4. Do not try to use humor.
5. Use specific, clear language that is familiar to the user.
6. If there is a lengthy pause while the computer is processing information, print a message on the screen indicating what is being done.

The puts( ) Function

The puts( ) function, put string, is used when a message is to be printed that does not contain any format specifiers. The puts() function accepts a single argument, the string that is to be printed. This string may be either a string literal or a character array. The format is:

```
puts(string);
```

This puts( ) function could be used in place of the printf( ) when displaying screen prompts. The output device for a puts( ) is normally the monitor, just the same as the printf( ).

Examples

```
puts("Press Any Key");
puts(name);
```

Self-Test

1. Assuming that CLS and LOCATE(r,c) have been defined, write the prompt screen to enter the following data:
Last Name:
First Name:
Phone:

Answers

1.
```
CLS;
LOCATE(10,10)
puts("Last Name:");
LOCATE(12,9);
puts("First Name:");
LOCATE(14,14);
puts("Phone:");
```

EXAMPLE PROGRAM

Write a program that will clear the screen and ask the user to enter their name and social security number. Output the information to the printer.

Notice that this program nicely divides into logical parts (see Figure 2-5). The first section sets up the screen form, then the information is gathered and then the information is sent to the printer.

The following table depicts the organization of this program.

Input (Screen)	Processing None	Output (Printer)
Name		Name
Social Security Number		SSN

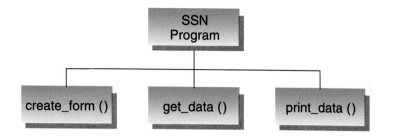

FIGURE 2-5
Hierarchy Chart for Social
Security Number
Program

```c
/*    A program that will create a screen form for
           entering employee information, get the
           data from the keyboard, and print the
           information on the printer    */

#include <stdio.h>
#define CLS printf("\033[2J");
#define LOCATE(r,c) printf("\033[%d;%dH",r,c);

void create_form( );
void get_data( );
void print_info( );

char name[20], social_sec_number[12];
/* remember the extra space for the null*/

void main( )
{
 create_form( );
 get_data( );
 print_info( );
}

void create_form( )
{
 /*              set up the screen "form"        */
 CLS;
 LOCATE(10,20);
 printf("Please enter your name:  ");
 LOCATE(12,20);
 printf("Social Security Number:  ");
}
```

```
void get_data( )
{
 /*              input the information          */
 LOCATE(10,50);
 gets(name);
 LOCATE(12,50);
 gets(social_sec_number);
}

void print_info( )
{
 /*              print the information          */
 fprintf(stdprn,"Name: %s\n",name);
 fprintf(stdprn,"SSN:  %s",social_sec_number);
 CLS;
}
```

Programming Style   Following the declaration of variables, a blank line is left to separate the declarations from the actual statements in the program. Although the program will run the same without the blank line, it improves readability of the program. Notice in the examples in this chapter that a blank line follows the preprocessor directives and another follows the declarations of the global variables prior to the main( ) function.

If the variables are declared inside a function we will leave one blank line between the variables and the first instruction.

```
void main( )
{
  int number;

  scanf("%d", &number);
  printf("The number entered is %3d\n", number);
}
```

Programming/Debugging Hint

Header Files

Just as the #include is used to access standard libraries, it may also be used to access your own collection of functions or definitions.

The #defines for the CLS and the LOCATE will be used in many programs. Rather than typing in the code in each one of the programs, you may wish to create your own header file.

The standard convention is for all header files to end with the extension .h. Therefore, the name for your header file should also use the .h extension.

To create a header file, type in the declarations that will be a part of the file into a text editor. This file will not contain a `main( )` function because when it is included in another program there would be two `main( )` functions. After you have typed the statements, save the file using an appropriate .h extension.

```
#define CLS printf("\033[2J")
#define LOCATE(r,c) printf("\033[%d;%dH",r,c)
```

Assume that this file has been created and saved as `mine.h.` In future programs we can use an include directive to incorporate the mine.h header file and the CLS and LOCATE will be a part of that program. The instruction would be:

```
#include "a:mine.h"
```

Notice that this include contains quotes instead of the normal braces around the header file name. The quotation marks allow the programmer to specify the path or drive where the file is located. In this example, the mine.h file should be located on the A: drive.

Reverse Image on the Screen

Sometimes you may wish to highlight a message or a prompt on the screen. This can be done by reversing the background and foreground colors. If you are printing in white characters on a black background, then the reverse image will place characters in black on a white background.

Reverse and normal video can be accomplished with ANSI escape sequences. It will be easier to use the sequences if we once again call on the preprocessor directive #define.

```
#define REVERSE printf("\033[7m")
#define NORMAL printf("\033[0m")
```

When you want to print in reverse, type REVERSE, call printf( ) - usually without a newline, and then type NORMAL.

```
REVERSE;
printf("Name:")
NORMAL;
```

The reverse image escape sequence may be used with either printf( ) or puts( ).

block
constant
data type
declaration
escape sequence

format specifier
global variable
identifier
local variable
macro

prompt
scope
string literal
symbolic constant
variable

CHAPTER SUMMARY

The information or data that is used in a program can be variable or it can be constant. The types of data in C are integer, long integer, float, double, and character.

When printing variables, with `printf( )` it is necessary to use a format specifier. The specifier tells the compiler the type of data as well as the way in which it should be formatted.

Data entry can be accomplished through the functions `gets( )` and `scanf( )`. Both of these functions allow us to get data from the keyboard. The scanf() can input various types of data and requires the use of specifiers. The `gets( )` is designed for the entry of string data.

String data is stored as an array of character data, containing one or more characters. Character arrays are terminated by a null character.

REVIEW QUESTIONS

1. Differentiate between a constant and a variable.
2. Name three data types available in C.
3. What is a symbolic constant?
4. Name two functions that can be used for obtaining data from the keyboard.
5. What is the purpose of the format specifier in a printf( ) statement?
6. List the rules for naming variables.
7. What two functions could be used to input string data?
8. What is a hierarchy chart and what is it used for?
9. Why would it be desirable to create a header file?

EXERCISES

1. Write a program that will allow students to input their name, major, and current number of units or credit hours. Make the name and major fields string while units should be a floating point. Send the data to the printer in the following format:

```
Name:     xxxxxxxxxxxxxxxxxxxx
Major:    xxxxxxxxxxxxxxxxxxx
Units:    ##.#
```

2. Create an invoice heading for the Ace Paper Company. The program should prompt the user for their name and address. The billing heading should print as:

```
              Ace Paper Company
              111 Main Street
              Richville, Ca
```

```
Bill To:   XXXXXXXXXXXXXXXXXX
           XXXXXXXXXXXXXXXXXX
           XXXXXXXXXXXXXXXXXX
```

3. Write a program that will clear the screen and print the prompts for first name, last name, and phone number. After all of the prompts have been written to the screen, locate the cursor after each prompt and input the necessary information. Do a print screen to show the screen with just the prompts and a print screen to show a completed screen.

4. Write a program that will print out a mailing label. The input screen should be designed to prompt for the following:

```
          Name:
          Title:
Street Address:
          City:
         State:
      Zip Code:
```

The label should be printed on four lines, with one blank line preceding the label and one blank line following it. It will be necessary to combine city, state, and zip code on a single line, and to print the appropriate comma and spaces.

Name
Title
Street Address
City, State Zip Code

5. Write a program that will create a cover sheet for any assignment.

   Input: Create a prompt screen that will ask for the author's name, course title, assignment number, and the date.

   Output: Center the appropriate information neatly on an 8 $\frac{1}{2}$ by 11 sheet of paper. Use a border around the information if you wish.

6. Write a program that uses reverse video for the prompts and normal video for the responses in a program that requests patient information.

   Input: First Name
                     Last Name
                     Street
                     City
                     State
                     Zip Code
                     Phone Number for Home
                     Work Number
                     Insurance Company

Policy Number
(Yes or No)
Hospitalized during past 12 months
Currently taking medication
Family history of heart disease
Family history of cancer

Output: Print a neatly designed report of the information to the printer.

7. Write a program that inputs both numeric and character data(string) to print up a current price update. Use the gets( ) for the string and the scanf ( ) to obtain the numeric data.

Input: The input will include the product name, the model number, the new price, and the effective date of the increase/decrease. Set up a screen to prompt for the information using reverse and normal video.

Output: Create a memo sheet to the attention of the salesperson giving the price update information.

HAYLEY OFFICE SUPPLIES

Using the data from the letterhead, create an invoice header. The invoice header will contain the company name and address for Hayley Office Supplies. It will also contain the name and address of the client. The client name and address will change on each invoice, so these fields will be input items. Use a variable for name, street address, city, state, zip code, and date.

Be sure to create appropriate prompt screens for the entry of the data.

Sample Output

Date: xx/xx/xx

Hayley Office Supplies
1111 Main Street
Chino, California 91710

Sold To:

Bob Smith
10252 Hale Ave.
West Somecity, CA 91111

CHAPTER

CHAPTER OBJECTIVES

By the end of this chapter, you should be able to:

■ **Recognize and be able to evaluate conditions using the relational operators.**

■ **Understand the significance of implied conditions.**

■ **Combine conditions using logical operators or nested conditions.**

■ **Discover the conditional operator available in C.**

■ **Perform string comparisons.**

■ **Create loops with the *while* statement.**

Iteration— Creating a Loop

- **Recognize the significance of comparisons of strings that may contain upper- or lowercase characters.**

- **Obtain loops with exit conditions using the *do* loop.**

- **Introduce *for* loops.**

- **Create a report program.**

CHAPTER OVERVIEW

All of the programs to this point have been sequentially executed. In this chapter, the concept of iteration will be introduced, allowing statements to be executed multiple times.

Relational operators will be introduced to create loops that use conditions to exit. The looping process will allow for conditions at the beginning or the ending of the loop.

Using loops we will be able to produce a report complete with heading, body of the report, and a summary.

relational operator An operator used in comparisons such as greater than, less than, or equal to (>, <, =).

Relational operators may be used to compare data items. It is possible to compare two variables or a variable and a constant. The comparison determines the relationship between the two fields.

The relational operators in C are:

<	less than	<=	less than or equal to
>	greater than	>=	greater than or equal
==	equal to	!=	not equal to

It is important to take note that the comparison for equality in C is denoted by the operator ==. If a single = is used, the result will be an assignment, not a comparison.

The not operator ! may be used to find the logical not of conditional expression.

Examples of conditions:

```
hours == 40.00     compare hours and 40 for equality
bonus != 1         check if bonus is NOT equal to 1
```

The relational operators may be used on character or numeric data. You may not use the operators on an array of characters. Comparisons of strings require the use of string functions.

Comparing Numeric Data

```
int count;

                count == 0

float number;

                number < 2000.00
```

expression A part of a statement.

These comparisons are **expressions** that will become a part of a statement. The expression is not followed by a semicolon because it is not a complete statement.

Comparing Character Data

```
item == 'x'
item != '\0'      checks for non-null character
```

To determine if the character condition is true or false, we compare the value of the character as it is positioned in the ASCII code table(for DOS machines). This means that numeric characters would come before uppercase characters, which are then followed by lowercase characters.

Selected ASCII Codes

0	NULL	38	&	60	<	
8	Backspace	39	'	61	=	
9	Tab	40	(	62	>	
10	Linefeed	41	)	63	?	
12	FormFeed	42	*	64	@	
13	Carriage Return	43	+	65–90	A–Z	
27	Escape	44	,	91	[	
32	Space	45	–	92	\	
33	!	46	.	93	]	
34	"	47	/	94	^	
35	#	48–57	0–9	95	_	
36	$	58	:	96	`	
37	%	59	;	97–122	a–z	

Examples

```
char letter1 = 'A';
char letter2 = 'a';
```

The expression

```
letter2 > letter1
```

is true because the ASCII code of 'A' is 65 while the code for 'a' is 97.

```
char symbol1 = '?';
char symbol2 = '!';
```

The expression

```
symbol1 > symbol2
```

is true because the ASCII code for ? is 63 while the ASCII code for ! is 33.

Self-Test

Are the following expressions true or false?

```
1. float num1 = 5.00;
   int num2 = 5;
      num1 == num2
```

```
2. char letter1 = 'A';
   char letter2 = 'C';
   letter1 > letter2
3. char letter1 = 'A';
   char letter2 = ' ';
      letter1 > letter2;
```

4. Are the following conditions true or false given that:

```
int count = 0;
float number = 15.75;
char  letter = 'x';
a. count < 10
b. number == 0
c. letter = 'x'
d. count !=0
```

Answers

1. True, the values are both equivalent.
2. False, C comes after A in the alphabet, which makes C greater than A
3. True, the space comes before the letter A in the ASCII code.
4. (a) True, count (0) is less than 10. (b) False, number is not equal to 0.
   (c) Careful, this assigns x to letter, rather than testing equality. C will still
   determine whether this is true or false, as will be explained next. (d.)
   False, count is equal to 0.

Implied Conditions—True or False

Following Boolean logic, a condition will be considered to be true if it returns a nonzero value—Ø will evaluate to false. This allows us to imply conditions in a sense.

```
amount != 0
```

If this condition is true, the computer will return a value of 1 while a 0 will be returned if the condition is false. Therefore, it would be possible to say:

```
amount      /*true if amount is not equal to 0*/
```

This will be true as long as amount is not equal to 0, because if the value of amount is not zero it is the same as a true, while a value of zero is equivalent to a false.

This means that in C, anything could be used as a condition, whether or not it contains a relational operator.

Example

```
x = 0        will be false.
```

0 is assigned to x, not compared to it. The value of x is then 0 which evaluates to false.

The Logical Operators

To test for multiple conditions, the relational operators may be combined together. The logical operators for combining conditions are:

```
&&        And
||        Or
||
```

The && operator requires that both conditions evaluate to true for the condition to test as true. With the || operator, only one condition needs to be true, but both may be.

```
amount == 0 || number == 3.0
```

This condition will test if amount is equal to 0 or if number is equal to 3. The condition will be true if either amount is 0 or if number is 3. It would, of course, be true if both amount and number are equal to 0 and 3 respectively. Conditions combined with || or && are frequently referred to as **compound conditions.**

compound condition
Combines more than one condition using and/or.

Precedence of And and Or in Compound Conditions

The && and || operators may be used together in the same expression if more than two conditions are to be tested. In this situation, it will be necessary to understand the precedence of operators to determine the results of the relational test. The && operator is of a higher precedence and the conditions around the && will be tested first to see if both are true.

The order of precedence can be overridden with the use of parentheses.

Examples

Assume that anum is 5, bnum is 6, and cnum is 7

```
anum < 5                                    false
bnum == 6                                   true
(anum < 5 || bnum == 6)                     true
(anum < 5 && bnum == 6)                     false
(cnum < 10)                                 true
(anum < 5 || bnum == 6 && cnum < 10)        true
```

```
(anum < 5 && bnum == 6 || cnum < 10)          true
(anum < 5 && bnum == b && cnum < 10)           false
```

Self-Test

Will the following conditions be true or false given that

```
int amount = 0;
float number = 3.0;
```

1. amount == 0 || number == 0.0
2. amount != number && amount == 0
3. amount > number && number < 10.0
4. amount = 0
5. amount == 0 && number < 10.0 || amount > number

Answers

1. True, amount is equal to zero.
2. True, amount is not equal to number and amount is equal to 0
3. False, amount is not greater than number. For an && to be true, both conditions must be true.
4. False, this assigns the value 0 to amount, and as a value 0 is false.
5. True, both && conditions are true, amount is 0 and number is less than 10. Since the and is evaluated first, it does not matter what the second condition on the or is, we already have one true for the or.

String Comparisons

As already indicated, strings cannot be compared using the relational operators. Instead they require the use of special functions designed for handling string data. The basic function used to compare strings is strcmp( ).

The format of strcmp( ) is:

```
strcmp(string1, string2)
```

The strings may be variables or literals. The function returns an integer greater than 0 if string 1 is greater than string 2, 0 if the strings are equal, or a negative integer if string 1 is less than string 2.

```
if(strcmp(salary_status,"salary") == 0)
    salary_pay( );
```

Notice that the test for equality checks for a 0. If you wish to test if two items are not equal the condition would be

```
strcmp(string1,string2) != 0.
```

It is also possible to compare a specified number of characters from each string with the `strncmp( )` function. The format is:

```
strncmp(string1, string2, number of characters)
```

The statement

```
(strncmp(item,"A11",3) == 0)
```

compares the first 3 characters of the variable item with the characters A11.

Comparing Strings and Ignoring the Case   C provides a function that will compare the contents of two strings without regard to the case of the two strings. When ignoring the case, the character 'A' would be considered to be equivalent to the character 'a'. This function is the `stricmp( )` function. The form is the same as the `strcmp( )` function which has two strings as the parameters.

```
stricmp(string1, string2)
```

where string1 and string2 may be string variables or string literals.

Example

```
char word[] = {"Almost"};
```

The expression

```
stricmp(word,"ALMOST") == 0
```

is true.

Finding the Length of a String   Sometimes it will be necessary to know how long a string is. Remember that the size set in the declaration is the maximum size of the array. The actual string value is terminated by a null character. The **string length** is the number of characters up to but not including the null character. To determine the actual string length use `strlen( )`. The format is

string length   Number of characters in a string.

```
strlen(string1)
```

The only parameter required by this function is the name of the string. It may be used as part of an assignment or part of a condition. The following example assigns the number of characters in name to the variable `string_size`.

```
string_size = strlen(name);
```

The `strlen( )` returns an integer, the length in bytes. Therefore, we can use the assignment operator to store this value in an integer variable, if desired.

We could also use the `strlen( )` function in a condition to determine if a string contained a specific number of characters.

```
strlen(name) != 0;
```

This condition checks to see if the name array contains a value. If name is empty it only contains the null and the `strlen( )` function would return a count of 0 which would make this condition false.

Self-Test

1. Is the following statement true or false?
   ```
   char name[] = "Mary Lou";
   ```
   ....
   ```
   strcmp(name,"quit") != 0
   ```
2. Code a condition that will be true if enter is pressed for the name prompt.
3. Write the expression that will compare the array name with the string "END" and return a match regardless of the case of the text that is entered into name.

Answers

1. True, the name is not equal to quit.
2. a. `strcmp(name,"") !=0`
   b. `strlen(name) == 0`
3. `stricmp(name,"END")`

Combining String Fields—Concatenation   The combining of string fields is known as **concatenation**. A longer string is formed that is the combination of string 1 and string 2.

```
strcat(string1, string2);
```

It might be necessary to have several successive `strcat( )` functions.

```
strcat(last_name, first_name);
```

The previous example does not put a space between the first and last names. It would be better to use:

```
strcpy(full_name,first_name);
strcat(full_name," ");
strcat(full_name,last_name);
```

String 1 must be large enough to hold all of the parts. If it is not you may have very unpredictable results. When C prints a string, it starts at the first character of

concatenation   Combining two string values.

the string and prints until it encounters a null character. If the field does not have a null, it will continue printing the next items in memory, whatever they may be, until a null character is found.

A partial string may be concatenated to a string by using the strncat ( ) function, which has the following format:

```
strncat(string1, string2, number of characters);
```

The specified number of characters from string 2 will be concatenated to string1.

To combine a last name with a first initial, the strcpy ( ) would be used along with the strncat ( ).

```
strcpy(name, last_name);
strcat(name, ", ");
strncat(name, first_name);
strcat(name,'.');
```

Self-Test

1. Code the statement(s) that will concatenate the address fields to combine the variables city, state, and zip so that the variable address will contain the city followed by a comma and a space, which will then be followed by the state, one space, and then the zip code.
2. What will the following print?

   ```
   char word1[] = "Programming";
   char word2[] = "Ready";
   char combined[20];
   . . . . . . . . . . . . .
   strcpy(combined, word2);
   strcat(combined, " to ");
   strncat(combined, word1, 7);
   printf("%s", combined);
   ```

3. Write the statement to concatenate the first five characters from word1 with word2.

Answers

1. ```
   strcpy(address,city);
   strcat(address,", ");
   strcat(address,state);
   strcat(address," ");
   strcat(address,zip);
   ```
2. Ready to Program
3. `strncpy(word2, word1, 5);`
   ```

loop Code which may be executed repeatedly as necessary.

To make our programs more useful, it is necessary to create a **loop** so that the instructions in the program can be repeated as many times as necessary to complete the job. If we were processing data for just one transaction, we probably would not need a computer or a program. In business applications we almost always need to repeat the program instructions numerous times.

Two of the loop constructs in C are the *do* loop and the *while* loop (see Figure 3-1). Both of these loop constructs will continue executing the loop instructions until a condition is met.

while tests the condition at the beginning of the loop while a *do* tests the condition at the end of the loop. In other words, the *while* has an **entry condition** and the *do* has an exit condition.

entry condition A condition at the beginning of a loop that determines when the loop will be terminated, possibly will never be executed.

exit condition A condition at the end of a loop that determined when the loop will be terminated: the loop will always be executed at least once.

With an **exit condition,** the condition to determine when to terminate the loop is at the end of the loop. The statement(s) inside a *do* loop **will always be executed at least once** before the condition is tested at the end of the loop.

A *while* loop will test the condition before the loop is entered, so it is possible that the statements in a while loop will never be executed.

The While Loop

The *while* loop is the loop form in C that has an entry condition. This means that the condition will be tested prior to the loop being performed. If the condition is true, the body of the loop will be executed. Otherwise, the program will continue execution at the statement after the loop.

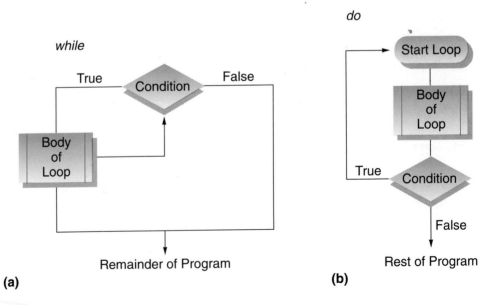

FIGURE 3-1
(a) Flowchart of while
(b) Flowchart of do

Format of the unblocked *while* loop

```
while(condition)
    statement;
```

This form of the *while* loop will *only execute one statement.* As a statement, the loop consists of only one statement prior to the semicolon.

Usually, the body of the loop will contain more than one statement. If more than one statement is to belong to the body of the loop, the statements must be blocked. Braces {} will be required to form the block around the body of the loop.

```
while(condition)
{
    statement;
    statement;....
}
```

It is an excellent technique always to use braces around the body of the loop. This will assure that the braces are not forgotten when more than one statement is intended to be included within the loop.

Do not place a semicolon after the while (condition) or the loop terminates at the semicolon. Then you would have an empty loop. If the condition has not been met, it will be an infinite loop because there is no way for it to end.

```
while(condition);      /* the loop contains no statements */
{
    statement;
}
```

Infinite Loops

You must be sure that there is some way for the condition to be met inside the loop or any loop could become infinite.

Example of possible infinite loop:

```
int number;

void main( )
{          /* an infinite loop
  scanf("%d",&number);
    while(number != 5)
      {
      printf("%d", number);
      }
}
```

This program will cause an infinite loop if 5 is not the number entered, because the `scanf( )` is not part of the loop and will only be executed one time.

To solve this problem we could create a block containing the `scanf( )`. This would appear as follows:

```
while(number != 5)
        {
          scanf("%d",&number);
          printf("%d",number);
        }
```

However, this will print 5 because the number will be printed before it loops back to the *while* where the relational test is made. This may not be what was intended.

This problem will be even more apparent with a test for a string condition.

```
while((stricmp(name,"quit")!=0)
{
      gets(name);
      printf("%-30s \n",name);
}
```

Once again, the condition is tested after the `printf( )` has been executed so "quit" will print before the loop is terminated.

priming input   The first input typically placed before the detail processing loop.

Priming Input   A better alternative would be to use a **priming input** and to put the `scanf( )` as the last statement in the loop. This means that the `scanf( )` at the end of the block of the loop will be the last statement to be executed before the condition is tested by the *while* condition. By obtaining input just before the end of the loop we can terminate execution of the loop as soon as the user enters the value we are testing for.

```
char name[20];

void main( )
{
      gets(name);                      /* priming input*/
      while(stricmp(name,"quit")!=0)
          {
            printf("%s\n",name);
            gets(name);         /*inputs next name*/
          }
}
```

This program gets a name from the keyboard and prints it on the screen. The program will loop until the name is equal to "quit".

Actually, the previous program will not get out of the loop because the program execution will not stop to allow for a name to be entered a second time. This is caused because the keyboard buffer contains data.

Flushing the Buffer for Strings in a Loop   When string data is entered in a loop, it is necessary to use the `fflush( )` to ensure that a new entry will be made through the loop each time. The `fflush( )` function can be used for any device but we will be concerned for now with the keyboard buffer. To empty the keyboard buffer place the command `fflush(stdin)` inside of the loop. A logical place to place this statement would be immediately prior to the `gets( )` function call.

Placing the Input Function Inside the Condition Expression   C does not limit the contents of the parentheses of the *while* to just a condition. It may be a complete statement as long as it contains a condition. Notice in the following example that the input function of `gets( )` is located inside the comparison. This causes the name to be entered, the string comparison to be made, and the loop condition to be tested in the same statement.

```
#include <string.h>
char name[20];

void main( )
{
        /*   all inputs for name are inside of condition */
        while(strcmp((gets(name)),"quit")!=0)
        {
            printf("%s\n",name);
            fflush(stdin);      /* clear buffer for name*/
        }
}
```

Self-Test

1. Code a *while* loop that will obtain print a number until 999 is entered.
2. What will the following print?

```
char word[10];
while(stricmp(word,"End")!=0)
    {
        printf("Hello");
        fflush(stdin);
        gets(word);
    }
```

3. Rewrite question two and place the gets( ) function call inside the condition.
4. Write a loop that will input a name and print the name until the Enter key is pressed.

Answers

1.
```
scanf("%d",number);
while(number <> 999)
    {
        printf("%d ", number);
        puts("Type in a number or 999 to quit);
        scanf("%d",number);
    }
```

2. Hello will print until End is typed regardless of case.

3.
```
char word[10];
while(stricmp(gets(word),"End")!=0)
{
    printf("Hello");
    fflush(stdin);
}
```
4.
```
char name[20];
puts("Enter a name ");
while(strlen(gets(name))!=0)
{
    printf("%-30s\n", name);
    puts("Enter a name or type Enter to quit");
    fflush(stdin);
}
```

Do Loop

The *do* loop provides a loop format in C containing an exit condition. Since the condition of the loop is tested after the body of the loop, the loop will always be executed at least one time. Therefore, even if the condition is false the body of the loop will be executed. This type of loop will be handy when we create menu programs. In most other situations, you will want to use an entry condition so that the user has a way out in case they do not want to execute this portion of the program.

The format for the *do* loop is:

```
do
{
}
while(condition);
```

Example

```
float balance = 0.0;
do
{
      printf("Balance:   %6.2f\n", balance)
}
while( balance > 0);
```

Output

```
0.00
```

The loop is executed one time because the condition is not tested until after the balance has been printed. If a *while* had been used in this instance, the loop would never have been executed.

```
float balance = 0.0;
while( balance > 0)
{
      printf("Balance:   %6.2f\n", balance);
}
```

Output

Nothing prints because the condition is false, not allowing the body of the loop to be executed.

Self-Test

1. What will the output be in the following?

```
do
{
      count = 0;
      printf("The count is %d\n", count);
}
while( count < 10);
```

2. What will the output be?

```
count = 0;
do
{
      printf("The count is %d\n", count);
      count = count + 1;
}
while(count < 10);
```

Answers

1. count is infinitely 0, because of the assignment.
2. ```
The count is 0
The count is 1
The count is 2
The count is 3
The count is 4
The count is 5
The count is 6
The count is 7
The count is 8
The count is 9
The count is 10
```

## for Loop

There is a third type of loop available in C that is used primarily with a counter when the number of times the loop is to be executed is known. Since, we have not yet discussed calculations, the first look at *for* loops will contain string functions.

A *for* loop consists of initialization, a condition, and an incrementation. The format is

```
for(initialization; condition; action-increment)
statement;
```

The three parts are separated by semicolons. All three parts are not required, but the semicolons must be there to distinguish the function of each part.

```
/*  A program combining a for loop and string functions */
#include <stdio.h>
char name[20],msg[10];
```
```

```
void main( )
{
    puts("Enter a name");
    gets(name);
    for(strcpy(msg,"Hello");strlen(name)!=0;strcpy(msg,"And again" ))
    {
        printf("%s %s\n",msg,name);
        puts("Enter another name or press ENTER to quit");
        fflush(stdin);
        gets(name);
    }
}
```

Output

```
Enter a name
Sue
Hello Sue
Enter another name or press Enter to quit
Brett
And Again Brett
Enter another name or press Enter to quit
```

The *for* statement in this example is:

```
for(strcpy(msg,"Hello");strlen(name)!=0;strcpy(msg,"And Again"))
{
}
```

The parts of the *for* are:

Initialization

```
strcpy(msg,"Hello");
```

Condition

```
strlen(name)!=0;
```

Action

```
strcpy(msg,"And Again");
```

The loop will initially set msg to "Hello" and the condition will be tested to see if there is a name (length of name not equal to zero). If the condition is met, the loop will be entered, and then msg will be changed to "And Again." *Note:* Similar to the *do* and the *while* loops, the *for* loop will contain only one statement if the braces are not used. Had the braces been omitted from the previous example, only the printf( ) for the name and the message would have been part of the loop. This would have caused an infinite loop.

Multiple Initialization, Condition, or Action   The *for* statement allows compound conditions. The other parts—initialization and action (usually increment)—may have multiple statements. The multiple statements within a part will be separated by commas, while the three parts are still separated by semicolons.

```
for(i = 0,n = 10;i < 5 && n > 5;i = i + 1,n = n - 1)
        printf("%d   %d\n", i, n);
```

There are two initializations in this example. The value of i is set to 0 and n to 10.

The condition is compound.

The actions increment i and decrement n.

Self-Test

1. Write a *for* loop that will print the even numbers from 0 to 100, using a loop variable called n.
2. What is wrong with the following loop?

```
for(i = 0, i < 10, i= i + 1)
        printf("Hello");
```

3. What is wrong with the following loop?

```
for(x = 5; x < 25; x = x + 1);
        printf("%d ",x);
```

4. What will the output be in the following?

```
for(num = 5; num > 0; num= num - 1)
        printf("%d ", num);
```

5. What will the loop do?

```
for(;;;)
        printf("Let's loop");
```

Answers

1. for(n = 0; n <= 100; n+=2)

    ```
    printf("%d ",n);
    ```

2. The parts of the loop should be separated by semicolons not commas. The compiler will interpret this to mean that there were three things for initialization but nothing for the condition or the action syntax error.
3. The semicolon after the *for* means that there are no statements inside of the loop. The printf( ) will only be executed one time after the loop is complete. The value of x at the time that the printf( ) is executed will be 25.
4. 5 4 3 2 1
5. The loop will print "Let's loop" forever. This is a legal loop since not all parts are required on the loop. However, there is no condition to exit the loop causing an infinite loop.

Nested Loops

Sometimes it will be desirable to nest loops, placing a second loop inside of another. The following example places one *for* loop inside of another.

```
void main( )
{
        int i, j;

        for(i=0; i< 3; i= i + 1)
           for(j=0; j<2; j= j + 1)
              printf("%d %d\n", i, j);
}
```

Output

```
0 0
0 1
1 0
1 1
2 0
2 1
```

In this case the value of i is set to 0 and the condition i less than three is tested. The second loop is executed setting the initial value of j to 0 which is less than 2. Therefore, the body of the loop is executed printing the current value of i and j (both 0).

The next step that will be taken is to increment j. The inner loop must be completed before control will be returned to the outer loop. In this case, j becomes 1 and the loop is executed printing i, still with a value of 0 and j with its value of 1. As j is incremented to 2, the condition of the inner loop becomes false and control is returned to the outer loop where i is incremented to 1.

When the inner loop is executed, it starts over again so j is once again initialized to a value of 0. This time the inner loop will print two lines with i = 1 both times while j = 1 and then j = 2.

The outer loop will execute a third time when i is incremented to 3 causing the inner loop to once again restart and be executed twice. This prints the next two lines where i = 2.

When i is incremented again to a value of three the condition on the outer loop becomes false and the loop will not be executed again.

Self-Test

1. What will the output be in the following?
```
for(a = 5; a < 10; a= a +3)
      for(b = 1; b < 3; b= b+1)
            printf("%d %d", a, b);
```
2. What will the output be?
```
for(i = 0; i < 3; = i +1)
      {
            printf("Outer Loop %d\n", i);
            for(j = 0; j < 2; j= j + 1)
                  printf("%d %d\n", i, j);
      }
```
3. Write a nested loop that will produce the following output:
```
1 2
1 3
1 4
2 2
2 3
2 4
```

Answers

```
1. 5 1
   5 2
   8 1
   8 2
2. Outer loop 0
   0 0
   0 1
```

```
    Outer loop 1
    1 0
    1 1
    Outer loop 2
    2 0
    2 1
 3. for(x = 1; x < 3; x=x+1)
      for(y = 2; y < 5; y=y+1)
         printf("%d %d\n", x, y);
```

A FIRST LOOK AT CALCULATIONS

The examples for the *for* loop included some addition operations. There is a shorter way to represent these calculations, which will be introduced with the calculation operators in the next chapter. For now we will use just the basic operators: + (add), − (subtract), * (multiply), and / (divide).

A REPORT PROGRAM

We now have the statements necessary to create a program to produce a report. This is one of the most common applications, since most business systems need several different reports.

Let's begin by considering the parts of a report. A report can be broken down into the heading, the body of the report, and the summary. The heading portion may contain a title and possibly column headings. The title may contain the date and page number.

The main body of the report is also called the **detail** portion. The detail portion of the report would contain an output line for each transaction. Although the titles would be only required once for each page, the detail lines will be repeated over and over. Therefore, the heading will precede the loop while the detail processing will be inside the loop.

detail The main body of a report; processing for an individual transaction.

The summary portion of the report contains items such as totals, averages, and item counts. The summary portion is optional depending on the needs of the particular situation. A report may also be a summary report which does not contain any detail lines but merely the summary information.

Calculations for totals must be performed during the detail loop while the information is available. Since each time that new data is entered into a variable the old value is lost, accumulations are done during the detail processing.

If we are to divide our report program into parts, it would be logical to divide it into the heading function, the detail function, and the summary function.

FIGURE 3-2
Hierarchy Chart—Report
Program

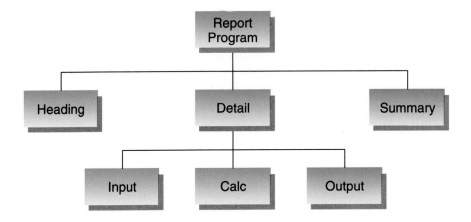

Heading( )
Detail( )
Summary( )

The detail portion of the report will process each record usingh a loop. This is the part of the program that will have the transaction input, processing, and detail output functions. These could be presented in hierarchy chart format as in Figure 3-2.

SAMPLE PROBLEM

In the burro race there are a number of entries, we need to create a report of the speed for each entrant and the average speed for all entrants. The report will consist of a title and appropriate column headings. The body of the report will contain the racer's name, time, and miles per hr.

Pseudocode

Heading Module
    Print the title
    Print the column headings

Detail Module
    print prompt screen and get time
    loop until no time is entered
        input racer's name

calculate miles per hour
add the time to the total time
add one to the number of racers
print a detail output line
redo prompt screen and get time for next person
end of loop

Summary Module
calculate the average
print the average

C Code

```
/*************************************************

Programmed By: A. Millspaugh
Purpose:Produce a report of times for a burro race including a summary
with the average time
------------------------------*/

/*  include the header files     */
#include <stdio.h>

/*   define symbolic constants          */
#define CLS printf("\033[2J")
#define LOCATE(r,c) printf("\033[%d;%dH",r,c)
#define DISTANCE 32

/*     declare variables and functions              */
void printheading( );
void processdetail( );
void printsummary( );
void prompt_screen( );
void input( );
void calc( );
void detailoutput( );
float time, mph, totaltime, avg;
int number_racers;
char name[20];
```

```
void main( )
{
  printheading( );
  processdetail( );
  printsummary( );
}

/*-------------------------------------------------------
prints out headings on the report
-----------------------------------------------------*/
void printheading( )
{
  fprintf(stdprn,"\t\t\tBurro Race Report\n\r");
  fprintf(stdprn,"\tRacer\t\tTime\tSpeed\n\n\r");
}

/*-------------------------------------------------------
input, process, and output each racer
-----------------------------------------------------*/
void processdetail( )
{
  prompt_screen( );
  while(time != 0)
    {
      input( );
      calc( );
      detailoutput( );
      prompt_screen( );
    }
}

/*-------------------------------------------------------
sets up screen and obtains priming input
-----------------------------------------------------*/
void prompt_screen( )
{
  CLS;
  LOCATE(5,25);
  puts("Burro Race");
  LOCATE (12,15)
  puts("Enter the finishing time or type 0 to Quit  ");
  LOCATE(12,15);
```

```
      puts("Racer's name:   ");
      LOCATE(10,60);
      scanf("%f",&time);
   }
   /*-------------------------------------------------------------
   obtains remainder of data
   -------------------------------------------------------------*/
   void input( )
   {
      LOCATE(12,40);
      fflushall( );
      gets(name);
   }


   /*-------------------------------------------------------------
   performs calculations for detail and accumulates totals
   for the summary
   -------------------------------------------------------------*/
   void calc( )
   {
      mph = DISTANCE/time;
      totaltime = totaltime + time;
      number_racers = number_racers + 1;
   }


   /*-------------------------------------------------------------
   prints the detail line
   -------------------------------------------------------------*/
   void detailoutput( )
   {
      fprintf(stdprn,"\t %-20s %5.1f %5.1f\n\r",name,time,mph);
   }


   /*-------------------------------------------------------------
   prints summary information at the end of the report
   -------------------------------------------------------------*/
   void printsummary( )
   {
      avg = totaltime/number_racers;
      fprintf(stdprn,"\n\tAverage Speed                          %5.1f\r\f",avg);
   }
```

Screen Output

```
Enter the finishing time or type 0 to quit    12.5
Racer's Name:                                  Jane King

Enter the finishing time or type 0 to quit    20
Racer's Name:                                  Kelly Dot

Enter the finishing time or type 0 to quit    11.2
Racer's Name:                                  Genie Ogland

Enter the finishing time or type 0 to quit    0
```

Report Output:

Burro Race Report

Racer	Speed	Time
Jane King	2.6	12.5
Kelly Dot	1.6	20.0
Genie Ogland	2.9	11.2
Average Speed	2.4	

Alternative Solution

Use the name as the primary input and test for the name in the *while* condition to determine when to quit.

3-5.c

```c
/*---------------------------------------------------------
Programmed By: A. Millspaugh
Purpose: Produce a report of times for a burro race
including a summary with the average time

---------------------------------------------------------*/
/*        include the header files    */
#include <stdio.h>

/*   define the symbolic constants    */
#define CLS printf("\033{2J")
#define LOCATE(r,c) printf("\033[%d;%dH",r,c)
#define DISTANCE 32
```

```c
/*          declare variables and functions      */
void printheading( );
void processdetail( );
void printsummary( );
void prompt_screen( );
void input( );
void calc( );
void detailoutput( );
float time, mph, totaltime,avg;
int number_racers;
char name[20];

void main( )
{
  printheading( );
  processdetail( );
  printsummary( );
}
/*-----------------------------------------------------------
prints out headings on the report
-----------------------------------------------------------*/
void printheading( )
{
  fprintf(stdprn,"\r\t\t\tBurro Race Report\n\r");
  fprintf(stdprn,"tRacer\t\tTime\tSpeed\n\n\r");
}


/*-----------------------------------------------------------
input, process, and output each racer
-----------------------------------------------------------*/
void processdetail( )
{
  prompt_screen( );
  while((strlen(gets(name)))   != 0)
          {
            input( );
            calc( );
            detailoutput( );
            prompt_screen( );
          }
}
```

```
/*-------------------------------------------------------------
sets up screen and obtains priming input
-----------------------------------------------------------*/
void prompt_screen( )
{
  CLS;
  LOCATE (5,25);
  puts("Burro Race");
  LOCATE (10,15);
  puts("Enter the racer name or press Enter to Quit  ");
  LOCATE (12,15);
  puts("Racer's time:  ");
  LOCATE (10,60);
}


/*-------------------------------------------------------------
obtains remainder of data
-----------------------------------------------------------*/
void input( )
{
  LOCATE (12, 40);
  scanf("%f",&time);
  fflush(stdin);
}


/*-------------------------------------------------------------
performs calculations for detail output and accumulates totals
for the summary
-----------------------------------------------------------*/
void calc( )
{
  mph = DISTANCE/time;
  totaltime = totaltime + time;
  number_racers = number_racers + 1;
}


/*-------------------------------------------------------------
prints the detail line
-----------------------------------------------------------*/
void detailoutput( )
{
```

```
        fprintf(stdprn,"\t         %5.1f         %5.1f\n\r""",name, time, mph);
}
/*------------------------------------------------------------
prints summary information at the end of the report
----------------------------------------------------------*/
void printsummary( )
{
    avg = totaltime/number_racers;                    %5.|f\r\f",avg)
    fprintf(stdprn,"\n\tAverage Speed
}
```

Sometimes when screen output is desired the screen must not be cleared immediately.

Pausing the Screen

A pause may be necessary after output has been written to the screen. If we do not have the program pause, the user may never have time to see the answer on the screen before the program continues on. When we clear the screen in the paint screen function, the answer would be cleared off before the user has a chance to see it.

There are many different routines to make a program pause. Of utmost importance is that the routine chosen gives the user control of how long the pause will be. We want the program to be user friendly and not have the machine controlling too much. In the work environment there are many interruptions that may keep the user from continuing immediately. The screen should remain until the user is ready to continue. For this reason, we will use a pause routine that prints a message at the bottom of the screen and halts execution until the user presses a key.

The pause routine will introduce two macros that are part of the `stdio.h` file, `getchar( )` and `getch( )`. The `getchar( )` macro gets one character from the default `stdin` stream. In our case, this means until one character is entered from the keyboard. The `getchar( )` requires Enter to be pressed before execution continues.

The `getch( )` macro is not standard ANSI C but exists in both the Microsoft and Borland standard input/output header files. Do not use this macro if the program is to be portable to other systems.

```
#define PAUSE printf("Press Enter to Continue"); getchar( );
#define PAUSE printf("Press any key to continue"); getch( );
```

When we reach a point in the program where we would like to have a pause we will call the LOCATE to position the "Press any key" message and then PAUSE.

```
LOCATE(22,38);
PAUSE;
```

It would also be possible to locate the "Continue" message in the same place and have the location defined as part of the definition. In order to do this, the definition for the LOCATE must precede the definition for the PAUSE.

```
#define LOCATE(r,c) printf("\033[%d;%dH",r,c)
#define PAUSE LOCATE(23,35);puts("Press Any Key to Continue");getch;
```

This example also uses `puts( )` instead of the `printf( )` function.

KEY TERMS

compound condition	exit condition	relational
concatenation	expression	operator
detail	loop	string length
entry condition	priming input	

CHAPTER SUMMARY

Comparisons of variables and/or constants may be made using relational operators. These comparisons will evaluate either a true or a false result.

When creating conditions testing string data, the comparison must be made using string functions instead of the relational operators. Strings may be compared in their entirely with only a specific number of characters, or with the case ignored.

More than one condition may be combined together using the and (&&) or the or (||) operator. When an *and* is used to combine conditions, both conditions must be true to yield a true result. However, the *or* only requires that one condition be true. Conditions may be used to control a loop.

A loop is a logic construct that allows for a statement or block of statements to be repeated. By using a condition, the programmer can determine when the loop statements will be executed and when the loop will terminate. The condition may be placed at the beginning of the loop (entry condition) using the reserved word *while*. In a *do* loop, it is possible that the loop will never be executed because the condition is tested before the loop is entered.

With a *do* loop, the condition is at the end of the loop(exit condition). Since the loop is not tested until the end of the loop, the statements in the loop will always be executed at least one time.

A report program typically will contain three major parts: the heading, the detail body, and a summary. Some reports may not contain a summary, while a summary report contains no detail lines. These parts can be used to form the basis of the structure of a report program.

REVIEW QUESTIONS

1. What is a loop?
2. What is the difference between a loop with an entry condition and a loop with an exit condition?
3. How many times will an exit condition loop be executed?
4. What is the purpose of the operators && and ||?
5. When two conditions are combined with an &&, when will the entire condition be considered true?
6. What are the primary parts of a report?
7. What is meant by a detail line?
8. In what part of the program—heading, detail, or summary—would you expect to find a loop?
9. How many times should a loop be executed?
10. What is the significance of uppercase and lowercase in string comparisons?

What will the output be in questions 11–14:

```
11. int num = 5;
      while(num++ < 10)
            printf("%d\n",num);
12. char letter;
      while(letter != 'a')
      printf("%c",letter);
13. int num = 5;
      while(++num < 10);
            printf("%d\n",num);
14. char letter;
      do
        {
            scanf("%c",&letter);
            printf("%c",letter);
        }
      while(letter != 'Q');
```

Note: Both detail and summary processing are part of the detail loop.

1. Write a program to produce a report of the total labor costs for FIXIT Construction.

    INPUT

    Create a prompt screen that will ask for the following
    information for each item:

    > Description of task
    > The number of hours
    > Cost per hour

    PROCESSING

    Detail: Calculate the total cost for each task.

    Summary: Accumulate the total labor cost.

    OUTPUT

    Headings: Include appropriate titles and column headings.

    Detail: Must contain the description, the number of hours, the cost per hour, and the cost for that line.

    Summary: At the end of the report, print out the total labor cost for all jobs.

2. Write a program to produce a billing report.

    INPUT

    Create a prompt screen that will input the following information for each
    customer:

    > First name
    > Last name
    > Account number
    > Amount billed

    PROCESSING

    Detail: None required.

    Summary: Accumulate the total amount billed and the number of customers.

    OUTPUT

    Heading: Include appropriate titles and column headings.

    Detail: Must contain the full customer name (concatenated together), the account number, and the amount billed.

    Summary: At the end of the report, print the total billing, the number of customers, and the average amount billed.

    Sample Data:

Jane Seemore	11821	28.31
Michael Millser	12061	320.00
Jennifer Longchamp	10932	102.50
Edward Catllin	12390	96.52

3. Write a program to produce a roster for the computer club that contains names and phone numbers, and a summary containing the number of members.

    INPUT

    Create a prompt screen that will include the following information for each
    member:

    > Last name
    > First name
    > Phone number

PROCESSING

Detail: None required.

Summary: Count the number of members.

OUTPUT

Heading: Use appropriate titles and column headings.

Detail: Full name and phone number; the name will be concatenated together as last name, followed by a comma and space, and then followed by the first name.

Summary: Print a line specifying the number of members.

Sample Output

The Computer Club
Membership Roster

Name	Phone Number
Ace, Annie	111-1111
Brown, Billy	222-2222
Cook, Crystal	333-3333
Number of members 3	

4. Write a program to generate and produce a report of subscription account numbers for a magazine. Each account number will consist of the first two letters of the last name, the first three digits of the zip code, and the expiration date.

INPUT

Create an input screen that will prompt the user for the following information:

Last Name:

First Name:

Zip Code:

Expiration Date:

Hint: Make the zip code type char[]. The expiration date may be in the form of 07/92 or Jul-92, whichever you prefer.

PROCESSING

Detail: Determine the account number by concatenating together the first two letters of the last name, the first three characters in the zip code, and the expiration date.

Summary: Count the number of accounts as they are processed.

OUTPUT

Heading: Use appropriate titles and column headings.

Detail: Name and account number, the name will be the last name concatenated with a comma and a space concatenated with the first name.

Summary: Print a line containing the number of records processed.

Sample Data:

Last Name	First Name	Zip Code	Exp. Date
Doe	Sam	11232	12/94
Smith	Carol	84567	08/94
Winters	Sharon	34571	08/95
Black	Tim	91763	11/95

Micro Magazine
Subscription Report

Name	Account Number
Doe, Sam	Do11212/94
Smith, Carol	Sm84508/94
Winters, Sharon	Wi34508/95
Black, Tim	Bl91711/95
Number of accounts processed 4	

5. Write a program using a loop to produce mailing labels for magazines. Use the data from program 4 but make up data for the street, city, and state. The labels will contain four lines, the account number on line 1 will be printed to the right. Names will be printed first name and then last. You may wish to concatenate the city, state, and zip code to eliminate extra spaces.

   INPUT
   Create a prompt screen that will enter the following information:
   Last Name:
   First Name:
   Street Address:
   City:
   State:
   Zip Code:
   Expiration Date:

   PROCESSING
   Detail: Concatenate the name and address fields as necessary. Create the account number as the first two characters of the last name, the first three digits of the zip code, and the expiration date.

   OUTPUT
   Labels:
   Sample Output:

                                                            B191711/95

              Tim Black
              1115 Second Avenue
              Montclair, CA   91763

6. Write a program to produce an invoice report for Widget Mfg. Company.

   INPUT   Create a screen to prompt for the following information:
   Product Description:
   Quantity:
   Cost:

   PROCESSING
   Detail: Calculate the extended price (unit price times quantity)
   Summary: Accumulate the total extended price At summary time, use a sales tax of 8% on the total price and add the sales tax to produce the total amount due.

   OUTPUT
   Headings: Use appropriate titles and column headings.
   Detail: The detail line will include the description, the cost, the quantity, and the extended price.

Summary: Print out the total of the extended prices, the sales tax, and the total amount due.

Test Data:

Blue widgets	1.45	17
Miniwidgets	.87	25
Gray widgets	1.40	18

HAYLEY OFFICE SUPPLIES

Using the invoice header created in Chapter 2, create individual customer invoices for sales for Hayley Office Supplies. Set up a loop that will input the appropriate information for a customer and then use a second loop to enter individual product information.

INPUT

Customer: Last Name (loop until enter is pressed)

First Name

Address: Street, City, State, and Zip Code

Product: Description (loop until enter is pressed)

Unit price

Quantity

PROCESSING

Find the extended price by multiplying the price by the quantity. Accumulate the total amount due.

OUTPUT

Heading: For each customer, print the invoice header.

Detail: Each detail line will include the product description, the quantity, the cost, and the extended price.

Summary: At the end of each invoice, print the total amount due.

CHAPTER 4

CHAPTER OBJECTIVES

By the end of this chapter, you should be able to:

- Calculate using binary and unary operators.

- Understand the importance and effect of precedence.

- Know how to assign values with operators.

- Combine relational operators into nested or compound conditional statements to increase the power and flexibility of the *if* statement.

- Use conditional statements to find the highest and lowest values in a group of data items.

Processing Data: Calculations and Decisions

CHAPTER OVERVIEW

Having learned how to declare variables and assign values, it is now important to find out how to perform calculations on those values. This will provide you with the ability to process the data and calculate the results of financial and mathematical formulas.

The processing of data often requires the use of an if statement to decide if the calculation or another operation should be performed, or to select a particular option to be performed. The if will be introduced in this chapter, along with a discussion on how to find the highest and lowest value in a series.

In the last chapter, relational operators were used in conditions to determine when to terminate a loop. These same operators can be used in conditional statements to determine whether or not a block will be executed. Statements that will be executed only if certain criteria are met can be coded using the if statement.

unary operator An operator requiring only one operand, such as increment and decrement.
operand One of the fields used in a calculation statement.
binary operator A calculation operator that requires two operands.

As with other languages, C has arithmetic operators for performing calculations. The operators for calculations are either unary or binary. A **unary operator** has only one factor or **operand** on which the operation is performed. The **binary operator** has two factors or operands.

Binary Operators

The binary operators are as follows:

+ (addition),
− (subtraction),
* (multiplication),
/ (division), and
% (modulus or remainder).

Using the assignment operator, we might write a C statement as follows:

```
tax = tax_rate * amount_of_purchase;
amount_due = amount_of_purchase + tax;
```

These statements call for a calculation to be performed and the result to be assigned to the variable on the left of the assignment operator.

Multiple operators may be used in a single calculation statement but attention must be paid to the **precedence** of the operators, that is the sequence in which the operators will combine with the operands. The operators follow the normal mathematical order of precedence when more than one operator is used in an expression.

precedence The sequence on which operations will be performed based on a predetermined hierarchy of operators.

Precedence of operators The order of precedence of the operators is, multiplicative operators from left to right, followed by additive operators from left to right.:

The multiplicative operators are as follows:

* Multiplication
/ Division
% Modulus

The additive operators are as follows:

+ Addition
− Subtraction

Of course, the order of precedence can be altered through the use of parentheses to indicate the desired sequence of calculations. Anything inside parentheses will be calculated first.

The following program shows several calculation statements and the use of parentheses with calculations.

```
int num = 5,answer;

void main( )
{
     /*    add 2 to the variable num */
     answer = num + 2;
     printf("%d\n",answer);

     /*    multiply 2 times the variable num */
     answer = 2 * num;
     printf("%d\n",answer);

     /*    multiplies 2 times num then adds num
              the value of num does not change  */
     answer = num + 2 * num;
     printf("%d\n",answer);
     /*      use parentheses to have num added to 2
              before multiplying by num        */
     answer = (num + 2) * num;
     printf("%d\n",answer);

     /*    use the modulus function to divide num by 2
              and store the remainder in answer   */
     answer = num % 2;
     printf("%d\n",answer);
}
```

Output

```
7
10
15
35
1
```

Notice the difference in answers with and without the parentheses. When there were no parentheses in the calculation, the precedence was determined by default. In this case, multiplication has a higher precedence and was therefore performed before the addition. The parentheses, however, caused the addition to be performed first on the next calculation.

Modulus

The **modulus** operator is used to find a remainder. It performs a division and then returns the remainder as the result of the operation. This operator is very handy when doing conversions that are not in base 10. When converting minutes to hours, any remainder will become a fraction of 60. Therefore, a decimal remainder is not easily understandable because it would relate to tenths or hundredths.

If we wished to convert minutes to hours we could divide the number of minutes by 60 and then use the modulus to determine the remaining number of minutes.

```
hours = minutes/60
minutes = minutes % 60
```

In the first calculation the whole number of hours will be placed in hours (assuming minutes is an integer field), the remaining minutes will then be placed into minutes.

Self-Test

What will be the results of the following calculations if

```
int num1 = 5, num2 = 2, num3 = 7;
```

1. num1 * num2 - num3
2. (num1 * num2) - num3
3. num1 % num2
4. num1 * 4 / num2
5. num1 * 4 % num2

Answers

1. 3
2. 3
3. 1
4. 10
5. 0

Unary Operators

C contains increment and decrement operators that will increase or decrease the value of a variable by one. The unary **increment operator** is ++ while the **decrement operator** is --.

Increment Operator If we were to use the expression `count++` the effect would be the same as the binary calculation `count = count + 1`.

Binary Operator	Unary Increment Operator
`count = count + 1;`	`count++;`

Both statements perform the same operation.

Decrement Operator Similarly the following statements are equivalent:

```
count--;
count = count -1;
```

Prefix versus Postfix The increment and decrement operators may be used as a part of another expression. It is then important to be able to determine exactly when the addition or subtraction operation will take effect in relation to the evaluation of the rest of the expression. The increment and decrement operators may be used either as a prefix or as a postfix. This means that the increment may be expressed as `count++` or `++count`.

count++ is a postfix while ++count is prefix increment. The placement of the operator determines the timing of the calculation. With a **prefix** increment the addition is done prior to the evaluation of the remainder of the expression or statement while a **postfix** operator evaluates the expression and then increments the variable.

Assume that count is 5.

```
x = count++;
```

The postfix operator will assign `count` to x and then increment `count`. Therefore, x will be 5.

```
x = ++count;
```

The prefix operator performs the increment first and then proceeds with the remainder of the expression or statement. In this case, `count` will be incremented to 6 and then will be assigned to x, leaving x with a value of 6.

The decrement operator may also be used as a prefix or a postfix as in `--count` or `count--`.

If count is 5 then

```
x = count--;
```

assigns 5 to x then decrements `count` to 4, whereas,

```
x = --count;
```

decreases `count` to 4 and then assigns the value of `count` to x, leaving x with a value of 4.

Another Look at Precedence The increment and decrement operators have a higher order of precedence than the binary operators that we have already considered. Be careful when evaluating expressions to understand the impact of this precedence.

```
int answer, count, num = 5;

void main( )
{
    /*  a postfix incrementer  */
    answer = num + count++;
    printf("%d\n",answer);

    /*  a prefix incrementer  */
    answer = num + ++count;
    printf("%d\n",answer);
}
```

Output

```
5
7
```

With the postfix incrementer `count` was 0 at the time that count was added to num. After that calculation, `count` was then incremented to 1. The prefix incrementer caused `count` to be increased from 1 (previous increment) to 2. After the increment, `count` was added to `num` giving a result of 7.

Self-Test

What will the results of the following calculations be, given that

```
int count, num = 5;
```

Note: Assume that each problem is a unique situation and `count` will be 0 and num is 5 before each problem.

1. count-- + num
2. count++ - num
3. --count + num
4. num % ++count
5. num++ / count--

Answers

1. 5
2. −5
3. 4
4. 0
5. Division by 0, which is an error.

Assignment Operators

Another category of operators in C is the assignment operators. These allow us to shortcut the writing of our code as the increment and decrement did. In fact, the unary increment and decrement operators are frequently considered to be assignment operators.

The **assignment operator** = which assigns the value of the expression on the right of the = operator to the variable on the left is already familiar. In addition, there are a +=, −=, *=, /=, and %=. These also require a variable on the left of the operator for the result of the operation to be stored in.

The expression x+=5 is equivalent to writing the assignment

```
x = x + 5;
```

Similarly, the other calculation operators can be combined with an assignment operator to produce a shortcut method of doing a calculation on a variable and then storing the value back into the same variable.

assignment operator The = used to store a value in a specific memory location or named data item.

Assignment Operators

=	Simple assignment
+=	Addition assignment
−=	Subtraction assignment
*=	Multiplication assignment
/=	Division assignment
%=	Modulus assignment
++	Unary increment
−−	Unary decrement

Some examples of the use of these assignment operators are:

```
total += sales;          /* add sales to the total*/
grade -= wronganswers;   /* subtract the incorrect
                            answers from the
                            grade*/
minutes %= 60;           /*finds the remaining
                            minutes after finding
                            hours   */
```

The next program uses the assignment operators to change the value of an integer called num.

```c
int num ;

void main( )
{
        num = 0;
        num += 5;
        printf("%d\n",answer);

        num = 1;
        num *= 5;
        printf("%d\n",answer);

        num = 1;
        num -= 5;
        printf("%d\n",answer);

        num = 10;
        num /= 5;
        printf("%d\n",answer);

        num = 10;
        num %= 3;
        printf("%d\n",answer);
}
```

num = num + 5

Output

```
5
5
-4
2
1
```

Placing the Assignment Operators in a Loop   The assignment operators may be used inside of loop statement as well as in the body of the loop. Consider the following example:

```c
void main( )
{
```

```
    float balance, entry;
    int i;

      /* Add 5 numbers to the balance    */
    for(i=0, balance = 0.0; i < 5; i++, balance +=entry)
    {
      puts("Enter a number ");
      scanf("%f"&entry);
    }
    printf("%6.2f", balance);
}
```

Precedence   The assignment operators, with the exception of the increment and decrement, have a lower order of precedence than the binary operators. This means, of course, that the binary operations will be performed first and then the assignment.

```
int number = 5;
number *=2 + 10;          number = number * 12
printf("%i",number);
```

The value of number that will be printed is 60. The 2 + 10 yields 12, which is then multiplied by 5 and assigned to number.

Self-Test

1. What values will be printed ?

```
int number1 = 10, number2;
number1 *= number2 = 4;
printf("%i%i",number1, number2);
```

2. What is the value of x?

```
int x=3;
x*=5-2;
```

Answers

```
1. number1 = 40
   number2 = 4
2. x = 9
```

Mixing Data Types in Calculations The binary arithmetic operators may cause a conversion of the data type depending on the operator and on the type of the operands. This conversion is known as an **arithmetic conversion.** Most of the operators will make all operands the same type. If an operand is of type char or short it will be converted to int. Basically, if two fields of different types are used, the compiler will "promote" the type of the operand from the less accurate data type to the more accurate type.

If there are mixed data types in your calculation statement you may be surprised by the results.

arithmentic conversion A predefined set of rules for converting data types during execution of a calculation involving multiple data types.

```
4-4.c
```

```
int intnum, intanswer ;
float floatnum, floatanswer;

void main( )
{
        floatnum = 3.5;
        intnum = 2;

        floatanswer = floatnum/intnum;
        intanswer   = floatnum/intnum;
        printf("float=%f,integer=%d\n",
                  floatanswer,intanswer);

        floatanswer = floatnum + intnum;
        intanswer   = floatnum + intnum;
        printf("float=%f,integer=%d\n",
                  floatanswer,intanswer);
}
```

Output

```
float = 1.750000, integer = 1
float = 5.500000, integer = 5
```

The data type of the integer was promoted or converted to type float because there were mixed types in the calculation. The operation was evaluated as 3.5/2.0. The assignment to an integer variable truncated the answer to an integer. Notice that the floating point number was not rounded to the nearest integer. Rather, the decimal portion was simply truncated. The result of the division was not rounded, only the integer portion was retained, which in this case was one.

Similarly, in the addition, the floating point calculation retained the decimal portion during the calculation and in the answer while the integer calculation truncated the decimal portion.

Self-Test

What will be the result of the following calculations given that

```
int intnum = 1, intanswer;
float floatnum = 7.5, floatanswer;
```

1. `floatanswer = floatnum - intnum;`
2. `floatanswer = intnum + intnum;`
3. `intanswer = floatnum;`
4. `floatanswer += intnum;`
5. `intanswer *= floatnum;`

Answers

1. 6.500000
2. 2.000000
3. 7
4. 8.500000
5. 7

The *sizeof* Operator   One operator in C is a word rather than a symbol. The *sizeof* operator is used to determine the number of bytes occupied by a given data element. It can be used to determine the size of a variable or a data type.

```
sizeof(data element);
```

Using the sizeof operator, it is possible to determine how many bytes of storage are used by a specific computer and compiler. This can aid in the portability of a C program.

```
sizeof(int);
```

In addition, this operator may be used on a variable or an array. When using the *sizeof* for an array, the number of elements in the array can be determined. This is different from `strlen()`, which tells the number of occupied positions within a character array.

Exponentiation   There is not an operator in C for raising a value to a power. This does not require an operator because exponentiation can be achieved by multiplying the number by itself the specified number of times. Rather than writing the code to do this, the ANSI function `pow()` may be used. The format for the `pow()` function is:

```
pow(the value to be raised, the power);
```

ARITHMETIC OPERATORS
103

It is illegal for both the value and the power to be equal to zero, and if the value is negative, then the power must be an integer. In order to use this function it is necessary to include the `math.h` file.

```c
#include <math.h>
void main( )
{
        int x=2,y=3,z;
        z = pow(x,y);
        /* z will be 2 raised to the power of 3 which
                         is 8  */

}
```

Self-Test

1. Write the statement to find 2 to the power of 10 and assign the answer to K.
2. Write the monthly compound interest formula in C.

$$\text{Compound Amount} = \text{loan amount} \times (1+\text{rate/12})^{(\text{number years X 12})}$$

Answers

1. `K = pow(2,10);`
2. `value = loan*(1+rate/12);`
   `power = num_years * 12;`
   `compound_amount = pow(value,power);`
   or
   `compound_amount =`
   `pow((loan*(1+rate/12)),num_years*12);`

Decisions—The If Statement

Sometimes it is necessary to execute certain commands or statements only when certain criteria (conditions) have been met. One of the ways this decision making can be accomplished in C is with the *if* statement (see Figure 4-1). The statement takes the following format:

```c
if(condition)
     statement;
[else
     statement;]
```

As with the loop statements, *if* only allows us to have one statement executed when the condition is true. If we wish to have more than one statement we must use braces {} to enclose a block of statements.

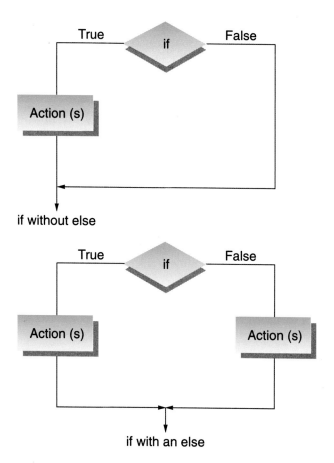

FIGURE 4-1
The if *Statement*

if without else

if with an else

The *else* is optional as indicated by the placement of the *else* in the square brackets. Not every *if* statement requires an *else*. If there is no *else* then the execution will begin with the next statement whenever the result of the condition is false. When an *else* is used, one or more statements will be executed when the resultant value of the condition is false. However, to have multiple statements for the false condition, we must once again use the braces to enclose the block.

The conditions used with an *if* are the same as those that are used in the loop conditions using the conditional operators, <, >, ==...

```
if(hours > 40)
  overtime( );
```

The overtime function is to be performed only if the hours exceed 40. If hours are not over 40, execution will begin with the statement following the ;.

The statement that is executed when the condition is true may be any C statement or function including input, output, your functions, or another *if*.

Note that the condition is enclosed in parentheses and that there is *no semi-colon after the condition*. If a semicolon was placed after the condition it would be interpreted in C that there are no statements to be executed when the condition is true. This will not cause a syntax error in C, it simply executes as a null statement—an *if* that does not control execution of any statements.

When the *else* clause is used, instruction(s) will be given that are to be performed if the condition is false. Remember that the *else* is optional. The *else* clause may also be followed by any instruction, including another *if*.

```
if(grade >= 70)
     printf("Pass");
else
     printf("No Pass");
```

Notice that in this example, there is a semicolon after both `printf()`s.

Sample program using an *if*:

```
void main( )
{
     int num = 10;

     if(num > 10)
          ++num;
     printf("%d",num); /*  not part of the if   */
}
```

Output

```
10
```

In this example the condition is false, num is *not* greater than 10. Therefore, the variable num was never incremented. Notice that `print( )` is not part of the *if* because there are no braces. The only statement that will be executed when the condition is true is ++num. Since the statement was false, num was not incremented and the execution continued with the statement following the *if* which is `printf( )`.

```
void main( )
{
     int num = 10;
     if(num > 10)
     {
          ++num;
          printf("%d",num); /*  part of if block */
     }
}
```

In this example, `printf()` will never be executed because `printf()` is part of the *if* which will only be executed when the condition is true. Since num is not greater than 10, neither the increment nor `printf()` are executed.

Once again it's always better to use braces when coding an *if* or an *if* with an *else*. The braces will make certain that all statements intended to be a part of the *if* are blocked with it.

Self-Test

What will the output be in the following?

```
1. num = 5;
   if(num++ < 10)
      {
         printf("Increment is after comparison");
      }
2. num = 5;
   if(num -- < 5)
      {
         printf("less than 5");
      }
   else
      }
         printf("not less than 5");
      }
3. if('c' == 'd')
      {
         printf("The letters are equal");
      }
4. balance = 1000;
   if( balance <= 0);
      {
         printf("It's all gone");
      }
```

Answers

1. Increment is after comparison
   The value of num at 5 is compared to 10, the condition is true, then the increment is made.
2. not less than 5
   The comparison is made first and 5 is not less than 5, num is then decremented to 4. The *else* will be executed because the statement is false.
3. Nothing will print.
4. It will print the statement. It does not matter what the balance is equal to because the condition has a semicolon after it, leaving an *if* with no

statements belonging to it. The print function is therefore not dependent upon the outcome of the condition.

nested if An *if* statement embedded within the block of another *if*.

Nested *If* Statements An *if* inside of an *if* is called a **nested *if*** and is used when more than one condition is to be tested. The second condition will be tested only if the first condition is true in the following example.

```
if(salary_status == 'h')
     if(hours > 40)
          overtime( );
```

The overtime( ) function will only be called if the first condition, salary_status equals h, is true; and the second condition, hours greater than 40, is also true.

A condition may be nested within the *if* or on the *else* portion of the *if* statement.

```
if(sex_code == 'm')
     if(age < 21)
          minor_male++;
     elseif(sex_code == 'f')
     if(age< 21)
          minor_female++;
```

When nesting an *if*, the *else* will belong to the last unmatched(no else) *if* regardless of indentation. In the previous code, the test for female will only be performed if it is a male, but not a minor. The best way to correct this example would be to use braces and indentations to clearly delineate what *if* statement the *else* belongs to.

```
if(sex_code == 'm')
{
     if(age < 21)
     {
       minor_male++;
     }
     else; \* no action if not minor male *\
}
else
}
     if(sex_code == 'f')
{
     if(age< 21)
     {
        minor_female++;
     }
```

```
        else;
        }
else
{
        printf(error_msg);
}
```

Compound Conditions   Another way of testing multiple conditions would be to use the logical operators && or | |.

```
if(salary_status == 'h' && hours_worked > 40)
        overtime( );
```

In this conditional statement both conditions must be true because of the && operator. If the salary status is hourly and the hours worked is greater than 40 then the overtime( ) function will be called.

As with the conditions used with loops, an && requires that both conditions be true, while an | | only requires one to be true. Also recall that the && has a higher precedence than the | |.

Example

```
int x,y,z;
x=y=z=1;
if(x > 0 && y = 1 || z = 0)
        {
        printf("True");
        }
```

This will print out True because the operators will bind as follows:

```
(x>0 && y = 1)  | |  z=0
```

After binding, the evaluation of the condition is from left to right. Once the solution is known the evaluation will end. Since x is greater than 0 and y is equal to 1, the first condition is true. The | | condition will never be tested because the final solution must be true at this point because one of the conditions in an | | is true.

Self-Test

1. Write a conditional statement using nested conditions that checks to see if an item is on the depreciation list (the char variable depreciate will contain a value of 'y'). If it is on the depreciation list, check if the depreciation type is straight line (the char variable type will contain the value 's'). If both conditions are true, give the instruction to execute the depreciation( ) function.

2. Answer the previous question using compound conditions.
3. Modify question number one to use string variables.
4. What will print in the following?

```
int a,b,c;
a=b=0;
c = 5;
if(c<10 || a = 0 && b != 0)
        {
        printf("True");
        }
else
        {
        printf("False");
        }
```

Answers

1.
```
if(depreciate == 'y')
        {
        if(type == 's')
                {
                depreciation( );
                }
        }
```

2.
```
if(depreciate == 'y' && type == 's')
                {
                {depreciation( );
                }
```

3.
```
if(strcmp(depreciate, "y") == 0)
        {
        if(strcmp(type, "s") == 0)
                {
                depreciation( );
                }
        }
```

4. True

the binding is c<10 || (a = 0 && b!=0)

The evaluation begins at the left, and after c < 10 is determined to be true, the evaluation will end.

conditional operator A ternary operator that can replace an *if* statement.

Conditional Operator   C provides a **conditional operator** that will express an entire conditional in a single statement. It is a ternary operator, meaning that it requires three operands: the condition, the action if true, and the action if false.

```
condition ? true : false
```

The assignment statement

```
a = x < 5 ? b : c;
```

can be read as

```
if x is less than 5 then a = b else a = c.
```

In this case the result of the condition is assigned to the variable a. If the condition is true then the value of b will be assigned to a; otherwise, the value of c will be assigned to a.

The conditional operator is the only ternary operator in C. Remember, there must be three parts to the operation: condition, action if true, and action if false. The first part is followed by a question mark and the other two parts are separated by a colon.

Self-Test

1. Using the conditional operator, assign a 0 to count if balance is less than 1000, otherwise count should be assigned 1.
2. Read the following condition:
   ```
   commission = sales < 50000 ? .05: .06;
   ```

Answers

1. count = balance < 1000 ? 0 : 1;
2. If the sales are less than 50,000, the commission will be .05, otherwise commission is .06.

Example

Write a banking program that will maintain a running balance of deposits and withdrawals to a noninterest bearing account. The program will use screen entry for the transaction type and for the amount. A detail report will be produced that prints a line for each transaction that specifies the type of transaction, the amount, and the current balance. The summary must include the number of deposits and the number of withdrawals (see Figures 4-2 and 4-3).

Input	Processing	Output
Transaction type:	Balance:	Transaction Desc.
d for deposit	Add if deposit	Amount
w for withdraw	Subtract withdraw	Balance
amount of transaction	Message if invalid	

FIGURE 4-2
Heirarchy Chart—
Banking Program

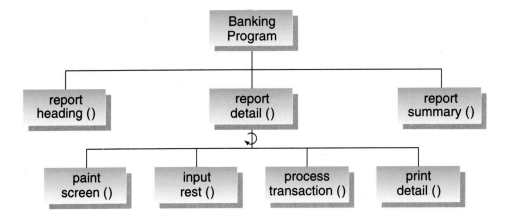

FIGURE 4-3
Screen Layout for
Banking Program

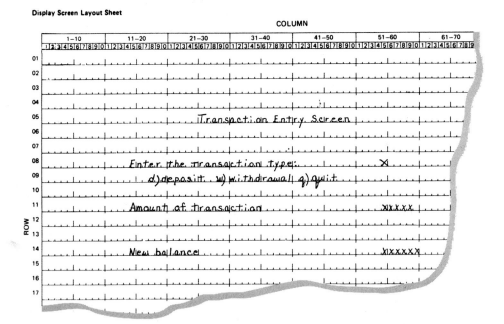

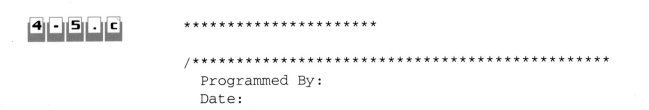

```
    Purpose:  Maintain an account balance providing
for deposit and withdrawal transactions. Use a
decision statement to determine appropriate
transaction. Data type and amount to be input from
the keyboard, report to the printer
*****************************************************/

/*    include header files as needed      */
#include <stdio.h>

/*    define symbolic constants           */
#define CLS printf("\033[2J")
#define LOCATE(r,c) printf("\033[%d;%dH",r,c)
#define PAUSE printf("Press Any Key to Continue"); getche( )

/*    declare variables and functions        */
float amount, balance;
int numberdeposits,numberwithdrawals;
char transaction, transdescription[9];


void main( )
{
    report_headings( );
    report_detail( );
    report_summary( );
}

report_headings( )
{
    fprintf(stdprn,"                    Transaction Report\n\n");
    fprintf(stdprn,"        Type          Amount         Balance\n"
}

report_detail( )
{
    paint_screen( );
    while(tolower(transaction) != 'q')
    {
            input_rest( );
```

```
                process_transaction( );
                print_detail( );
                paint_screen( );
        }
        CLS;
}

void paint_screen( )
{
        CLS;
        LOCATE(5,25);
        printf("Transaction Entry Screen");
        LOCATE(8,15);
        printf("Enter the transaction type:");
        LOCATE(9,18);
        printf("d) deposit  w) withdrawal  q) quit ");
        LOCATE(11,15);
        printf("Amount of Transaction");
        LOCATE(14,15);
        printf("New Balance");

        fflush(stdin);
        LOCATE(8,55);
        scanf("%c",&transaction);
}

void input_rest( )
{
        LOCATE(11,55);
        scanf("%f",&amount);
}

void process_transaction( )
{
        if(tolower(transaction) == 'd')
                {
                        strcpy(transdescription,"Deposit");
                        numberdeposits++;
                        balance += amount;
                }
```

```c
        else
                if(tolower(transaction) == 'w')
                {
                        strcpy(transdescription,"Withdraw");
                        numberwithdrawals++;
                        balance -= amount;
}

        else
            {
              strcpy(transdescription,"Invalid");
              LOCATE(19, 30);
              printf("Invalid transaction type");
              LOCATE(20,30);
              PAUSE;
            }

}


void print_detail( )
{
    if(strcmp(transdescription,"Invalid") != 0)
    {
      LOCATE(14,55);
      printf("%6.2f", balance);
      LOCATE(20,30);
      PAUSE;
      fprintf(stdprn,"    %-10s %15.2f %16.2f\n",
              transdescription, amount, balance);
    }
}

void report_summary()
{
    fprintf(stdprn,"\n Number of deposits %d",numberdeposits);
    fprintf(stdprn,"\n Number of withdrawals %d\n",numberwithdrawals);
}
```

Output

Transaction Report

Type	Amount	Balance
Deposit	100.00	100.00
Withdrawal	5.00	95.00
Withdrawal	20.00	20.00
Number of deposits	1	
Number of withdrawals	2	

Highest/Lowest Logic Using the *If* Sometimes it is desirable to find the largest or the smallest value from a group of data that has been entered or processed. Since the values of the variables change each time we process a new record in the detail processing loop, it would be impossible to wait until after the loop to determine the smallest or largest value.

By the time we reach the summary or totals portion of our report program, the only values left in memory are from the last record that was input and processed. Therefore, if we want to perform a comparison to find the maximum and minimum value it must be done during the loop process.

To find the maximum value we need to compare each time through the loop to determine if this record contains the highest value so far. If we keep track of the highest value "so far," when we reach the end of the detail loop we will have found the maximum value— whether it was in the first record, the last record, or any one in between.

```
if (grade > maxgrade)
  maxgrade = grade;
```

We need to store this highest value and then use it in the comparison each time through the loop. To make sure that we are comparing to a small value, we normally need to initialize the variable for the highest value to 0, assuming all values to be compared are positive numbers. If the highest value begins at 0, we can be certain that the first record to be processed will become the highest so far. Likewise, the variable to hold the smallest value must be initialized to a large value to be sure that the records being processed will actually contain a smaller value than where the variable started. Another alternative would be to initialize both the highest and lowest comparison variable to the value in the first record, because it definitely is the highest and the lowest at the time that the first record is processed.

Let's look at the detail processing to find the highest, lowest, and average grade on an exam. The input will contain the student name and the exam grade. We will also print out the name of the individual with the highest grade.

Assume that:

```
int maxgrade = 0; mingrade = 999;
char name[20]; maxname[20];
```

```
void detail_processing()
{
      paint_screen( );   /* designs screen, obtains
      name */while(strlen(name) != 0)
      {
           input_grade( );
           calculations( );
           print_detail( );
           paint_screen( ;
      }
}

.....

void calculations( )
{
      if(grade > maxgrade)
      {
           maxgrade = grade;
           strcpy(maxname, name);
      }
      if(grade < mingrade)
      }
              mingrade = grade;
      {
      count++;                /*   accumulate grade, count*/
      totalgrade += grade;
}
```

The comparison for the small grade cannot be an *else* of the first condition. Just because a grade is not the largest does notg mean that it will automatically be the smallest, which is what an *else* implies. Most of the grades being processed will probably not be the smallest or the largest so far.

The summary function for this grade example might be coded as follows:

```
summary( )
{
      average = totalgrade/count;
      printf("Average:       %3d\n",average);
      printf("Highest Grade:   %3d\n",maxgrade);
      printf(" by             %20s\n",maxname);
      printf("Lowest Grade:    %3d\n",mingrade);
}
```

This logic does not account for two names both having the highest grade. The way it is written, the first record processed that contains the highest grade will have the name stored in maxname. If anyone else has an equal score it would not be greater and would not do anything. We will not attempt to solve this issue right now.

Self-Test

1. Write the decision statement to find the name of the person with the highest amount of sales, given the following variables:
   ```
   char name[20], highname[20];
   float sales, highsales;
   ```

Answers

1.
   ```
   if (sales > highsales)
   {
     highsales = sales;
     strcpy(highname, name);
   }
   ```

Precedence of Assignment, Logical, and Relational Operators

Expressions can be combined in C to make very complex statements. This fact makes it necessary for the programmer to understand the way in which operators will **bind** (combine according to precedence) and how expressions will be evaluated.

bind The order in which operands are combined according to the precedence of operators.

All operators on the same line have equal precedence and will be evaluated

Precedence of Operators

Operator	Associativity
( ) [ ] . −> ++ −− sizeof * / %	left to right*
+ −	left to right
< > < => =	left to right
== !=	left to right
&&	left to right
| |	left to right
?:	right to left
= *= += /= %= −=	right to left

*Except unary operators which are right to left.

according to the appropriate associativity. The following examples are not realistic and demonstrate poor programming practice. However, they are designed as an exercise in understanding the underlying significance of the precedence of operators.

Combining logical operators and assignment operators:

```c
void main( )
{
    int num1, num2, num3, answer;

    num1 = num2 = num3 = 0;
    answer = num1 || num2 && !num3;
    printf("%d", answer);
}
```

Output

```
0
```

First: num1 || (num2 && (!num3))

The && is FALSE   (False(0) and true(not zero))

Second: 0 || False

The || is FALSE   (False or False)

Third: Since the expression evaluates to false, it has a value of 0 which is assigned to answer.

Combining assignment and increment operators

```c
void main( )
{
    int num1, num2, answer;

    num1 = num2 = answer = 5;
    answer += -num1++ - ++num2;
    printf("%d %d %d", num1,num2,answer);
}
```

Output

```
6 6 -6
```

First: answer += −(num1++) − (++num2)
          5+= −(5) - 6
          answer = −6
          num1 = 6 (note the − is a unary operator)
          num2 = 6

Combining Increment and Logical Operators:

```
void main( )
{
    int num1, num2, num3;

    num1 = num2 = num3 = 5;
    num1++ || ++num2 && num3++;
    printf("%d %d %d", num1,num2,num3);
}
```

Output

```
6 5 5
```

First: (num1++) || ((++num2) && (num3++))
num1 is 5 which is True

Since the statement can be evaluated at this point to definitely be TRUE because of the ||, the num2 and num3 will not be evaluated

num1 becomes 6
num2 and num3 remain 5

After these examples, you may ask yourself, "Who would write a statement or expression like these examples?" C provides the ability to nest functions, operations, and expressions within each other. The important thing is to understand exactly how these will be evaluated. It is feasible that an increment may be used with a relational operator. If so, what happens?

Take a look at the next realistic application.

```
if(remainder %= HRS_PER_PERSON > 0)
    ++people_needed;
```

This statement attempts to find if any partial (remainder) of a person was needed, rounding up if even a fraction remains. Unfortunately, the relational operator has a higher precedence than the assignment operator, which means that the expression will be evaluated as follows:

First:	HRS_PER_PERSON > 0 is probably true which results in a value of 1 being used with the modulus.
Second:	Dividing by 1, there will be no remainder, assigning a value of 0 to remainder.
Finally:	The expression will evaluate to 0 which will be considered false. The increment will never take place.
To Solve:	if((remainder %= HRS_PER_PERSON) > 0) ++people_needed; Use parentheses to override the precedence Or, better yet, do not mix assignments with conditionals.

```
remainder% = HRS_PER_PERSON;

if(remainder>0)
{
   ++people_needed;
}
```

Self-Test

1. What will the value of num1, num2, and num3 be?
   ```
   int num1,num2 = 0, num3 = 1;
   num1 = num2++ == num3;
   ```
2. What will be the value of num1, num2, and num3?
   ```
   int num1,num2,num3;
   num1=num2=num3=1;
   num1 *= num2 == num3 ? num2++ : num3++;
   ```

Answers

1. ```
   num2 = 1 , but not at the time of the comparison
   num3 = 1
   num1 = 0 because == causes an equality test
   which is false
   ```
2. ```
   num1 = 1 because 1*=1
   num2 = 2, incrementing after the assignment
   num3 = 1, since condition is FALSE num3 does
   not change
   ```

Programming Style

When working with the arithmetic operators, the computer will follow the order of precedence. However, the use of white space will make it easier for the programmer to read and may affect the interpretation of the operators. Consider the following example:

```
answer=amount+++balance;
```

The three plus signs represent an increment and an addition operator. But there is still a question as to whether this means there is a postfix increment on amount or a prefix increment on balance. It could be written as:

```
answer = amount++ + balance;
```

or

```
answer = amount + ++balance;
```

Without the whitespaces, it will be interpreted with the increment attached to amount.

```
int amount = 0;
int balance = 5;
int answer;

void main( )
{
    answer=amount+++balance;
    printf("answer %d\n",answer);
    printf("amount %d\n",amount);
    printf("balance %d",balance);
}
```

Output

```
answer 5
amount 1
balance 5
```

From this output, we can conclude that balance of 5 was added to amount of 0 and stored in answer. After that amount was incremented to 1. Now we will try the same program with whitespaces.

```
int amount = 0;
int balance = 5;
int answer;

void main( )
```

```
{
     answer = amount + ++balance;
     printf("answer %d\n",answer);
     printf("amount %d\n",amount);
     printf("balance %d",balance);
}
```

Output

```
answer 6
amount 0
balance 6
```

The answers changed because now the increment operator belongs to `balance`. In this instance, `balance` was incremented to 6 and was then added to `amount`. The value of `amount` never changed.

Because of the interpretation issue as well as to improve the readability of the code we will leave a space before and after each arithmetic and assignment operator.

KEY TERMS

arithmetic conversion	**decrement operator**	**postfix**
assignment operator	**increment operator**	**precedence**
binary operator	**modulus**	**prefix**
bind	**nested** *if*	**unary operator**
conditional operator	**operand**	

CHAPTER SUMMARY

There are a large number of operators in C. For calculations, we have both unary and binary operators. When using the operators, it is extremely important to understand the priority of each of the operators.

Data can be manipulated using the arithmetic operators. Variables can be changed using the assignment operators. String data still requires the use of string functions.

Another important factor in processing data is the ability to use conditions to determine what action is to be taken. The *if* statement provides this capability. The conditional *if* may be combined with an *else* as needed. Multiple conditions may be tested using compound conditionals or through the use of nested *if* statements. One application of the conditional statements is the determination of a maximum or minimum value in a range of data.

In addition to the *if* statement, C also contains an operator for doing conditions. The conditional operator is the only one that contains three operands.

1. Name the operator necessary for the following operations:
   a. Postfix increment
   b. Modulus
   c. Multiplication
   d. Multiplication assignment
   e. Division
2. What will be the result of the following if = 5 (for each problem start with x = 5)
   a. ++x;
   b. x −= 2;
   c. x++ *= 2;
   d. x+++3;
3. What importance is the precedence of operators to calculation results?
4. How can the order of the precedence be altered in a calculation statement?
5. What function is used to assign a string to a string variable?
6. How can a portion of a string be appended to another string?
7. What is meant by a nested *if?* A compound *if?*
8. Why must the processing for a high–low comparison be performed during the detail portion of the processing?
9. What will the output be in the following:

```
void main( )
{
      int num1, num2, num3;

      num1 = num2 = num3 = 5;
      num1++ || ++num2 && num3++;
      printf("%d%d%d", num1,num2,num3);
}
```

EXERCISES

1. Write a program that will determine the number of packages of strip paneling required to do each wall in a room, if each package contains 13 square feet of paneling. The walls to be covered are 8 feet high. Input the length of the wall.

        Preprocessor Constant: HEIGHT

   Input:
           Client last name:
           Client first name:
           North wall size:
           South wall size:
           East wall size:
           West wall size:

   Processing:
           Calculate the number of packages for each wall. Calculate the total number required (round up for any partial package).

OUTPUT

Heading:

Include the customer name.

Detail:

Specify wall and number of packages.

Summary:

Total the number of packages required.

2. Calendari Publications is having a special promotion for its sales staff. A bonus of 5% will be paid for all sales over $2000.00, in addition to the normal commission rate of 10%. Write a program that will input the amount of sales and the salesperson's name, and that will calculate the normal commission rate and the bonus rate. Print out a statement that includes the company name, the salesperson's name, and the amount of sales, the commission, and the bonus. At the end of the report, print out the total commissions, the total bonuses, and the average commission. Also print out the name of the salesperson with the highest sales.

Input:

Salesperson's last name:
Salesperson's first name:
Amount of sales:

Processing:

Determine if a bonus is to be paid. Find total commission for each salesperson. Accumulate totals for sales, commission, bonus, and total commission. Count the number of salespeople. Determine who has the highest sales.

OUTPUT

Heading:

Use appropriate titles and column headings.

Detail:

Print out the salesperson's name (concatenated with first initial and last name), the amount of sales, the amount of bonus, the commission, and the total compensation.

Summary:

Print out bonus, commission, and total compensation. Print out the average total compensation per salesperson. Print the name of the salesperson with the highest sales.

Sample Output:

Calendari Publications
Sales Commission Report

Name	Sales	Commission	Bonus	Total
J. Jon	1700.00	170.00	0.00	170.00
F. Hong	2655.00	265.50	132.75	398.25
C. Marquez	2000.00	200.00	0.00	200.00
Total	6355.00	635.50	132.75	768.25

Highest sales: F. Hong
Average Commission: $256.08

3. Write a program that will determine that rate for straight line depreciation for an asset item.

Input:

The program must prompt the user to enter the asset name, the asset cost, the life in years, and the salvage value. Create an appropriate input screen using reverse image for the input prompts.

Processing:

The formula for the annual rate for straight line depreciation is:

$$\frac{\text{Cost} - \text{Salvage Value}}{\text{Life in Years}}$$

OUTPUT

Send an output report to the printer that contains the necessary information as follows:

Whatever Corporation
Depreciation Schedule

Description of asset:	xxxxxxxxxxxxxxxxxx
Cost basis:	$xxxx.xx
Salvage value:	$xxxx.xx
Life in years:	xx
Annual depreciation:	$xxxx.xx

Sample Data: Use the following information to test your program.

Description	Cost	Life	Salvage
Desk	842.12	10	25

(If your calculations are correct, the result will be 81.7.)

4. Write a program to calculate a grade average for a student. The prompts should ask for the student's name, two test scores, and three program grades. The tests are worth 50% of the grade and the programs are worth 50% of the grade.

Input:

Student name:

Two test scores:

Three program grades:

Processing:

Find the average by taking 50% of the sum of the tests, divided by 2, and add that to 50% of the sum of the programs divided by 3. Find the name and average of the student with the highest grade. Find the overall average grade for all students.

OUTPUT

Heading:

Course title and appropriate headings.

Detail:

Student name, test scores, program grades, average.

Summary:

Highest name and student average. Average grade for all students

5. Write a program to find the area of a rectangle.

Input:

Length and width.

Output:

The area of the rectangle.

Processing:

Multiply the length by the width.

6. Write a program to determine bowling averages, handicaps, and female high series, male high series, female high game, and male high game.

Input:

Bowler's name:

Score for game 1:

Score for game 2:

Score for game 3:

Male or female:

Processing:

Find the bowler's average for the three games.

Find a handicap of 80% of 200 by subtracting the average from 200 and multiplying by 80%. Find the highest:

Game for this bowler

Female series (total of three games)

Male series

Female high game

Male high game

OUTPUT

Heading:

Use appropriate titles and column headings.

Detail:

Print out the bowler's name, three scores, average score, high game, and handicap.

Summary:

Print out highest female series, male series, female high game, and male high game.

7. Write a program to determine overtime hours based on an 8-hour day.

Input:

Employee name:

Start time:

End time:

Processing:

Find the number of regular hours, the overtime hours, and the total hours for each person.

Find a total of the regular hours, the overtime hours, and the total hours for all employees.

OUTPUT

Heading:

Use appropriate titles and column headings.

Detail:

The detail line will include the employee name, regular hours, the overtime hours, and the total hours.

8. The elementary school PTA is having a fundraiser selling chocolate bars. The students will receive bonus gifts based on the number of cases of candy that they sell. In addition,

the class that sells the most will receive an ice cream party sponsored by the room mothers.

Input:
For each student, input the student's name, the number of cases sold, and the room number.

Processing:
The first two cases receive 10 points toward the prize list, while the third through fifth case will earn 15 points. All cases beyond five will receive 20 points each. Find the class that has the highest number of points.

OUTPUT

Heading:
Use appropriate titles and column headings.

Detail:
Print out a detail line for each entry that contains the name and the number of points earned.

Summary:
At the end of the report, print out the classroom that earned the most points.

Test Data:

Name	Cases Sold	Room #
Annie Ace	3	5
Barney Boy	5	2
Clara Cool	1	5
Danny Dare	20	6
Eric Early	7	5

9. Modify the grade report from Exercise 4 to print out a numeric average and an alphabetic grade. The loop will test for the student name and will exit when an enter has been pressed.

Input:
The input will include the name, two test scores, and three program grades.

Processing:
The grading scale will be:

 90-100 A   80-89 B   70-79 C   60-69 D   <60 F

OUTPUT

Heading:
The report will contain appropriate title and headings.

Detail:
Each detail line will include the student name, the numeric average, and the letter grade.

Summary:
At the end of the report, include a line indicating the numeric grade average for the class and the number of students included on the report.

HAYLEY OFFICE SUPPLIES

Write a program to calculate the merchandise turnover rate and the average inventory. The average inventory is found by finding the average of the beginning inventory and the ending inventory. The merchandise turnover rate can be determined by dividing the cost of the goods sold by the average inventory amount. Assume that Hayley Office Supplies had a beginning inventory of 27,000 and an ending inventory of 32,500. The cost of goods sold is 148,672.

CHAPTER

5

CHAPTER OBJECTIVES

By the end of this chapter, you should be able to :

■ Use a *switch* statement as an alternative to the *if*.

■ Create menus through the use of the *switch* statement.

■ Design and code menu programs that call submenus.

■ Access other executable programs and return to the menu program.

■ Use colors on the screen.

Creating Menu Programs Using the Switch Statement

CHAPTER OVERVIEW

Another alternative to the if statement for determining whether or not selected statements will be executed is a switch statement. Switch allows for different "cases" to be tested. Switch and case will be covered as well as the break statement.

This chapter will introduce programs that are controlled by a menu. Although the if statement could be used to determine which option has been selected, the switch statement will provide an easier approach. An additional advantage of the switch is the ability to do some automatic validity checking with a default statement.

The use of screen colors will be covered for those that have color capabilities and wish to use them.

⑨ ❶ ❷ ❸ ④ ⑤ ⑥ ❼ ❽ ⑨ ❶ ❷ ❸ ④ ⑤

Another decision-making tool in C is the *switch* statement. This statement allows a variable to be tested for several various possible values called **cases**. There also is a built-in error checking factor, called **default,** that may be used when none of the cases have been met. Each *case* may contain statements that are to be executed when a condition is met. These statements could involve calling other functions, providing a method of performing a conditional branch.

The format of the *case* statement is:

```
switch (expression or variable)
{
 case value:
      statement(s);
 case value:
      statement(s);

  .
  .
  .

 default:
      statement(s);
}
```

case Reserved word to specify a possible value for a variable and the appropriate actions to be taken.
default Automatic action to be taken if not specified otherwise.

Break

break Reserved word to exit an *if* or *switch.*

A **break** statement must be used to indicate the end of the statement(s) for each case, or the execution of the program will continue to flow through the remaining cases without testing the case conditions. When a *break* is encountered, execution continues with the statement following the closing brace of the *switch* statement.

The *default* case will be executed if none of the other cases produced a match with the expression.

Suppose that we have a variable called choice that will determine which function should be executed. If the value of choice is A then the add_record(   ) function will be executed, D will cause the delete_record( ) function to be performed and E will cause the edit_record( ) function to be executed. All other entries will be invalid.

```
switch (choice)
{
  case 'A':
      add_record( );
      break;
  case 'D':
      delete_record( );
      break;
```

```
   case 'E':
      edit_record( );
      break;
   default:
      error_rtn( );
}
```

Notice that the default statement is `error_rtn( )`. This will be executed if a choice other than A, D, or E is selected.

More than One Alternative for a Case

It is possible to have more than one value allowed for each case. Perhaps the `add_record` function could also be accessed with a lowercase 'a' or the number one. Then we could change the code to

```
case 'A': case 'a': case '1':
add_a_record( );
break;
```

All of the values for choice must be enclosed in single quotes presuming that choice is of type *char*.

The *switch* statement may also be used on numeric variables. The value following the word case must then be numeric constants of type float or integer depending on the type of variable that is being tested. A range of numbers cannot be tested with the case, only individual values.

Self-Test

1. What, if anything, is wrong with the following?

```
switch(answer)
    case 'y'
      {
          ycount++;
          printf("Yes");
      }
    case 'n'
      {
          ncount++;
          printf("No");
      }
```

2. What will print in the following?

```
int count = 0;
while(count++ < 3)
```

```
        {
            switch(count)
              {
                    case 1:
                       printf("1");
                    case 2:
                       printf("2");
                    case 3:
                       printf("3");
                    case 4:
                       printf("4");
                    default:
                       printf("Oops\n");
              }
        }
```

3. What will print in the following:

```
int count = 0;
while(++count < 3)
{
        switch(count)
          {
                case 1:
                   printf("1");
                case 2:
                   printf("2");
                case 3:
                   printf("3"):
                case 4:
                   printf("4");
                default:
                   printf("Oops\n");
          }
}
```

4. What will print in the following?

```
int count = 0;
while(count < 3)
{
```

```
switch(++count)
    {
        case 1:
           printf("1");
        case 2:
           printf("2");
        case 3:
           printf("3"):
        case 4:
           printf("4");
        default:
           printf("Oops\n");
    }
}
```

5. What will print in the following:

```
int count = 0;
while(count < 3)
{
    switch(count++)
      {
        case 1:
           printf("1");
        case 2:
           printf("2");
        case 3:
           printf("3");
        case 4:
           printf("4");
        default:
           printf("Oops\n");
      }
}
```

Answers

1. There are three problems with the code:
   (1) There should be a set of braces around all of the cases. The open
   brace should follow the *switch* statement before the first case and the
   closing should be at the end of the set of cases or after the default (if
   there is one, default is not required).
   (2) There should be a colon after the value for each case 'y':
   (3) The statements for each case need not be in braces but there should
   be a break statement. The execution continues until a break is found.

2. 1234Oops
   234Oops
   34Oops

   There is no break so it falls through every statement after it is true. Count starts with a value of 1 because it was incremented after the condition on the while.

3. 1234Oops
   234Oops

   In this instance, count is incremented before it tests the condition on the loop so the switch is only executed two times.

4. 1234Oops
   234Oops
   34Oops

5. Oops
   1234Oops
   234Oops

   Notice that, in this case, the value of Oops is printed because count has a value of 0; the first time the *switch* statement is executed, count will be incremented after the test is made.

Example Program   Modify the transaction balance program from Chapter 4 for deposits and withdrawals from a noninterest-bearing account using the *switch* statement. The planning will remain the same but a *switch* will be used instead of the *if*.

Input Transaction Type:	Processing Balance:	Output Transaction Desc.
d for deposit	Add if deposit	Amount
w for withdraw	Subtract withdraw	Balance
Amount of transaction	Message if invalid	

The processing function will become:

```
void process_transaction( )
{
    /*    select action depending on transaction    */
    switch(transaction)
        {
          case 'd':
          case 'D':
            strcpy(transdescription,"Deposit");
            numberdeposits++;
            balance += amount;
```

```
      break;
         case 'w':
         case 'W':
             strcpy(transdescription,"Withdraw");
             numberwithdrawals++;
             balance -= amount;
      break;
         default:
          strcpy(transdescription,"Invalid");
          LOCATE(19, 30);
          printf("Invalid transaction type");
          LOCATE(20,30);
          PAUSE;
         }
}
```

Self-Test

1. Write a *switch* statement that will print "Hello World" to the printer or to the screen.

Answer

```
1. char option;
   scanf("%c", &option);
   switch(option)
   {
        case 'S': case 's':
            printf("Hello World");
        case 'P': case 'p':
            fprintf(stdprn,"Hello World");
   }
```

Using the switch *for a Range of Values*

The *switch* statement is not designed to use for a range of values using relational operators. Multiple values need to be listed as we did earlier. This does not help in situations using floating point numbers where we need to test a continuous range. The *if* would, of course, be available. However, in some situations a little manipulation will make the *switch* feasible.

Consider the example of converting numeric grades to a letter grade using percents. If everything between 90 and 100 is an 'A', we could list each integer. A lot of code, but it still does not work for a value such as 95.4. If the grade is divided by 10, then the first digit could be used in the cases.

```
/*----------------------------------------------------
       determine the letter grade from a numeric grade
            using the scale:
                     90-100   A
                     80-89    B
                     70-79    C
                     60-69    D
                     < 60     F


----------------------------------------------- */

   float grade;
   int intgrade;
   char ltrgrade;

   void main( )
   {
    puts("Enter numeric grade");
    scanf("%f",&grade);

    /*  divide the grade by 10 to get first digit */
    intgrade = grade/10;

    switch (intgrade)
    {
     case  9:
     case 10:
     ltrgrade = 'A';
     break;
     case 8:
     ltrgrade = 'B';
     break;
     case 7:
     ltrgrade = 'C';
     break;
     case 6:
     ltrgrade = 'D';
     break;
     default:
     ltrgrade = 'F';
    }
    printf( "%3.1f %c\n", grade, ltrgrade);
   }
```

Output

```
Enter numeric grade
76
76.0  C
```

Self-Test

1. Write the statement to evaluate the pay rate for the following piecemeal pay rate system. The pay per unit is determined by the number of units produced. Once the number of units produced is determined, that rate will apply to all units for that individual.

# Units	Rate Per Unit
Less than 200	.40
201–500	.50
Over 500	.65

Answer

```
1. units /= 100;
   switch (units)
   {
        case 0: case 1:
             rate = .4;
             break;
         case 2: case 3: case 4:
             rate = .5;
             break;
         default:
             rate = .65;
   }
```

MENU PROGRAMS

One of the most useful applications of a *switch* statement can be the creation of a menu routine. A **menu** is a program that displays several different options that may be selected. In an earlier example, a variable called `choice` was tested to determine what function should be performed. This is an example of a menu.

menu A list of options.

```
switch (choice)
{
  case 'A':
     add_record( );
     break;
```

```
   case 'D':
      delete_record( );
      break;
   case 'E':
      edit_record( );
      break;
   default:
      error_rtn( );
}
```

Notice that if the case matches an 'A' that the `add_record( )` function will be performed followed by a `break`. This results in the *switch* statement being exited after the appropriate action has been taken. The *default* `error_rtn( )` function will only be performed if `choice` is not an 'A', 'D', or 'E'.

Structure of a Menu Program

In creating a menu program, the menu must be displayed, an option will be selected and the proper function executed, and then the program will return to the menu until the user elects to quit.

The `main( )` function for this type of program will differ from the report program structure that has been used in the previous programs. The `main( )` must contain a loop that will not be exited until the user selects the quit option.

```
void main( )
{
    while(choice != '0')
    {
    printmenu( );
    getchoice( );
    }
    CLS;
}
```

The `printmenu( )` function will clear the screen and display all of the options. The `getchoice( )` allows the user to enter a selection and then executes a *switch* statement.

After any option from the menu is executed, the control of the program will return back to the `main( )` function because of the loop. The menu will continue to print until the loop is terminated by the selection of the "quit" option on the menu.

Sample Program

Write a menu program that will allow the user to either find the average of a series of numbers or to find the square of a number (see Figures 5-1 and 5-2).

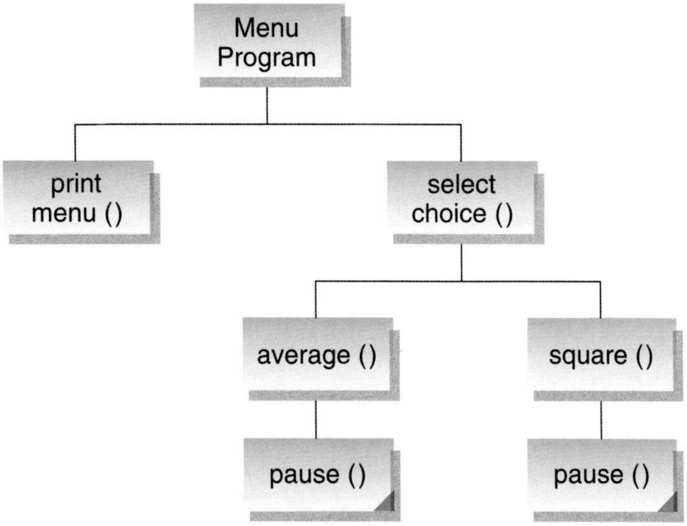

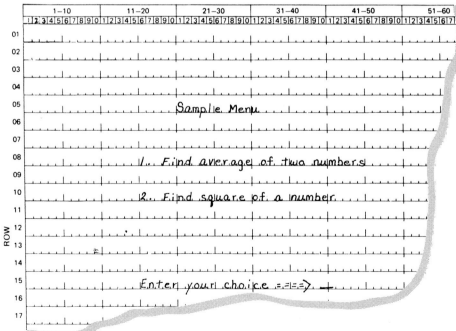

FIGURE 5-1
Hierarchy Chart—Menu
Program

Display Screen Layout Sheet

COLUMN

FIGURE 5-2
Screen Layout for Menu

5-3.c

```
/* -------------------------------------------------------------
Programmer Name:
Date:
Purpose:  a menu program that allows options for
          averaging or squaring two numbers
------------------------------------------------------------ */
#include <stdio.h>

/*   Set up Symbolic Constants for Cursor Control
#define CLS printf("\033[2J")
#define LOCATE(r,c) printf("\033[%d;%dH",r,c)
#define PAUSE LOCATE(23,35);puts("Press Any Key to Continue");getch();

char choice;
void printmenu( );
void getchoice( );
void average( );
void square( );

void main( )
{
    /*      loop until 0 is selected for exit    */
     while(choice != '0')
     {
     printmenu( );
     getchoice( );
     }
}

/*-----------------------------------------------------
clear the screen and print the menu
-----------------------------------------------*/
void printmenu( )
{
    CLS;
    LOCATE (5,20);
    puts("Sample Menu");
    LOCATE (8, 15);
    puts("1. Find Average of two numbers");
```

```
          LOCATE (10,15);
          puts("2. Find Square of a number");
          LOCATE (12,15);
          puts("0. Quit");
          LOCATE (15,15);
          puts("Enter your Choice ====>");
}

/*-------------------------------------------------------
    input menu option from the keyboard and branch to the
                appropriate module - prints an error message
                if an invalid option is selected
---------------------------------------------------------*/
void getchoice( )
{
     LOCATE (15, 40);
     scanf("%d",&choice);
     switch (choice)
     {
      case '1':
        average( );
        PAUSE;
        break;
      case '2':
        square( );
        PAUSE;
        break;
      case '0':
         CLS;
        break;
      default:
        LOCATE (19,18);
        puts("You must enter a NUMBER (1-3)");
        PAUSE;
      }
}

/* ------------------------------------------------
      inputs and finds the average of two numbers
--------------------------------------------------  */
void average( )
```

```
{
  float num1, num2;

  CLS;
  LOCATE (10,20);
  puts("Enter first number     ");
  LOCATE (10,43);
  scanf("%f", &num1);
  LOCATE (12,20);
  puts("Now the second number ");
  LOCATE (12,43);
  scanf("%f",&num2);
  LOCATE (14,20);
  printf("The average is %4.2f",(num1+num2)/2);
}

  /*-----------------------------------------------------------
          inputs a number and finds the square
-------------------------------------------------------------*/
void square( )
{
    float num1;

  CLS;
  LOCATE (10,20);
  puts("Enter a number  ");
  LOCATE (10, 35);
  scanf("%f",&num1);
  LOCATE (12,20);
  printf("The square of %4.2f is %4.2f", num1, num1 * num1);
}
```

Output

```
Sample Menu
1. Find Average of two
numbers
2. Find Square of a number
0. Quit
```

Using Letters or Numbers for Menu Options

Menus often are created that allow the user their choice of entering a letter or a number to make a selection. This can be done by declaring the option variable as character and then using a list of multiple cases for the switch statement. Remember to use the `fflush( )` to clear the buffer before the option is entered.

```
char option;

fflush(stdin);
scanf("%c", &option);

switch (option)
{
    case '1':
    case 'A':
    case 'a':
      average( );
      break;
    case '2':
    case 'S':
    case 's':
        square( );
      break;
    case '0':
     case 'Q':
    case 'q':
      choice = '0';  /*   to exit the main( ) loop */
      CLS;
      break;
    default:
      LOCATE (19,18);
      puts("You must enter a NUMBER or LETTER");
      PAUSE( );
}
```

To make it clearer to the user that the A is an option, the letter could be capitalized, placed in parentheses, displayed in bold, italics, or in a different color. To use bold, italics, or colors, see the programming tip.

```
        Sample Menu
1 A)verage of two numbers
2 F)ind Square of a number
0 Q)uit
Enter Your Choice =======>_
```

Self-Test

1. Write the *switch* statement for the following menu.

```
        Trimet Auto Inc.
   1 E)nter a sale transaction
   2 D)isplay daily report
   3 P)rint weekly report
   0 Q)uit
   Enter your option =====>_
```

2. Why does the main( ) contain a loop printing the menu?
3. If the loop terminates with an option of 0, what happens if someone types Q to quit?
4. Why is the PAUSE used at the end of each module that displays to the screen?

Answers

1.
```c
char option;

fflush(stdin);
scanf("%c", &option);
switch (option)
{
    case '1':
    case 'E':
    case 'e':
       entersale( );
       break;
    case '2':
    case 'D':
    case 'd':
       displaydaily( );
       break;
    case '3':
    case 'P':
    case 'p':
       printweekly( );
       break;
    case '0':
    case 'Q':
    case 'q':
       option = '0';  /*   to exit the main( ) loop */
```

```
        CLS;
        break;
    default:
        LOCATE (19,18);
        puts("You must enter a NUMBER or LETTER");
        PAUSE;
}
```

2. The only way to exit a menu program should be through the menu or an assigned function key that will terminate the program. Until that time, the menu should be reprinted and another option selected.
3. The condition in the loop in main( ) must contain compound conditions or the '0' can be assigned to the option variable in the switch statement.
4. Since the function will return to the loop that reprints the menu, any data that is printed on the screen will be cleared. The PAUSE macro allows the user to determine when to go back to the menu.

Menu Hints

It is better to use a character type for the selection variable even if the options are all numbers. The *default* will print messages for any invalid characters. Even if the menu only lists numerical option, some user may attempt to type a letter.

The quit option should be consistent from one menu to another. If a menu has multiple levels, they should be connected with an option to return to the previous menu. This menu option should also always be consistent. When using numbers for the options, consider using an option of zero(0) for the quit and return to previous menu options.

Self-Test

1. Write the switch statement for the following menu:

```
E)nter Production Orders
P)rint Daily Schedule
B)illing Information
W)eekly Report
Q)uit
```

2. What could be done in the previous example if a second item began with the same letter, for example:
                        Produce Weekly Report
3. Why does the quit option require a case in the *switch* statement when there is no function to be executed?

Answers

1. switch(choice)

```
{
      case 'E':
            production( );
            break( );
      case 'P':
            schedule( );
            break;
      case 'B':
            billing( );
            break;
      case 'W':
            report( );
            break( );
      case 'Q':
            CLS;
            break;
      default:
            error_rtn( );
}
```

2. Highlight any letter within a word to indicate that the option may be selected with that choice.
3. If the case was not included for the quit option, the program would execute the default routine when the quit was selected.

MULTIPLE LEVEL MENUS

The *switch* may be used multiple times for multiple menus within a program. The hierarchy chart (see Figure 5.3) for the option containing the menu would contain another loop similar to the mainline loop. However, the lower menu level should return to a previous menu—there should only be ONE EXIT from the program.

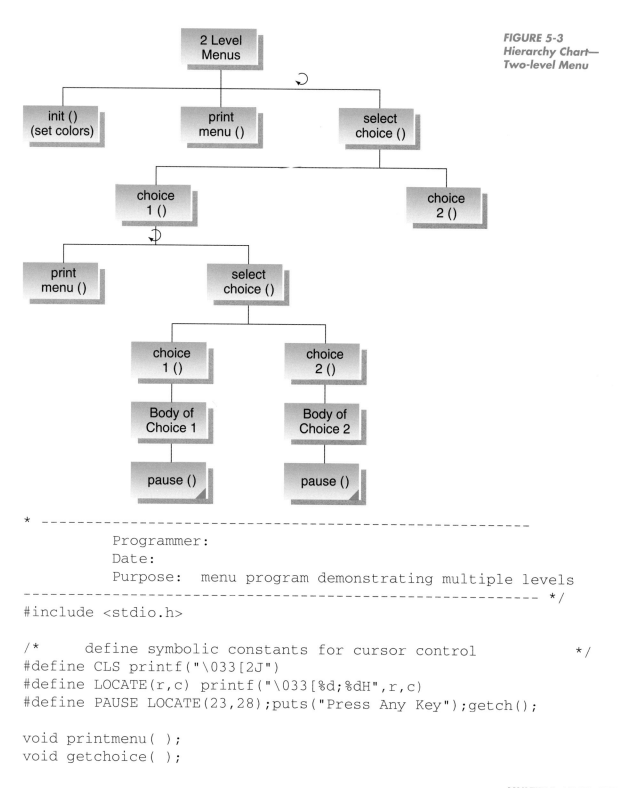

FIGURE 5-3
Hierarchy Chart—
Two-level Menu

```
*       ----------------------------------------------------------
        Programmer:
        Date:
        Purpose:  menu program demonstrating multiple levels
----------------------------------------------------------- */
#include <stdio.h>

/*      define symbolic constants for cursor control              */
#define CLS printf("\033[2J")
#define LOCATE(r,c) printf("\033[%d;%dH",r,c)
#define PAUSE LOCATE(23,28);puts("Press Any Key");getch();

void printmenu( );
void getchoice( );
```

```
void choice1( );
void printmenu2( );
void getchoice2( );
char choice, option;

void main( )
{
   /*     Print the menu and execute a choice until choice is quit */

      do
      {
         printmenu( );
         getchoice( );
      }
      while(choice != '0');
}


/*-----------------------------------------
            Prints Main Menu
--------------------------------------*/
void printmenu( )
{
      CLS;
      LOCATE(5,20);
      puts("Sample Menu");
      LOCATE(8, 15);
      puts("1. Choice 1");
      LOCATE(10,15);
      puts("2. Choice 2");
      LOCATE (12,15);
      puts("0.  Quit");
      LOCATE(15,15);
      puts("Enter your Choice (0-2)===>");
}


/*-----------------------------------------------------------
    inputs choice from keyboard and executes appropriate option
------------------------------------------------------------*/
void getchoice( )
{
      LOCATE(15,43);
```

```
          fflush(stdin);
          scanf("%c",&choice);
          switch (choice)
          {
           case '1':
             choice1( );
             break;
          case '2':
             CLS;
             LOCATE(12,30);
             puts("Choice 2");
             PAUSE;
             break;
          case '0':
             CLS;
             break;
          default:
             LOCATE(16,15);
             puts("You must enter a valid choice");
             PAUSE;
          }
}


/*-----------------------------------------------
        represents choice 1 from the main menu
        which will create a loop for a secondary menu
-----------------------------------------------*/
void choice1( )
{
        do
        {
          printmenu2( );
          getchoice2( );
        }while(option != '0');
}


/*---------------------------------------------------------
   Print secondary menu, allow option to return to
previous menu
------------------------------------------------------- */
void printmenu2( )
```

```c
{
    CLS;
    LOCATE(5,20);
    puts("Sample Menu Level 2");
    LOCATE(8, 15);
    puts("A. Choice A");
    LOCATE(10,15);
    puts("B. Choice B");
    LOCATE (12,15);
    puts("0.  Return to Previous Menu");
    LOCATE(15,15);
    puts("Enter your Choice ======>");

}


 /*-------------------------------------------------------------------
   gets menu option and takes proper action
-------------------------------------------------------*/
void getchoice2( )
{

    LOCATE(15,41);
    fflush(stdin);
    scanf("%c",&option);
    switch (option)
    {
     case 'A': case 'a':
       CLS;
       LOCATE(12,30);
       puts("Choice A");
       PAUSE;
       break;
     case 'B': case 'b':
       CLS;
       LOCATE(12,30);
       puts("Choice B");
       PAUSE;
       break;
     case '0':
       CLS;
       break;
```

```
default:
    LOCATE(16,15);
    puts("You must enter a valid choice");
    PAUSE;
}

}
```

When multiple menus are used it becomes apparent that there must be a better way. A single menu function could be used and then an array of the option names included. This will require passing values to a function that will be discussed in Chapter 6. Arrays are covered in Chapter 7.

Running Executable Files or DOS Commands from the Menu

The C program can "shell" out to the operating system using the `system( )` function. The program can be requested to run another program (an .EXE, .BAT, or .COM file) or to perform a DOS command. (This command is portable to UNIX machines, but, of course, they will not understand DOS commands. To make the switch it would be necessary to substitute, for example, IS for DIR.) The `system( )` function uses the following format:

```
system("string instruction to operating system");
```

The string must be enclosed in quotes, and may contain the name of an EXE, BAT, or COM file or a DOS command.

```
system("CH5EX6");
system("CLS");
```

One problem that you may encounter with the system command is that it does not work from within the editor environment. The program containing the `system()` function call will compile and link without errors. However, in order for the `system()` call to be performed, the program must be called from the DOS prompt.

```
/*
Programmer: A. Millspaugh
Date:
Purpose:  demonstrate the ANSI C code to "shell" out
to the operating system (DOS)    */

#include <stdio.h>
#include <stdlib.h>
```

```
void main( )
{
    puts("Hello to you from C");    /*  print from C */
    system("dir b:/w");             /*  print from DOS */
    puts("...and back to C");       /*  print from C  */
    return 0;
}
```

After creating a file called system.exe:

```
C:> system
```

Output

```
Hello to you from C
Volume in Drive B has no label
Volume Serial Number is 2A4F-16CA
Directory of B:\

RETURN    BAT      NAMES    FUNCTION  WK3
EXER1B
README             LETTERS
    6 File(s)     686500 bytes free
```

This function may be used to make a menu program "tie together" several individual programs. At this point, you could create a menu that would run any of the previous programs that have been written for this course.

PROGRAMMING/DEBUGGING HINT

Reverse Video

Another way to accentuate options or prompts is to incorporate reverse video (sometimes called reverse image). The reverse video will work on all DOS system monitors. To do this you can incorporate the reverse video escape sequence within the print line to the screen or use a #define.

To place the 1 and the A in reverse image for the line

1. Average

we could use the following printf( ).

```
printf("\033[7m1. A\033[0mverage");
```

This statement turns on reverse video before the 1 and sets the print back to normal after the A. This might be clearer if we break it down as follows:

```
#define    REVERSE printf("\033[7m")
#define    NORMAL  printf("\033[0m")
REVERSE;
printf("1. A");
NORMAL;
printf("verage");
```

Using Screen Colors in a Program

The colors on the screen can be changed using the same type of escape sequences that have been used for locating the cursor position, for clearing the screen, and for displaying reverse image. Of course, the colors only applies to color monitors. It will work on CGA, EGA, and VGA monitors.

The easiest way to display color is to set up some preprocessor directives, although you could just use the escape sequence directly in the `printf( )` format string.

The available definitions are for a change in the foreground or the background color. Therefore, the letters BKG or FG will be included in the name to indicate background or foreground.

```
#define BLACKFG printf("\033[30m")
#define BLACKBKG printf("\033[40m")
#define REDFG printf("\033[31m")
#define REDBKG printf("\033[41m")
#define GREENFG printf("\033[32m")
#define GREENBKG printf("\033[42m")
#define YELLOWFG printf("\033[33m")
#define YELLOWBKG printf("\033[43m")
#define BLUEFG printf("\033[34m")
#define BLUEBKG printf("\033[44m")
#define MAGENTAFG printf("\033[35m")
#define MAGENTABKG printf("\033[45m")
#define CYANFG printf("\033[36m")
#define CYANBKG printf("\033[46m")
#define WHITEFG printf("\033[37m")
#define WHITEBKG printf("\033[47m")
```

You need to define whatever colors you will be using in the preprocessor directives, or keep all of them in your header file. If you want your entire program to run in a specific set of colors, set them in the `initialization( )` function. For any screen that would be different, the settings should be changed at the beginning and reset at the end of a specific function.

Try the following code for practice.

```
#define BLUEBKG        printf("\033[44m")
#define WHITEFG        printf("\033[37m")
#define CLS            printf("\033[2J")
#define LOCATE(r,c)    printf("\033[%d;%dH",r,c)

void main( )
{
    CLS;
    BLUEBKG;
    WHITEFG;
    LOCATE(10,38);
    puts("Menu");
}
```

Any other print statements in this program will print in the new set of colors, white characters on a blue background, until another color change is made.

Boldface and Italics

There are escape sequences to place the display in boldface or italics. These are similar to the color commands in that they end with an 'm'.

```
#define BOLD printf("\033[1m")
#define ITALICS printf("\033[2m")
#define BLINK printf("\033[5m")
```

Printers

All of the escape sequences are for screen use only, they do not affect printed output. There are sets of codes that may be found in a printer manual that can control the style, font, and size of a character, as well as the portrait or landscape orientation.

KEY TERMS

break	**default**
case	**menu**

CHAPTER SUMMARY

In situations where a variable needs to be tested for several different values, the variable may be tested using a *switch* statement. The *switch* statement contains possible values that may be contained in the variable, each of which is called a *case*. In the case that none of the actual values tested for were met, a *default* may be specified.

Once the condition has been met, all of the following statements will be executed without further testing, until a *break* statement is encountered.

A menu program can be written easily through the use of a *switch* statement. The values in the *switch* correspond to the possible selections from the menu. The statements or functions to be executed will be determined by the value selected.

Using the `system( )` function in C allows a program to temporarily "shell" to the operating system. The program may then execute another program or perform an operating system command.

The ANSI codes provide the capability of using colors, or reverse video, on the screen. Other capabilities include boldface and italics.

REVIEW QUESTIONS

1. When would a *switch* statement be preferable over an *if* statement?
2. Can a compound condition be used with a *switch*?
3. Why is the option of 0 suggested for the quit in a menu?
4. Why is the break statement necessary inside of the *switch* statement?
5. What would the main( ) function of a menu program consist of?
6. A menu program will execute one of various options, how will the program be terminated?
7. What statement easily allows the function for the correct option to be selected and executed?
8. Why would it be necessary to pause execution of a program?
9. What code can be used to pause the execution of the program?
10. How can a menu option contain another menu?

EXERCISES

1. Write a menu program that will list your favorite movies by category. The menu should contain at least comedy, romance, and musical categories and an option to exit. When the choice is made a function will be executed that displays the appropriate information neatly on the screen. If exit is chosen, clear the screen before leaving the program. You will need to use a pause function or macro before returning back to the menu from each display function.
2. Write a menu program that displays a company's current assets and liabilities. The menu will offer the choices of displaying assets, displaying liabilities, or of exiting. Use the following information in creating your display screens. Be sure to pause before returning to the menu. (*Optional:* Include values for each item.)

Assets:
    Cash
    Accounts receivables
    Building
    Office furniture
    Office supplies

Liabilities:
    Accounts payables
    Building loan
    Office expenses
    Utility expenses

3. Create a menu program that displays a list of resort destinations along with an option to exit. For each resort, create a display screen that will include suggested hotel, dining recommendations, activities, and the approximate price range for each.

4. Create a menu program with at least three options and an exit that displays information about your favorite hobby or interest.

5. Write a landscape program that will display a menu of plants appropriate for: shade, sun, drought, freeze. Each option should list the names of flowers, shrubs, vegetables, or trees appropriate to the specified conditions.

6. Write a menu program that will display the meeting time and date for the following clubs. Be sure to add an option to exit.

    Computer Club
        First and third Tuesdays
        11:00–12:00
        Building 26D-4
    Alpha Gamma Sigma
        Second and fourth Wednesdays
        Noon
        Third Thursday evening
        7:00 p.m.
        Student center
    Forensics
        Every Wednesday
        1:00
        Department offices

7. Write a program that will calculate and print a report for monthly utility bills for the Genie Electric Company. The rates for usage are on an escalating scale depending on the units used.

Rates:

Up to 300 kilowatt hours	=	10.151 cents per KWH
301 to 500	=	14.11 cents per KWH
Over 500	=	16.80 cents per KWH

Input:
Customer last name:
Customer first name:
Starting reading:
Ending reading:

Output
Appropriate title and column headings for name and amount due.

Detail lines to include customer name and amount due

Summary—average usage, total billings

8. Write a menu program that will run the programs that you have written for the previous chapters.

9. Write a program that will allow the user to:

    a. Format a low-density diskette.

    b. Format a high-density diskette.

    c. Copy files.

    d. Display disk directory.

    e. Quit.

    Submenus:

        Option 1, 2, and 4: Allow an option for Drive A, Drive B, or Drive C, and return to previous menu

        Option 3: Allow options for all files or for a specific file. Also allow an option to return to the previous menu.

10. Write a program that allows options to convert to or from metric measurements.

HAYLEY OFFICE SUPPLIES

Write a menu program that will allow letterhead to be printed (Chapter 1, Case Study), customer invoices to be prepared (Chapter 3, Case Study), or merchandise turnover to be calculated (Chapter 4, Case Study).

The menu must contain an appropriate title. Use an option of 0 to exit the menu. Each option should allow the user to type in a letter or a number to select the option. If color is available, use different colors for the characters that can be used to select from the menu. If no color is available, use boldface print, or use low-intensity white and high-intensity white.

CHAPTER

CHAPTER OBJECTIVES

By the end of this chapter, you should be able to:

■ **Examine and use the different storage methods available for data.**

■ **Understand the visibility and scope of data items and functions.**

■ **Use local variables by being able to pass arguments to functions.**

■ **Differentiate between arguments and parameters.**

■ **Define functions via prototypes to specify the data type for parameters and to indicate data type for return values.**

■ **Create functions that return values to a calling function.**

More Details about Functions and Variables

- **Understand the concepts of cohesion and coupling to provide a properly structured relationship between functions.**

CHAPTER OVERVIEW

C provides the capability to access and deal with data in many ways. This chapter will introduce more of the items that introduce this flexibility into the language. These topics include the storage type of data items, the visibility of variables, and the ability to pass values to and return values from functions.

It is possible to specify exactly how data should be stored in the C language. The storage type affects the visibility and scope of the data. The possible storage classes are auto, static, register, and extern.

Auto

auto Storage type for local varible.

The default storage of data for local variables is auto. An **auto** variable is created when a block is entered and is destroyed at the exit of the block. An auto variable does not "remember" what value it had last time it was in the function because each time the function is entered the variable is assigned a new memory location and initialized as specified. If an *auto* variable is not initialized, its value is undefined.

```
calculate( )
{
    int number;
    float amount;

. . . . . . . .
}
```

Both number and amount have a storage type of *auto* by default. There will be no initial value and the final value will not be retained after the calculate( ) is exited.

Static

static A storage classification allowing a local variable to retain its value and same memory location from one execution of a function to the next execution.

To keep the values of local variables from being destroyed when the function or block is exited, the variables may be assigned the storage type of *static*. A **static** variable maintains the value from one execution of the block to the next.

If a counter was created in a function to determine how many times the function was executed, the counter would be destroyed every time the function was left if it was an *auto* type. This would not work properly because the value of the counter would not increase. In this situation, the variable could be defined as static.

The value of a **static** variable remains for the life of the program. A *static* variable is automatically initialized to 0. The value of the *static* variable is only visible within the block in which it was defined.

```
accumulate( )
{
static int count;   /* the value of count will be
retained */
```

```
        count++;
. . . . . . . . . . . .
}
```

Another application of static is the declaration of the global variables. If static is used outside of a function, the variable can only be accessed by the program it is declared in. Other global variables could be accessed by other programs when the programs are tied together through a program list.

Register

A **register** is used to store integer variables at the best speed. In many compilers, the storage register causes the value of the variable to be stored in a CPU register. If there is no room for the variable as a *register,* it will become type *auto* with no harm to the program other than not gaining in speed.

register A storage type for local integer variables used to increase speed of execution.

The storage type of *register* is very common because of its advantages without any other change to the data. The *register* storage can reduce the size as well as improve the performance of a program.

```
calculate( )
{
        register number;
        float amount;
. . . . . . . . . .
}
```

The variable `number` will be given storage in a *register* if possible; otherwise, it will become *auto*.

Extern

An external storage type is designated with the keyword **extern**. The external variable is a global variable defined at the external level of any source file that makes up the program. The word extern used inside of a block is only a reference to a variable that has been defined at the external level.

extern Storage type for global variables or data items declared in another program.

An *extern* variable may be declared before the main or between any of the functions. It is visible to all functions that follow the point where it was defined. By referencing the *extern* variable in an earlier function, the variable can become visible to that function. If a local variable is defined with the same name as an external variable, the variable name will refer to the local variable and the global variable is no longer visible to that block.

```
extern int number;
void main( )
{
```

```
        extern int number;
        .....
}
```

Since number was declared as *extern* prior to `main(  )`, *extern* within `main` is for information only.

```
void main(  )
{
        extern int number;
        ......
}

function1(  )
{
}

extern int number;

function2(  )
{
}
```

The external variable `number` is visible after it is declared: therefore, it is visible to `function2(  )`. By the explicit request, it is also visible to `main(  )`.

Summary Table of Data Storage Types

Storage Type	Visibility	Initialization	Lifetime
auto	Local	No	Function
static	Local	Yes	Program
register	Local	No	Function
extern	Global	Yes	Program

Storage Types for Functions

Functions may also have the storage type specified. Functions will always be global in their visibility but they may be specified as *extern* or *static*. A *static* function is visible only within the source file where it is defined. Another *static* function in another source file does not conflict with one of the same name in a different source file.

Extern functions are visible within all source files that make up the program list unless it is later declared as *static*. All functions are *extern* by default.

Summary Table of Function Storage Types

Storage Type	Visibility
static	Only within local source code
extern	To all files in the program list

Self-Test

1. Why would a programmer use the storage type of register as opposed to letting the storage default to auto?
2. Write the declaration that would make the variable total_cost be of type float with a storage type of static.
3. What is the advantage of declaring a variable to be of type static?
4. What will be the initial value of the following variables:
   a. `extern float total;`
   b. `register number;`
   c. `auto char letter;`
   d. `static int number;`
   e. `static char letter = 'c';`

Answers

1. A register storage can significantly improve the speed and performance of a program.
2. `register float total_cost:`
3. The storage type static allows the value of a local variable to be retained from one execution of a function to the next. It should be used in instances where the data is not to be initialized every time the function is performed.
4. a. 0, external variables are automatically initialized to 0 or NULL.
   b. Not initialized.
   c. Not initialized.
   d. 0, static variables are also automatically initialized.
   e. 'c', variables can always be initialized as they are declared to the value desired by the programmer

VISIBILITY OF VARIABLES

Local variables are only visible to the function in which they are declared. This is known as the **scope** of the variable. Frequently a local variable is more appropriate than a global variable. There are many instances when a variable or a value will be used in only one function. If a *for* loop is being used within a function it is not necessary to have the loop index variable visible to any other function.

scope Visibility of a variable or function.

```
void printit(int size)
{
   int i;
    for(i=0; i> size: i++)

.....etc..
```

It is possible in C to have different variables with the same name that exist at the same time. This could be caused by having a local variable and an external variable by the same name. Within the function that contains the local variable, that local value would be accessed and the external variable would remain unchanged. It is also conceivable that a block within a function will have a variable that is only visible to that block.

To take a closer examination of the concept of visibility of a variable, we will look at a program that has nested blocks, with variables declared at different points.

Please type this program in and execute it on your system.

6.-1.c

```
int num = 1;       /* external variable */

void main( )
{
   printf("%d\n",num);
   { int num = 2, num2 = 3;     /* local num*/

     printf("%d  %d\n",num,num2);
        {
         int num = 0;          /* another num */

         printf("innerblock %d   %d\n",num,num2);
         }         /*end of block with num of 0 */
         /* now print num again */
         printf("%d\n",num);
         }
     printf("%d\n",num);
   }
```

Output

```
1
2   3
innerblock 0   3
2
1
```

This example makes it clear that the same variable name or identifier could be used for different variables. This can be of an advantage to us, when we are sharing functions from one program to another. However, you will certainly agree that this is not something that would be desirable to do intentionally within the same program.

Self-Test

1. What is the value of total when it is printed?

```
float total = 0.0;
void main( )
{
   calc( );
   printf("%6.2f\n",total);
}

void calc( )
{
     float total =  6.5;

total *= 2.0;
}
```

2. What takes priority within a function, the local or the external variable, if both have the same name?

Answers

1. 0.00, the total that is declared in calc( ) is not visible to main( ).
2. The local variable is visible inside the function. Outside the function, the external variable of the same name would be visible.

FUNCTION CALL BY VALUE

When calling a function, local variables can be used to provide more flexibility for the program. As the functions are created they may be stored in our own libraries or header files for use by other programs. With internal variables, the function can process data as instructed and return a value without having any affect on other portions of the program. Each module then acts independently and programs may combine existing functions together. This is basically what we have been doing by using the standard library functions and passing values called **arguments** to them.

arguments A value being received by a function: enclosed in parentheses in the function header.

```
scanf("%d",&number);
```

Think about the scanf( ) as an example. Inside the parentheses there are two or more arguments, separated by commas. The fprintf( ) has 3 or more arguments while the gets( ) has only one.

The number of arguments is determined by the needs (expectations) of the function that is being called. The scanf( ) function needs a format and an address. The variables that will hold the arguments in the called function are called **parameters.**

parameter A value being sent when calling a function.

The functions that we have created so far have not had any arguments inside the parentheses and none were expected. Since we were using global variables, the data was visible to all functions.

Passing Values to a Function

Values may be passed to a function by placing the variable name to be passed inside of the parentheses of the sending function and the variable name to receive it inside parentheses on the calling function.

```
void main( )
{
      int number = 5;
      printit (number); /*  number is an argument */
}

printit(int num)    /* num is the parameter */
etc.
```

When the parameter is received, the data type must be specified and should match the argument that was passed. The two variables number and num are different memory locations, they may or may not have the same name as illustrated below.

6-2.c

```
void printit(int number); /* specifies the function will
                             receive an integer and return
                             nothing */
void main( )
{
    int number; /* a local variable number */

    puts("Enter A Number ");
    scanf("%i", &number);

    /*  send the value of the number to printit( ) function */
    printit(number);
```

```c
    /* the original value of number has not changed */
    printf("The value of number in main( ) is still %d\n",number);
}


void printit(int number)
{
    /* the variable number is local to the printit() function, although
       it contains the value of number which was passed, it is a copy
       of the number and occupies a new memory location   */

    printf("The number is %d \n", number);
    number *= number;     /* changes the value of local number only */
    printf("Number squared is %d \n", number);
}
```

Output

```
Enter a number
5
The number is 5
Number squared is 25
```

The value of number in main( ) is still 5

Notice that the same variable name was used for both the sending and the receiving variable. Although both local variables were called "number", they refer to separate memory locations. Passing a variable only passes the value of the variable, a copy of the data, not the actual memory location.

The name of the variable does not need to be the same. The next program is exactly the same except that a different variable name was used.

```c
void printit(int num);

void main( )
{
    int number; /* a local variable number */

    puts("Enter A Number ");
    scanf("%i", &number);

    /*  send the value of the number to printit() function */
    printit(number);
```

6-3.c

```
    /* the original value of number has not changed */
    printf("The value of number in main( ) is still %d\n",number);
}

void printit(int num)
{
    /* the variable number is local to the printit() function,
although
    it contains the value of number which was passed, it is a copy of
    the number and occupies a new memory location  */

    printf("The number is %d \n", num);
    num *= num;    /* changes the value of local number only */
    printf("Number squared is %d \n", num);
```

More than one value may be passed to a function. The types may be different, because each receiving variable must have the type specified. The values will be received in the same sequence that they are sent.

```
void passletters(char a, char b);

void main( )
{
    char letter1 = 'a', letter2 = 'b';

    passletters(letter2, letter1);
}

void passletters(char ltr1, char ltr2)
{
    printf("%c  %c\n", ltr1, ltr2);
}
```

Output

```
b  a
```

Self-Test

1. Write the function header for percent( ).

```
void main( )
{
    int numcorrect, numpossible;

    percent(numcorrect, numpossible);
}
```

```
_____

{
    int percentage;

    percentage = (numcorrect/numpossible*100);
    printf("Percent correct %d %%\n",
percentage);
}
```

2. What is wrong with the following function headers?

   a. `void percent(int numcorrect, int numpossible);`

   b. `void calc_pay(hours, rate)`

3. Write a function that will receive two integer numbers and find and print the average of the two numbers.

void total(int num, int number)

Answers

1. `void percent(int numcorrect, int numpossible)`
2. a. Because of the semicolon after the statement, it must be assumed that this is a call to a function. When parameters are passed, the data type is not specified.

   b. There is no semicolon, so this must be a function header. The function header must indicate the type of data for each field.
3.
```
void average(int num1, int num2)
{
    printf("The average is %i \n", (num1 +
num2)/2);
}
void average(int num1, num2)
{
  float avg;
  avg = (num1 + num2)/2;
  printf("The average is %i \n", avg);
}jkjpi
```

In order for a function to return a value to a calling function the reserved word *return* must be used. The *return* may contain a value or an expression. The value or the result of the expression will be sent back to the location where the function was called. Now let's create a function that will pass two values and return the average of the numbers.

```
int average(int num1, int num2);
int average;

void main( )
{
    int x=5, y=7;

    printf("The average of %d and %d is %d",
            x,y,average(x,y));
}

int average(int num1,int num2)
{
    return((num1+num2)/2);
}
```

[Handwritten annotations: "returns", "call forret", "5-7 copied to x,y=par", "parameter", "sent to function"]

This program calls a function called average( ) which contains two arguments and two parameters. The arguments x and y are local integer variables that are visible only in the main( ) function. The values of the two variables are sent to the average( ) function.

In the function called average( ), there are two variables, num1 and num2, that receive the data values. The storage for these parameters are different memory locations than x and y. The parameters must be declared before the opening brace of the function. ANSI C allows for the data type of the parameters to be declared inside of the function name such as:

```
average(int num1, int num2)
```

Each parameter must have its own type listed. Older C code will frequently have the data type specified on a separate line before the opening brace.

```
average(num1, num2)
int num1, num2;
{ .....
```

If there were any other variables that would be used by the average( ) function they will be declared inside the braces.

The *return* function causes the answer of the calculation to be sent back to the requesting location in the program. In this case, the requesting location was the call to average in the `printf( )` function. The call to `average( )` could also have been an assignment statement. The next program works exactly the same as the last.

```
void main( )
{
  int avg, x = 5, y = 7;

  avg = average(x,y);
  printf("The average of %d and %d is %d",
                x,y,avg);
}

float average(int num1,num2)
{
  int avg;

  avg = (num1 + num2)/2;
  return(avg);
}
```

The avg in the `average( )` function is a different memory location than avg in the `main( )` function. avg was declared inside the braces of the `average( )` function because it is a local variable for that function and not an argument of the function.

Using the Return Value from a Function

The value that is returned from a function may be used in an assignment statement as it was earlier or within another function as the return from `average( )` was used in a `printf( )`. Many variations are possible.

Consider the use of the return value within a condition, perhaps a condition that is part of a loop. This would be no different than nesting `gets( )` inside the loop conditions in earlier chapters.

Self-Test

1. Write a function that will receive the length and the width of a rectangle (in feet) and will return the square footage.
2. Write a function that will calculate merchandise turnover rate, using the formula:

   Turnover = average inventory/cost of goods sold

   (Input beginning inventory, ending inventory, and cost of goods as local variables and return the turnover as integer.)

Answers

```
1. int square_feet(int length, int width)
   {
        return(length * width);
   }
2. int find_turnover ( )
   {
int begin_inventory, end_inventory, cost, turnover;


puts("Enter Beginning Inventory: ");
scanf("%i", &begin_inventory);
puts("Enter Ending Inventory:     ");
scanf("%i", &end_inventory);
puts("Enter Cost of Goods Sold:    ");
scanf("%i",&cost);

turnover = ((begin_inventory + end_inventory)/2)/ cost;
return(turnover)
}
```

DATA TYPES FOR FUNCTIONS

The return value of a function is integer by default. In the last example this was fine because the function was working with integer variables. However, to find the average of float data the return value would need to be of type float.

The function may be declared to be of type float in the variable declaration area. This is sometimes referred to as a **prototype.** The return type will be specified again when the function is coded. The format for a prototype is:

```
return-type name-of-function(parameter-type
parameter name..)
```

There may be as many parameters as needed but each will have the data type specified before the variable name. The parameter name is actually a local variable to be used within the function.

The return type indicates the data type for the value that will be returned from the function

```
float average(int num1,int num2);
```

declares a function called `average` that receives two integer parameters and will return one floating point value.

```
float average, find_average(float num, float num2);

void main(void)
{
    float x=5, y=7;

    printf("The average of %d and %d is %d",
            x,y, find_average(x,y));
}

float find_average(float num1,float num2)
{
    return((num1+num2)/2);
}
```

Remember that a function may only return one value. Functions may return any data type. Arrays and functions may not be returned.

Example

Write a program that will calculate the letter grade when the numeric grade (float) is entered. (Use the *switch* statement.)

6 - 5 . c

```
/*-----------------------------------------------------------
A program to determine the letter grade from a numeric grade using the
scale:
                90-100   A
                80-89    B
                70-79    C
                60-69    D
                < 60     F

----------------------------------------------------------- */

char find_lettergrade(float x);  /* prototype for function */

void main( )
```

```c
{
    float grade;

    puts("Enter numeric grade");
    scanf("%f",&grade);

    printf( "%3.1f %c\n", grade, find_lettergrade(grade));
}

/* ----------------------------------------------------
                 finds the letter grade
   ------------------------------------------------ */
char find_lettergrade(float grade)
{
    int intgrade;
    char ltrgrade;

    /*  divide the grade by 10 to get first digit */
    intgrade = grade/10;

    switch (intgrade)
    {
      case  9:
      case 10:
      ltrgrade = 'A';
      break;
      case 8:
      ltrgrade = 'B';
      break;
      case 7:
      ltrgrade = 'C';
      break;
      case 6:
      ltrgrade = 'D';
      break;
      default:
      ltrgrade = 'F';
    }

    return(ltrgrade);
```

Self-Test

1. Give the prototype declaration and the function header for a function that will receive two floating point values and will return a floating answer.
2. Write the statement to find a total of extended_prices, send the variables quantity and unit_price as arguments.

```
float calc_extended_price(int qty, float price)
{
   /* multiply quantity by price to find extended
amt   */
        return(price * qty);
}
```

3. Write a function that will calculate merchandise turnover rate, using the formula:

Turnover = average inventory/cost of goods sold

(Input beginning inventory, ending inventory, and cost of goods as local variables and return the turnover as float.)

Answers

```
1. float function_name(float parameter1, float
   parameter2);
2. total += calc_extended_price(quantity,
   unit_price);
3. float find_turnover( )
   {
        int begin_inventory, end_inventory, cost;
        float turnover;

        puts("Enter Beginning Inventory: ");
        scanf("%i", &begin_inventory);
        puts("Enter Ending Inventory:    ");
        scanf("%i", &end_inventory);
        puts("Enter Cost of Goods Sold:   ");
        scanf("%i",&cost);

        turnover = ((begin_inventory +
                        end_inventory)/2)/ cost;
        return(turnover)
   }
```

Example

Input	Processing	Output
Name	Check if hours > 40	Name
Hours	Calculate pay	Hours
Rate		Rate
		Pay

The following example will demonstrate the use of local variables in a report program. The program calculates pay, considering overtime at time and one half for the hours over 40 (see Figure 6-1 on page 180).

```c
#include <stdio.h>
#define CLS printf("\033[2J")
#define LOCATE(r,c) printf("\033[%d;%dH",r,c)
void report_heading( );
void report_detail( );
voiid report_summary( );
void prompt_screen( );

/*   specify that the functions will return type float, not int */
float enternumber( );
float calc_pay( );

void main( )
{
    report_heading( );
    report_detail( );
    report_summary( );
}

void report_heading( )
{
  fprintf(stdprn,"                              ABC Payroll Company\n");
  fprintf(stdprn,"          Name                Hours           Rate
Pay\n\n");
}


/*---------------------------------------------
                Prints the headings
-----------------------------------------------*/
void report_detail( )
{
    char name[20];
    float hours, rate, pay;
```

```
      prompt_screen( );
                                    /*    loop until an enter is pressed */
      while( strlen(gets(name)) !=0)
      {
        hours = enternumber(12);
        rate = enternumber(14);
        fprintf(stdprn,"%-30s %5.2f %6.2f %6.2f\n",name, hours, rate,
                                         calc_pay(hours,rate));
        prompt_screen( );
      }
}

/*------------------------------------------------
                  creates data entry screen
--------------------------------------------------*/
void prompt_screen( )
{
  CLS;
  LOCATE(5,35);
  puts("ABC Payroll Program");
  LOCATE(10,12);
  puts("Name:");
  LOCATE(12,12);
  puts("Hours:");
  LOCATE(14,12);
  puts("Rate:");
  fflush(stdin);          /* clear buffer for next name */
  LOCATE(10,30);
}

/*   ----------------------------------------------
    The enternumber function is used to enter the float values for the
          hours and for the rate, the row to use in the LOCATE is
          passed as an integer value
    ---------------------------------------------- */

float enternumber(int row)
{
    float num;

    LOCATE (row, 30);
    scanf("%f", &num);
    return(num);
}
```

```
/*------------------------------------------------
                  Calculates the pay
-----------------------------------------------*/
float calc_pay(hours,rate)
 float hours, rate;
{
  float pay;

  if( hours > 40)
  {
     pay = 40. * rate + (hours-40)*1.5*rate;
  }
  else
  {
     pay = hours * rate;
  }
  return(pay);
}



/*------------------------------------------------
                  prints at end of the report
-----------------------------------------------*/
void report_summary( )
{
 fprintf(stdprn,"\n ************* End of Report
*************");
}
```

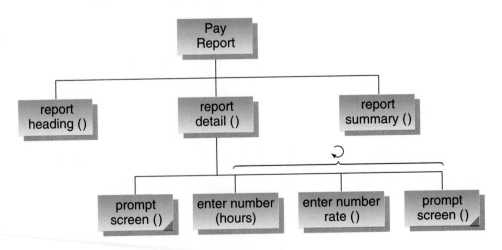

FIGURE 6-1
Hierarchy Chart—Pay Report

Self-Test

1. Why was it necessary to declare the enternumber( ) and calc_pay( ) functions in the example program?
2. Write the contents of the return( ) for the following code:

```
findcount ( )
  {
       static count;

       count++;
       return(                              );
}
```

3. Could the count++ be combined with the return?

Answers

1. If the data type is not specified for a function, the default return value will be integer.
2. `return(count);`
3. Could have been

   `return(++count);`

   because the contents of a return may be a variable or an expression.

COHESION AND COUPLING

The purpose of breaking down a program into functions was specified in Chapter 1 as a method of dividing the program into logical parts. More consideration needs to be given to this point.

The statements within a function should relate to each other. This relationship is referred to as the **cohesion** of a module or function. The cohesion should be based upon the purpose of the statements within the function.

cohesion The relationship of statements within a function.

A function that is used to print out a detail line of output will have several different types of statements. These might include checking the line count to see if a new page is needed: calling a `heading ( )` function, if necessary: adding to the line count: and printing the detail line. The statements are related in their purpose, producing the detailed output portion of the report.

Cohesion does not mean putting all *if* statements together and all `printf ( )` functions together. This would make no sense logically.

In addition to cohesiveness, the well-structured program will also contain functions that are not affected much by what occurs within another function. The measure of the interdependence of one function with another is referred to as **coupling.**

If functions are not interrelated, then a change or update to one function should not have an effect on other functions. This "loose" coupling will aid in the maintenance of the well-written program. Frequently, some change needs to be made in a program, perhaps in the formula for calculating a commission. This change should not affect the other modules besides the calculation portion of the code, such as the output design.

The best programs should have very cohesive functions with very little coupling between functions. This relationship aids in the debugging as well as the maintenance of code.

Self-Test

1. Give an example of a cohesive function for initialization. What is the relationship between the statements?
2. Would the acceptance of the system date in initialization be unacceptable for proper cohesion?

Answers

1. The initialization module sets beginning values, may get the date from the system, load a table, or access the first record. The statements in initialization are those that will be executed one time.
2. Since the date will not likely change during the execution of the program, it needs only to be accepted from the system a single time. The fact that it is "set up" or a one-time only item makes the acceptance of the date appropriate for the initialization procedure.

PROGRAMMING/DEBUGGING HINT

One error message indicates that something must be an lvalue. Data items may be referenced as lvalues and rvalues.

Lvalues versus Rvalues

lvalue The left side of an assignment statement: must represent a memory location.
rvalue The value on the right-hand side of an assignment statement: may be a value or a memory location.

An **lvalue** refers to a location in memory that may be changed. The variable on the left side of an assignment statement is an example of an item that must be an lvalue. Any value may be an **rvalue.** The terms lvalue and rvalue come from the assignment statement.

```
number    =        5;
LVALUE             RVALUE
```

Another way to visualize this is that the left side represents the address of the variable and the right side is the value that will be stored at that address. Thinking of it in this way, you could picture each variable as having a name, an lvalue, and an rvalue.

```
int num1 = 5;
float num2 = 5.0;
```

Variable	Lvalue	Rvalue
num1	location of num1 in memory	5
num2	location of num2 in memory	5.000000

These terms will take on more significance when we deal with pointers in Chapter 9. Pointers allow us to access data by its location.

The name of a string (a character array) is not an lvalue because it does not refer to a specific location where a value may be stored. The name of the array is really the memory address of the first element in the array. This is why the assignment operators may not be used on string data: rather, they are handled with the string functions.

```
char name[10];
name = "Mary"; /*  Error  */
```

This statement is illegal, causing an error message similar to:

```
Left Side Must be an LVALUE
```

KEY TERMS

argument	**extern**	**register**
auto	**lvalue**	**rvalue**
cohesion	**parameter**	**scope**
coupling	**prototype**	**static**

CHAPTER SUMMARY

In C it is possible to specify the type of storage that will be used for a variable or a function. This storage type may affect the visibility of the variable, the initial value of the variable, and maybe even the speed of execution of the program.

Variables of the same name may occur in a program at different levels or within different blocks. The most local variable takes precedence over any global or other local variables of the same name.

Functions may send a copy of the value of a variable by passing the variable as an argument to another function. The value being received is called a parameter. In addition, functions may return an expression or value to the location from which the function was called.

When dividing programs into modules or functions it is important to consider the relationship of statements within a module (cohesion) and the interrelationship between modules (coupling). Cohesion should be very strong while coupling should be loose.

The term lvalue refers to a location where something may be assigned. What is being assigned is the rvalue. The rvalue may be a value or an address.

REVIEW QUESTIONS

1. What is the difference between an auto and a static variable?
2. Name and describe the possible storage types of local variables.
3. What is the default storage type for global variables? For local variables?
4. Explain when and why a register would be used.
5. Why do the variable names that are passed as arguments not need to be identical to those variable names used as parameters on the receiving function?
6. Differentiate between cohesion and coupling. Which one should be tight? Which one loose?
7. What is indicated by the error message—not an lvalue?

EXERCISES

1. Write a program to calculate a grade average for a student using local variables for the calculation results. The input will ask for the student name and will prompt for two test scores and three program grades. The tests are worth 50% of the grade and the programs are worth 50% of the grade.

   Input:
   Student name:
   Two test scores:
   Three program grades:
   Processing:
   Find the average by taking 50% of the sum of the tests divided by 2 and add that to 50% of the sum of the programs divided by 3. Find the name and average of highest student. Find the overall average grade for all students

OUTPUT

Heading:

Course title and appropriate headings.

Detail:

Student name, test scores, program grades, average.

Summary:

Highest name and student average. Average grade for all students.

2. Write a program to find the area of a rectangle using local variables.

Input:

Length and width.

Output:

The area of the rectangle.

Processing:

Multiply the length by the width.

3. Write a program to determine bowling averages, handicaps, and female high series, male high series, female high game, and male high game. Use local variables wherever possible.

Input:

Bowler's name:

Score for game 1:

Score for game 2:

Score for game 3:

Male or female:

Processing:

Find the bowlers' average for the three games. Find a handicap of 80% of 200 by subtracting the average from 200 and multiplying by 80%. Find the highest:

game for this bowler.

female series (total of three games).

male series.

female high game.

male high game.

OUTPUT

Heading:

Use appropriate titles and column headings.

Detail:

Print out the bowler's name, three scores, average score, high game, and handicap.

Summary:

Print out highest: female series, male series, female high game, and male high game.

4. Write a program with a loop to create a monthly loan payment chart for a range of loan amounts and interest rates. Use local variables. Create interest rates from column for 10% to 12% in increments of 1/2%. Print out a line of loan payment amounts for loans in the amount of 100,000 to 200,000 in increments of 10,000. Print out charts for a 15-year loan and for a 30-year loan.

The formula to calculate monthly payments:

$$\text{payment} = \text{principal} * \text{Rate} * \frac{(1 + \text{Rate})^{\text{number of periods}}}{((1 + \text{Rate})^{\text{number of periods}} - 1)}$$

30 Years			Loan Payment Chart		
Loan Amount	10%	10.5%	11%	11.5%	12%
100000	877.57	914.74	952.32	990.29	1028.61
110000	965.33	1006.21	1047.56	1089.32	1131.47
120000	1053.09	1097.69	1142.79	1188.35	1234.34
130000	1140.84	1189.16	1238.02	1287.38	1337.20
140000	1228.60	1280.64	1333.25	1386.41	1440.06
150000	1316.36	1372.11	1482.49	1485.44	1542.92
160000	1404.11	1463.58	1523.72	1584.47	1645.78
170000	1491.87	1555.06	1618.95	1683.50	1748.64
180000	1579.63	1646.53	1714.18	1782.52	1851.50
190000	1667.39	1738.00	1809.41	1881.55	1954.36
200000	1755.14	1829.48	1904.65	1980.58	2057.23

5. Write a program to print out the portion of a monthly loan payment that goes for principal and for interest. Allow the user to input the loan amount, the annual interest rate in decimal form, and the term of the loan in years. Use the formula for monthly payment from Exercise 4. The amount of interest for a payment is simple interest found by multiplying the outstanding balance by the interest rate per month. The principal applied is the monthly payment minus the interest portion. To calculate the new outstanding balance, subtract the principal from the previous balance.

Sample Screen:

```
Loan Amortization Entry
```

Please input the following:

Loan amount:

Annual interest (in decimal form):

Term of loan (in years):

Sample Output Design:

```
Loan Amortization
```

```
Loan amount:    xxxxxxxxx
Interest rate:  xx.x%
Length of loan: xx
```

Payment Number	Payment Amount	Principal	Interest	Remaining Balance
xx	xxxx.xx	xxxx.xx	xxxx.xx	xxxxxx.xx

6. Modify Program 5 by inputting the beginning month and year of the loan. Print out the month and year for each payment instead of the payment number.

HAYLEY OFFICE SUPPLIES

Modify the Merchandise Turnover Problem (Chapter 4) to:

1. Use local variables as appropriate.
2. Specify the storage class for the variables as they are declared.
3. Include a function that has a return type other than integer.

CHAPTER OBJECTIVES

By the end of this chapter, you should be able to:

■ Understand the concepts behind creating an array in C.

■ Access individual elements within an array.

■ Visualize a multidimensional array as an array of arrays.

■ Search for information using binary and serial search techniques, including use of the ANSI bsearch( ).

■ Sort data in an array using a simple sort algorithm or the qsort( ) function.

Arrays: Single and Multidimensional

CHAPTER OVERVIEW

The use of arrays can speed the processing of data and provide methods of storing data for processes such as sorting. This chapter will introduce the concept of single and multidimensional arrays. Arrays will be accessed using the for *loop to process the data for loading the table, doing calculations on all elements, and for printing the values within the array.*

Performing searches will be covered by creating functions as well as accessing existing functions. The difference between a serial search and a binary search will be discussed along with the advantages or limitations of each. Since the binary search requires sorted data, the qsort( ) *function will be demonstrated.*

SINGLE DIMENSION ARRAYS

array A data item that contains multiple values.

An **array** is a data structure that can hold a list of values as opposed to the variables, which, so far, have contained one value at a time. An exception to this has been string data, which actually is an array of type character. With an array it is possible to store an entire list of values at one time. One data name is assigned along with the maximum number of elements that the array will contain. Each **element** of an array contains a separate value.

element A single value within an array.

string[]

P	r	o	g	r	a	m	\0

```
char string[8] = "Program";
     is the same as:
char string[ ] = {'P','r','o','g','r','a','m',NULL};
```

The square brackets [] used to give the length of a string field are the notation for an array. In the declaration the brackets may contain the maximum number of elements in the array.

Declaring an Array

Arrays may be string or they may be of any numeric data type or data structure. A numeric array is defined similarly to the way that strings have been defined. An integer array called number with 10 elements would be defined as:

```
int number[10];
```

Initializing an Array

An array can be initialized at the time it is declared by enclosing the list of elements inside of braces. If the items are string or character, they must also contain quotes.

```
     int number[5] = {1,2,3,4,5};
     char letters[6] = {'a','b','c','d','e', NULL};
or   char letters[6] = {"abcde"};
```

If the char arrays are to be accessed as a string they must allow one extra position for the null character as previously covered. When the character array is initialized using the double quotes "" around the string, a null will automatically be placed at the end of the string.

If the array is to be a local variable and to be initialized as it is declared, some compilers require it to be of storage type static.

```
static int quantity[5] = {77,54,88,92,7};
```

Initializing an Array of Unspecified Size

When an array is being initialized as it is being declared it is not necessary to specify the size of the array if it does not need to be larger than the number of elements being initialized.

```
int number[ ] = {1,2,3,4,5};
```

At run time the size of the array will be determined to be five elements.

```
char msg[ ] = "Press Any Key to Continue";
```

This msg will be allocated the appropriate number of elements and will allow a position for a null character.

Partially Filled Array

An array does not need to be filled, so more elements may be specified than are actually used. It would be legal to say

```
int number[5] = {1,2,3};
```

There is now room for two more elements. This feature will be very important when an array needs to be declared and the size is unknown. One technique would be to use a symbolic constant for the maximum number of elements and then declare the array using the symbolic constant.

```
#define MAXITEMS 100
float account_balance[MAXITEMS];
```

Subscripts

When a single value within the array is to be accessed, the position of the element must be specified. The position number of the element is called a **subscript** and is the offset(distance in values) from the beginning of the array. Since the subscript points to a position within the array, the subscript must be an integer value. The subscript is also placed in [].

Given the declaration:

```
int number[10]={10,20,30,40,50,60,70,80,90,100};
```

subscript Position of an element within an array, starting with the first postion at 0.

10	20	30	40	50	60	70	80	90	100
[0]	[1]	[2]	[3]	[4]	[5]	[6]	[7]	[8]	[9]

The actual elements in the array are numbered from 0 to 9. C always starts arrays at a base element position of 0. If we wanted to access the third position in the array number, we would use a subscript of 2.

```
printf("%d", number[2]);
     would print 30
```

The first element is at subscript 0, the second at subscript 1, and the third at subscript 2.

Self-Test

1. Given the following array, what is the value of num[3]?

   ```
   int num[5] = {2,4,6,8,10};
   ```

2. What is the subscript for the last element in the array num[5]?
3. Declare a char array called zipcode that can contain an extended zip code with 9 characters and a hyphen.

Answers

1. 8
2. 4
3. ```
   char zipcode[11];
   /*    don't forget a space for the null */
   ```

FOR LOOPS AND ARRAYS

When accessing an array, a loop is frequently required that will increment the subscript position each time through the loop. The subscript, an integer variable, will change for each iteration of the loop. This can be handled easily with a *for* loop.

A loop would be appropriate for entering data into the array, finding a total of all of the elements in the array, or outputting each position in the array. These tasks all call for repeated access to the array, changing the subscript each time.

To print every element in an array of 10 integers, the following loop could be used.

```
int i, number[10] = {2,4,6,8,1,3,5,7,9,0};
for(i=0; i<10; i++)
```
```

```
{
    printf("%d\n"; number[i]);
}
```

Output

```
2
4
6
8
1
3
5
7
9
0
```

The value of i is first initialized to 0, the condition is tested, and since i is less than 10 the loop will be executed. After the loop statement is executed, the value of i is incremented, and the condition is once again tested. The loop will continue to be executed until the condition is false.

The previous loop example works well with arrays in C. First, set the subscript variable to 0, which, of course, will point to the first element in the array. Since the elements in the array are numbered from 0, the last element is actually one less than the size of the array. As a result, the condition is tested as less than the size of the array which assures us that the loop will terminate when the end of the array has been reached. Notice that the condition is not <=, which would cause the loop to access one location in memory beyond the array.

```
int numbers[10];
for(i = 0; i < 10; i++)
{   process the array };
```

Both numeric and character arrays can be accessed one character at a time.

```
#define MAXITEMS 100
......
int i;
float account_balance[MAXITEMS];

/*          find the total for account_balance   */

for(i=0; i< MAXITEMS; i++)
{
total += account_balance[i];
}
```

Actually this could be condensed, but it would become more difficult to read:

```
/*                  find the total for account_balance    */
for(i=0; i < MAXITEMS; total += account_balance[i++]);
```

Remember that the character array contains a null character at the end, which allows us to access the entire array by using the array name as a string expression. This cannot be done with numeric arrays. If we accessed the numeric array by its name we would get the address of the first position of the array. We will discuss the reason for this in the next chapter.

```
int num[5] = {1,2,3,4,5}, i;
char letters[6] = {'a','b','c','d','e'};
char word[6] = {"abcde"};


void main( )
{
  /* Print out array elements          */
  for(i=0; i<5; i++)
  {
     printf("%d %c %c\n",num[i],letters[i],word[i]);
  }
     /*   try to print entire array      */
     printf("%d %s %s\n",num,letters,word);
  }
```

Output

```
1 a a
2 b b
3 c c
4 d d
5 e e
3792 abcde abcde
```

Notice that both character arrays act the same whether they were initialized as individual characters or as a string. The 3792 on the last line of output is the address of the array num and may differ if the program is executed again.

Using a for Loop on Partially Filled Arrays

Sometimes all of the elements in the array may not be filled. In this case we would need two conditions: one to test the size of the array and another to determine if we have reached the number of elements that are being used.

```
#include <stdio.h>
```

```
void main( )
{
     char city[15];
     int i;
     printf("Enter City:      ");
     gets(city);

/*     test for end of array or last character */

     for(i=0;  i < 15,  city[i]  != NULL;  i++)
          printf("%c\n",city[i]);
}
```

Output

```
Enter City:      Chicago
C
h
i
c
a
g
o
```

```
#include <stdio.h>

void main( )
{
     char city[15];
     int i;
     printf("Enter City:      ");
     gets(city);

/*     test for end of array or last character */

     for(i=0;  i < 15,  city[i]  != NULL;  i++)
          printf("%c\n",city[i]);
}
```

Output

```
Enter City:      Hacienda Heights
H
a
c
i
e
n
d
a

H
e
i
g
h
t
```

```
void main( )
{
     char city[15];
     int i;
     printf("Enter City:     ");
     gets(city);

/*   terminate loop when the character is an i   */

     for(i=0; i < 15, city[i] != 'i'; i++)
         printf("%c\n",city[i]);
}
```

Output

```
Enter City:      Chicago
C
h
```

In the first example, the loop continues until it reaches a null. If more than 15 characters are typed for the city name, the loop would terminate when the end of the array is reached. The s at the end of Hacienda Heights is never printed.

The third example checks for the character i. Note than when the value of city[i] is equal to the character i, the loop is terminated. Because of this only the C and the h were printed.

Self-Test

1. Write the loop that will print out each of the elements in the array

   ```
   int grade[10];
   ```

2. Write the loop that will find the average of all of the elements in the array

   ```
   int grade[10];
   ```

3. What will the following print?

   ```
   #include <stdio.h>

   void main( )
   {
     static char city[] ="Chino";
     int i;

   /*     test for end of array or last character
   */

         for(i=0; i < 15, city[i] != NULL; i++)
             printf("%c\n",city[i]);
   }
   ```

Answers

1. ```
   int i;
   for(i=0; i < 10; i++)
   {
         printf("%d", grade[i]);
   }
   ```

2. ```
   int i;
   for(i = 0; i < 10; i++)
   {
         total += grade[i];
   }
   printf("%d",total/10);
   ```

3. ```
   C
   h
   i
   n
   o
   ```
   ```

multidimensional array An array with multiple subscripts.

Arrays may have multiple levels of subscripts. A **multidimensional array** may be pictured as being an array of arrays. In memory, one array is followed by the next array. The first subscript refers to which array and the second subscript references the element within the array.

```
int num[3][5];
```

refers to an array that has three arrays with five elements in each array. With a multidimensional array of characters, there is a "list" or array each containing a "string".

```
char word[12][5];
```

sets up the storage for 12 words with 5 letters in each.

Initializing Multidimensional Arrays

Multidimensional arrays may also be initialized as they are declared. The initialization will have sets of braces within braces.

```
int num[3][5] = {
              {1,2,3,4,5},
              {6,7,8,9,10},
              {11,12,13,14,15}
              };
```

The inner sets of braces are not required. They may be used for clarity when reading the initialization. If there were no braces, the first five elements would fill up the first row, the second five the next row, etc. This would not work properly in some cases where an entire row may not be filled.

```
int num[3][5] = {
              {1,2,3},
              {6,7,8,9,10},
              {11,12,13,14,15}
              };
```

If the braces had been omitted in this case then the 6 and the 7 would have been placed in the first row of the array, which is not what was desired.

When declaring character arrays, it will be easier to eliminate the inner braces because we have the quotes to delimit the string. A string is an array of characters. The following two examples will accomplish the same thing.

```
char word[12][6] = {
                {"one"},
                {"two"},
                {"three"}
                };

char word[12][6] = {
                "one",
                "two",
                "three"
                };
```

Accessing a Two-Level Array with Nested Loops

Since the two-level array requires two subscripts, the array can be accessed with nested loops. The loops will be used when all elements of all arrays are to be processed.

```
int num[3][5] = {
                {1,2,3,4,5},
                {6,7,8,9,10};
                {11,12,13,14,15}
            };

void main( )
{
    int x,y;

    for(x=0; x<3; x++)
    {
    for(y=0; y<5; y++)
        printf("%d  ",num[x][y]);
    }
}
```

Output

```
1 2 3 4 5 6 7 8 9 10 11 12 13 14 15
```

The order of the loops will affect the sequence in which the array is accessed. Consider the following:

```
void main( )
{
    int x,y;
    int num[3][5] = {
                                {1,2,3,4,5},
                                {{6,7,8,9,10};
                                {{11,12,13,14,15}
             };


    /*    Print out first element in each array, then
            second in each array etc.          */

  for(y=0; y<5; y++)
  {
    for(x=0; x<3; x++)
      printf("%d  ",num[x][y]);
  }
}
```

Output

1	6	11	2	7	12	3	8	13	4	9	14	5	10

Self-Test

1. Write the statements to find the sum of the elements in the following array.

   ```
   float   sales[5][7];
   ```

2. What will print?

   ```
   int num[3][5] = {
                       {10,21},
                       {67,89,10}
                       {11,12,13}
                   };

   void main( )
   {
   ```

```
          int x,y;

     for(x=0; x<3; x++)
     {
        for(y=0; y<5; y++)
        {
           printf("%d   ",num[x][y]);
        }
        printf("\n");
     }
}
```

Answers

```
1. int x,y;
   float total;
   for(x=0, total = 0; x<5; x++)
   {
        for(y=0; y<7; y++)
        {
             total+= sales[x][y];
        }
   }
2. 10   21   0   0   0
   67   89   10  0   0
   11   12   13  0   0
```

Example Program

Write a program that will create a report of daily sales. Each day's sales are to be listed along with the percent they represent of the weekly sales.

Use an array to hold the daily sales. The array must be of type float with 7 elements assuming that there are sales seven days a week (see Figure 7-1).

Input:

Sales for each day

Processing:

Find total of sales

Divide total by 7 to find average

Output:

Average sales

```
/*----------------------------------------------------

     Programmed By:
     Date Written:
     Purpose:  Produce a sales report on the printer
               that lists each days total sales and the
               percent each day is of the total sales
----------------------------------------------------*/


#include <stdio.h>
#define CLS printf("\033[2J")
#define LOCATE(r,c) printf("\033[%d;%dH",r,c)

char day[7][10] = {"Sunday", "Monday", "Tuesday",
          "Wednesday","Thursday","Friday","Saturday"};
float sales[7], total, percent;

void main( )
{
 heading( );
 detail( );
 summary( );
}

/*----------------------------------------------------
        Print the headings on the report
-------------------------------------------------- */
void heading( )
{
   fprintf(stdout,"\t\t\t\t\Daily Sales Report\n\n");
   fprintf(stdout,"     Day              Percent of
              Total");
}

/*----------------------------------------------------
          Produce Detail Lines of report
---------------------------------------------------*/
void detail( )
{
```

```
    int i;

    paint_screen( );
    for(i=0; i<7; i++)
    {
      input_sales( );
      add_to_total( );
    }
}

/*-------------------------------------------------
      prints the prompts on the data entry screen
---------------------------------------------------*/

void paint_screen( )
{
    int i;
    CLS;
    LOCATE(5,20);
    puts("Daily Sales Input");
    for(i = 0; i < 7; i++)
    {
     LOCATE(10+i,15);
     printf("%s",day[i]);
    }
}

/*-------------------------------------------------
          inputs the sales data
---------------------------------------------------*/
void input_sales( )
{
    LOCATE (10+i, 30);
    scanf("%f",&sales[i]);
}

/*-------------------------------------------------
      calculates total  sales
---------------------------------------------------*/
void add_to_total( )
{
```

```
     total+=sales[i];
}


/*--------------------------------------------------
           produces summary portion of the report
-----------------------------------------------*/
void summary( )
{
  for(i=0;  i<7;  i++)
  { percent = sales[i]/total*100.;
    fprintf(stdout,"\t%-15s%6.2f percent\n," day[i],percent);
  }
  fprintf(stdout,"\n\tTotal Sales      $%5.2f",total);
}
```

Some things to notice:

1. The locate inside of the loop, row is 10 + i. Each time through the loop the screen prompt will be located one row lower with the first line printing at row 10.
2. Two identical loops, one for input and calc, one for print. Two loops were used, the first one entered the data and added the sales to the total. Since we had to find the total before we could print the percent of total, the print could not be a part of the same loop. Another loop was needed to access each element in the array to print it out.
3. The array of strings, there are two subscripts. One for length of each string, one for the number of elements which was 7 for the number of days

The loops did not have to use the same variable, but it is more efficient to declare an integer to be used as a subscript and reuse it for each loop. The i is ini-

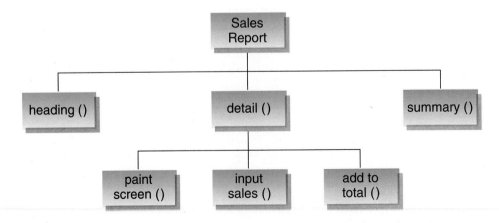

FIGURE 7-1
Hierarchy Chart—Sales
Report

tialized each time a new loop is entered. You may prefer to use a different integer variable name that is more descriptive, such as index or subscript.

ACCESSING DATA IN AN ARRAY

Data in an array can be accessed through **direct access** or **indirect access**. In direct access the subscript is known and the element may be found through the use of the subscript number. With indirect access the subscript number must be determined.

An example of direct access would be an account number assigned starting with 0 to correspond to the position within the array.

```
char client[9][7] =
{"Adams","Baker","Doe","Evans","Jones",
               "Mills", "Nguyen", "Olsen", "Smith"};
```

0	Adams
1	Baker
2	Doe
3	Evans
4	Jones
5	Mills
6	Nguyen
7	Olsen
8	Smith

If the client's "account number" is known, their name could easily be accessed. For example, account number 7 relates to Olsen. If the account numbers were not sequential or if the account number is not known, a search is needed to **lookup** the appropriate data.

Searching an Array

A **search** is used to match an item with another item from a list (array) or from a file. There are two types of search logic: a serial search and a binary search.

A **serial search** compares each item in the list sequentially with the key field. **Key field** refers to the item to be found. In a serial search the key field will be compared to the first item in the array. If it does not match, the subscript will be incremented and the key field will then be compared to the next element in the array. If the item to be found was located in the last element in the array, it would have been necessary to compare the key field with every element in the array. With a 100-element array, it may take 100 comparisons to find a match.

search Lookup a value within an array or file.
serial search A lookup that begins with the first element in the array and compares each item unitl a match is found.
key field The data item used in performing a search or sort operation.

A binary search is faster but requires that the data be sorted in order prior to the search. With a binary search on a list of 100 elements, the maximum number of comparisons is seven. A **binary search** of a sorted list compares the item in the middle of the list with the item to be found, the key field, and then determines whether the middle item is too large or too small or a match. The next comparison will then be with the middle item in the appropriate half of the list, the top half if the middle element was too small, or the lower half if the middle element was too small. The search will continue to divide the remaining elements in half and then compare with the next middle item until a match is found.

binary search A table loop of sorted data that begins the search in the middle of the data.

Serial Search Consider two arrays: the first array will contain account numbers and the second array will contain client names. Then we will create a search routine that will locate a name given the account number.

```
int account[9] = {10,20,30,45,55,65,75,85,99};
char client[9][7] = {"Adams","Baker","Doe","Evans","Jones",
                     "Mills", "Nguyen", "Olsen", "Smith"};
```

Subscript	Account	Last Name
0	10	Adams
1	20	Baker
2	30	Doe
3	45	Evans
4	55	Jones
5	65	Mills
6	75	Nguyen
7	85	Olsen
8	99	Smith

Notice that each of the arrays have the same number of elements. The account numbers belong to the corresponding name. Account 30 is the third account number and Doe is the third name. Two is the subscript for both elements, therefore we can see that the elements and subscripts correspond between the two arrays. These could be called **parallel arrays** because of the correspondence between them.

To search for a name to match an account number, first look for the position of the account number within the first array. Next, print the corresponding position within the second array.

parallel arrays Multiple arrays in which the elements of one array are related to the elements in the same position within another array.

Pseudocode

Set a found switch to No.

Ask for the account number key.

In a loop, compare the key with each element in the account number array until end of array or item is found

If a match is found:

Set the found switch to Yes.

Print the corresponding name (same subscript) from the client array.

Exit the loop.

At the end of the loop:

Check if the found switch is still set to No. If it is then no match was found.

Pause the screen to display the name or the not found message.

The search function to find the name associated with an account number is as follows:

7-5.c

```
void search( )
  {
     char found = 'n';    /* set found switch to no */

     CLS;
     LOCATE (10,20);
     puts("Account Number  "); /* prompt for key field */
     LOCATE (10,35);
     scanf("%d", &account_in);  /*  input key field     */
      /*   loop sequentially through the loop comparing
             the key with each element in account array */

     for(i=0; i<9 && found == 'n'; i++)
     {
       if(account_in == account[i])
          {
           LOCATE (12,20);
           found = 'y';
           printf("Client:      %s", client[i]);
          }
     }
     if (found == 'n')
          {
           LOCATE (12,20);
           puts("Client not found - check number );
          }
     PAUSE;
}
```

Self-Test

1. Write the search routine to find the room number when a course name is entered. Assume that the following arrays have been declared and initialized.

```
int roomnum[5] = {112, 4, 310, 308, 17};
char course[5][6] = {     "COBOL",
                          "BASIC",
                          "CICS",
                          "RPG",
                          "C"};
```

2. How would the function change if we knew the room number and were looking for the course that meets in that room?

Answers

1.
```
void search( )
{
     char found = 'n';

     CLS;
     LOCATE (10,20);
     puts("Course Name   ");
     LOCATE (10,35);
     scanf("%d",&course_in);
     for(i=0; i<5 && found == 'n'; i++)
     {
        if(strcmp(course_in, course[i])== 0)
           {
            LOCATE (12,20);
            found = 'y';
            printf("Room Number:     %d",roomnum[i]);
           }
     }
     if (found == 'n')
           {
            LOCATE (12,20);
            puts("Course not found - check spelling );
           }
     PAUSE;
}
```

2. Change the key to ask for the room number. Change the comparison to com-pare the key with the room number array. Print the }corresponding course name.

Binary Search A binary search in C can be accomplished via the `bsearch( )` function. This function will perform a binary search on a sorted array with a specific number of elements each with a specific width. You must specify the base of the array to be searched and a key field to be searched for. In order to access the `bsearch( )` function you must include the `stdlib.h` header file.

The format of the `bsearch( )` is

```
bsearch(key,base,num,width,compare);
```

The **key** is the item to be searched for; **base** is the name of the array; **num** gives the number of elements in the array; **width** is the width in bytes of each item in the array; and **compare** is a function that performs the comparison.

The `bsearch( )` returns the address of the item if a match is found, otherwise the function returns a character. The actual search and looping takes place in the function from the header file. The loop will work properly because the size of the array is being passed to the `bsearch( )` function.

The compare function will be used by the binary search but is defined by the programmer. This is necessary in order to specify the type of data that is going to be compared. The `compare( )` function must return an integer:

Negative	if element1 < element2
Zero	if element1 = element2
Positive	if element1 > element2

Example

Suppose we have a list of department names and a list of department numbers. We can use the `bsearch( )` to find the position of the department name if we enter a department name to be found.

Subscript	Department #	Department Name
0	331	Accounting
1	633	Information Services
2	425	Marketing
3	124	Production
4	515	Sales

The account numbers are in alphabetic order making it possible to do a binary search by account number. The return value of the binary search will be assigned to a field to hold an address of the character where the match was found. The concept of addresses and pointers will be discussed in more detail later. For now, accept that the declaration to hold the address will be:

```
char *result;
```

The assignment will be:

```
result = bsearch(key,department,5,sizeof(key),compareit);
```

The key will be the same size as a single department name in the array because it will hold the name of the department to be found. The compare function is `compareit( )` as defined within the program. Since the department names are of type `char[ ]`, `compareit( )` uses the `strcmpr( )` function.

When a match is found, the address of the department name will be known within the department name array. The difference between the beginning of the array and the match must then be divided by the number of characters in each element to find the subscript

```
subscript = (result - department)/sizeof(department[0])
```

This subscript may then be used to find the corresponding position within the department number array.

7-6

```
/*---------------------------------------------------
    Programmed By:
    Date Written:
    Purpose:        Find the department number by entering
                    department name using a binary search
------------------------------------------------------*/
#include <stdio.h>
#include <stdlib.h>
#include <string.h>

char key[21], department[5][21] = { "Accounting",
                                    "Information Services",
                                    "Marketing",
                                    "Production",
                                    "Sales"};
char *result;
int  deptnum[5] = {331, 633, 425, 124, 515};
int compareit( );

void main( )
{
  printf("Enter Department Name:    " );
```

```
      gets(key);

      result = bsearch(key,department,5,sizeof(key), compareit);

      if(result == NULL)
        printf("Item not found\n");
      else
          printf("Department number is %d",
                   deptnum[(result-department)/sizeof(key)]);

/* note that the function returns an address if found - must
     convert that to number of positions in the array to find
     subscript in parallel array    */
}



/*---------------------------------------------------
          compare function to be used by bsearch()
-----------------------------------------------------*/
intcompareit(char  item1[ ], char item2[ ])
{
    return(stricmp(item1, item2));
}
```

Example 2

Reverse the situation, and lookup the department number to determine the department name. The data needs to be arranged in order by department number, because the search will be performed on that field.

Subscript	Department #	Department Name
0	124	Production
1	331	Accounting
2	425	Marketing
3	515	Sales
4	633	Information Services

The key field will now be of type integer because the search is for a department number. The compare function must also be modified to work with integer numbers. The * operators will be explained soon.

```
/*-------------------------------------------------------
      Purpose:   Find the department name when the
                 department number is entered, using a bsearch( )
--------------------------------------------------------*/
#include <stdio.h>
#include <stdlib.h>
#include <string.h>

char department[5][21] = { "Production",
                    "Accounting",
                    "Marketing",
                    "Sales",
                    "Information Services"};
char *result;
int  key, deptnum[5] = {124, 331, 425, 515, 633};
int compareit( );

void main( )
{
  printf("Enter Department Number:    " );
  scanf("%d",&key);

  result = bsearch(&key, deptnum, 5, sizeof(int), compareit);

  if(result == NULL)
    printf("Item not found\n");
  else
     printf("\nDepartment name is \%s",department[(result-deptnum)]);

  /* note that the function returns a pointer to address found - must
     convert that to number of positions in the array to find subscript
     in parallel array    */
}


/*-------------------------------------------------------
          compare function to be used by bsearch()
--------------------------------------------------------*/
int compareit(int  item1[], int item2[])
{
   return(*item1-*item2);
}
```

Self-Test

1. Write the bsearch( ) to find the client name from the example in the linear search logic section.
2. Why is the *sizeof* operator preferable to just keying in the size of an element in the array?

Answer

1. `bsearch(account_in, account, 10, sizeof(account_in),compare);`

2. The size of data types may differ from one type of machine to another, the sizeof operator provides greater portability.

Sorting Data in an Array

In order to put data into sequential order, either ascending or descending, a sort may be made. The sort will work on either numeric or string data depending on whether relational operators or the string functions are used.

The sort may be coded in the program or the quicksort function called `qsort( )` may be used. Let's look at the logic for doing a sort first, then we will consider the `qsort( )` function. Either sort may be used on the array prior to performing a `bsearch( )`.

An Exchange Sort An exchange sort routine is about the easiest sort logic to follow. It is efficient if the array has fewer than 10 elements which, of course, is not very often. We will do an example with a 10-element array called num.

```
void sort( );
void printarray( );

num[5] = {456,123,781,213,377};
void main( )
{
  printarray( );      /* print array before sort  */
  sort( );            /* sort the array           */
  printarray( );      /* print the sorted array   */
}

/*-----------------------------------------------------------------
```

```
                perform an exchange sort on an array
---------------------------------------------------------*/
void sort( )
{
   int a,b, temp;

   for(a =0;a<4;a++)
   {
     for(b = a+1;b<5++)
       {
         if(num[a] > num[b])
           {
             temp = num[a];          /* store in temporary */
             num[a]=num[b];          /* exchange the values */
             num[b] = temp;
               }
         }
     }
}


/*-----------------------------------------------------
              print contents of array
---------------------------------------------------------*/
void printarray( )
{
   for(a=0<5;a++)
    printf("%d ",num[a]);
   printf("\n");
}
```

Output

```
456
123
781
213
377
123
213
377
456
781
```

Using the `qsort( )` Function

The `qsort( )` function, which is located in `stdlib.h`, is used for performing a quick sort. The sort arguments are similar to those used in the `bsearch( )` function.

```
qsort(base,num,width, (compare) ( ));
```
(handwritten above width: width of elements)

The base gives the name of the array to be sorted. The num is the number of elements in the array, and the width is the width of each element in the array. The `compare( )` function is one from your program and can use whatever name you wish.

Example

```
/*              use the qsort() function to sort */
#include <stdlib.h>      /*   ANSI */

char name[5][6] = {"Mary","Bob",
    "Laura","Susan","David"};

int compare(char arg1[ ],
        char arg2[ ]);
void printarray( );

void main( )
{
  printarray( );
  qsort(name,5,6, compare); /* call to stdlib.h sort
*/
  printarray( );
}


/*----------------------------------------------------
        compare for the qsort( )
-----------------------------------------------------*/
int compare(char arg1[ ],char arg2[ ])
{
    return(stricmp(arg1,arg2));
}


/*----------------------------------------------------
        print contents of the array
-----------------------------------------------------*/
```
(handwritten: 7-9.c)
(handwritten near David: 1 null)

```
int printarray( )
 {
  int i;

  for(i=0;i<5;i++)
    printf("%s ",name[i]);
  printf("\n");
  return(0);
}
```

Output

```
Mary Bob Laura Susan David
Bob David Laura Mary Susan
```

The qsort( ) function could also take advantage of the operators or functions within C to determine the width and the number of elements.

```
qsort(name,sizeof(name),sizeof(name[0]),compare( ));
```

The compare function in qsort( ) **and** bsearch( ) The function used for comparison should return a 1 if the value of the first element is greater than the value of the second. If the two values are equal then a 0 will be returned and a −1 if the value of the first is less than the second.

For string comparisons, strcmp( ) takes care of this very nicely. When doing numeric comparisons, we may use the following compare functions. The pointer (*) notation will be discussed in Chapter 9.

```
int compare( unsigned *elem1, unsigned *elem2 )
{
    if( *elem1 > *elem2 )
      return 1;
    else if( *elem1 < *elem2 )
      return -1;
    else
      return 0;
}
```

or

```
int compare(int *num1, int *num2)
{
   return(*num1-*num2);
}
```

Let's take a look at another example that performs a quick sort on an array of integers. The compare function is different than the one that we used on the names in the earlier example.

```c
#include <stdlib.h>

int num[5] = {3,4,1,2,5};
int compare( );

void main( )
{
   int i;

   qsort(num,5,sizeof(int),compare);
   for(i = 0; i< 5; i++)
      printf("%d  ",num[i]);
}

/*-----------------------------------------------------

     compare function for integers,
     returns 0 if equal
-------------------------------------------------------*/
compare(int *num1, int *num2)
{
   return(*num1 - *num2);
}
```

Self-Test

1. Write the bubble sort loop to sort the 100 elements in an array called numint[].
2. Write the qsort call for sorting the 100 elements in an array called numint[].

Answers

```c
1. for(a =0; a<100; a++)
       {
          for(b = a+1; b<99; b++)
            {
               if(numint[a] > numint[b])
                  {
                     temp = numint[a];
                     num[a]=numint[b];
```

```
                                  numint[b] = temp;
                              }
                  }
          }

      2. qsort(numint, 100, sizeof(int), compare);
```

PROGRAMMING/DEBUGGING TIP

Another unique thing about an array in C is that the subscript and array name can be reversed. What?? Consider the following code segment:

```
int a[3] = {550,661,772};

void main( )
{
      int i= 2;

      printf("a[i] = %d\n", a[i]);
      printf("i[a] = %d\n", i[a]);
}
```

Output

```
a[i] = 772
i[a] = 772
```

KEY TERMS

array	indirect access	parallel arrays
binary search	key field	search
direct access	lookup	serial search
element	multidimensional array	subscript

CHAPTER SUMMARY

An array is a type of data structure that can contain multiple values at the same time. Another way to think of an array is as a variable that contains a list of values.

Each value is called an element within the array. In order to specify which element we are referring to, every access to the array must include a subscript. A subscript is an index to a position within the array. The subscript must evaluate as an integer value but it may be a constant, a variable, or an expression.

A *for* loop can be used to access an array using the subscript as a variable. Multidimensional arrays require multiple subscripts to reference each of the dimensions. A two-dimensional array may be considered to have rows and columns and would require a subscript to specify the row and a subscript to specify the column. To accomplish access to the entire array, you may use nested *for* loops.

Data can be accessed from an array either directly or indirectly. With direct access, the subscript is known from some other factor or variable. For example, the month portion of the date contains an integer that could directly refer to the appropriate position in an array of month names.

Indirect access requires a search operation. This search may be either binary or serial. A binary search requires that the arrays be sorted in order prior to the search. With a serial search, the elements of the array are accessed sequentially. The search will frequently be performed on one array and then the subscript used to reference the same position in a "parallel" array.

To put the elements in the array in order, they must be sorted. This can be accomplished by writing a routine or by calling the C qsort ( ) function.

REVIEW QUESTIONS

1. What is an array?
2. Define the term *subscript.*
3. What constitutes a legal value for a *subscript?*
4. Why is the *for* loop a natural for accessing array elements as opposed to a *while* loop or a *do* loop?
5. Given an array declared as int quantity[10]:
    a. What is the subscript of the first element?
    b. What is the subscript of the last element?
6. What happens if a processing loop attempts to access a subscript larger than the size of the array?
7. What will the termination test be for a *for* loop to access a 25-element array, assuming the loop starts with i = 0?
8. Give the array size for the following multidimensional values.

```
{
    {1,3,5,7},
    {2,4,6,8},
    {9,9,9,9},
}
```

9. What are the subscripts of the value 4 in the array values in Question 8?
10. Give the subscript for the value 4 in the previous array, if the array is accessed as a single-dimensional array.

11. Why is it possible in C to handle a multidimensional array as though it were a single dimension?

12. How many elements can an array hold?

13. When and how can an array be initialized?

14. What is the subscript of the first element of an array?

15. How is a multidimensional array stored in memory?

16. If an array has been declared as

```
int number[5][6];
```
   how can the first element of the second array be accessed?

17. What occurs during a sort process to the elements in an array?

18. How can the values of two elements be swapped during the sort process?

19. What type of sort is the sort function contained in the C library?

EXERCISES

1. Write a program for a grocery checkout. The program will produce a receipt containing the description, qty @ unit price, and the extended price. At the end of the receipt include the subtotal, the amount of tax, and the total amount.

   Tables:

   Create tables to contain the product code, the description, and the unit price. The first character of the product code determines the department. The variety and liquor departments are taxable.

   Departments:

1	Bakery
2	Deli
3	Produce
4	Dairy
5	Variety
6	Liquor
7	General Foods

   Input:

   The input screen will be designed to include the store name. The program will prompt for the product code and the quantity. (The product code must be verified as valid by confirming that it is in the table before asking for the quantity.)

   Output:

   Each detail line will include the description, the extended price, and tx if the item is taxable. If a quantity of more than one has been requested, print a line with
   qty @ unit price

Product Code	Description	Unit Price
101	Whole wheat rolls—doz.	1.79
102	Croissants—pack of 4	1.29
103	Carrot cake	5.27
201	Potato salad	1.19
202	Ham	3.49
301	Lettuce	.79
302	Onions	.49
303	Potatoes	1.29
401	Whole milk	.98
402	Cottage cheese	.79
501	Cold tablets	2.50
502	Pencils	.59
601	Beer	2.99
701	Tomato soup	.49

Calculations:

Use a sales tax rate of 6% for taxable items.

Sample Output:

```
         Your Neighborhood Grocers
    Lettuce                 .79
        2 @ 1.29
    Potatoes              2.58
    Cold tablets          2.50        tx
    Subtotal              5.87
    Tax                    .15
    Total                 6.02
```

2. Write a program that will find the yearly total for each year, the quarterly average for the same quarter over the three years, and the yearly averages for sales for 1990 through 1992.

Sample Data:

```
int sales[3][4] = {
                    {5000,5025,6800,3750},
                    {5555,5050,7000,4590},
                    {6000,6000,6700,7000}
                 };
```

Sample Output:

Year	Sales
1990	20575
1991	22195
1992	25700
Yearly average:	$22823

Quarterly Averages

1st Qtr	2nd Qtr	3rd Qtr	4th Qtr
5518	5358	6833	5113

3. Write a program that will produce a list of the sales for each salesperson and print out the percent of total sales that each salesperson has maintained.

Input:
Place the names of the salespeople and the amount of sales into 2 arrays.

Output:
Produce a report of the salespeople and percentages. Use appropriate titles and column headings. Each detail line should include the salesperson's name, the amount of sales and the percent of total sales.

Processing:
Accumulate the total sales for all salespeople and use the total as the base by dividing the individual's sales by the total sales and multiplying by 100.

4. Write a menu program that will find telephone numbers or give a listing (screen or printer) of all names and phone numbers.

Array:
Initialize parallel arrays with names and phone numbers.

Option 1:
Enter a name and use a serial search to locate the appropriate phone number. Print the number on the screen and pause execution.

Option 2:
Prompt for screen or printer output. Produce a list as desired on the screen or on the printer, allowing for multipage or multiscreen output.

5. Write a menu program to retrieve information about project due dates.

Array:
Initialize parallel arrays containing project titles and completion dates.

Option 1:
Allow the user to enter a project title and have the completion date displayed on the screen.

Option 2:
Allow the user to enter a date and list all projects that are scheduled for completion as of that date. In testing, be certain to have duplicate dates.

6. Write a program that tallies total calendar sales for each girl in a Girl Scout Troop.

Array:
Create an array that contains the girls' names and an array to accumulate the total sales.

Input:
Enter the girls' names and the quantities sold.

Output:
Produce a report that lists the total sales by girl. The report should contain appropriate titles and column headings. Each detail line will print a girl's name and the total number sold by that girl. Print a summary line containing the total sold for all girls.

Processing:
Add the quantity sold to the proper element in the total sales array for the girl making the sale.

TEST DATA
Girls:

Laurie, Julie, Christine, Heather, Lisa

Sales:

> Laurie, 5
> Julie, 5
> Heather, 4
> Lisa, 10
> Christine, 7

7. Modify program 6 to print the names on the report in alphabetical order along with the proper total calendars sold for each girl.

8. Write a program to track the responses to an interactive survey about potential success in a programming course. A summary report will be produced on the printer at the conclusion of the program to indicate the number of responses that were received for each response for each question.

> **Initialization:** Load an array to hold the following questions:
> Do you attend class consistently?
> Do you read the text thoroughly?
> Do you test short programs to understand concepts?
> Do you do assignments promptly?
> Do you chart before coding?

> **GATHERING RESPONSES**

> **Welcome Screen:** Create a screen that will welcome the survey respondent and prompt for their name. Loop until no name is entered.
>> a. Print a screen containing a question from the array and possible answers.

> **Sample:**
> Programming success survey: Do you do test short programs to understand concepts?
>> 1. Never
>> 2. Occasionally
>> 3. Usually
>> 4. Frequently
> Enter NUMBER for your response _
>> b. Add 1 to an appropriate two-dimensional table according to the question number and the response.

> **Print the Report:**
> At summary time, print the table and the accumulated responses for each question.

HAYLEY OFFICE SUPPLIES

Create parallel arrays to store the product items and to store the aisle numbers where the products can be found.

1. Write a program that will "lookup" the aisle number when the product description is entered. Use the `strncmp( )` to compare the number of characters entered with the table entry—for example, if pen is entered, a match should be found for pens and pencils.

2. Modify the program to use a binary search. Sort the array, if necessary.

Sample Data

Product	Aisle
Staples	11
Notebooks	8
Pens and pencils	1
Desk chairs	17
Computers	16
Typewriters	16
Printers	16
Drafting tables	17
Forms	8
Calendars	9
Diskettes	15

CHAPTER

CHAPTER OBJECTIVES

By the end of this chapter you should be able to:

■ Define fields within a record using a structure.

■ Distinguish between a structure and a union.

■ Combine structures and unions as needed.

■ Determine the amount of storage required by either a structure or a union.

■ Define new data types using the *typedef*.

■ Represent data in integer form with *enum*.

■ Access the tm structure declared in the time.h file.

Aggregate Data Types: Structures and Unions

CHAPTER OVERVIEW

In business, data is most frequently referred to according to the hierarchy of file, record, and field. In C, a unit of multiple fields that are associated with each other may be represented using structures. This provides the ability to access an entire record or an individual field. Another derived data type that allows a single storage area to contain different types of data is a union. We will examine these as well as the typedef in this chapter.

A very useful structure that is defined in the time header file is used to represent the system time. Accessing this structure will provide the capability of using a date in a program, such as in the title of a report.

AGGREGATE DATA TYPES

aggregate data types A data type that contains a declaration of more than one item; includes structures, unions, and enum.

An **aggregate data type** is one that may contain more than one type of data. The *struct, union,* and *enum* data types in C are derived aggregate data types. The *typedef* allows programmers to create their own data types.

Structures

structure An aggregate data type consisting of a group of fields.

A **structure** allows us to combine several variables together and to treat them as a single unit. You might be familiar with the concept of a record containing several fields of data. We could refer to the group of data by the record name or we can refer to an individual field. This is also true of structures.

A structure may combine as few or as many fields as desired, and the fields may be of any type or combined types. The format for defining a structure is:

```
struct [tag]
{
    field 1;
    field 2;
    .....
} [variable_name1, variable_name2,...];
```

tag Gives a name to an aggregate data type; does not reserve memory.

The structure tag is a name given to the new data type created by this definition: the tag is optional. The **tag** does not reserve memory for a variable but merely gives a name to the structure that may be referred to later in the program. The structure declaration may contain a variable name associated with this structure type; the variable name does create a variable and reserves memory.

If other variable names are to be declared to be of a structure type at a later point in the program then it is necessary to have a structure tag.

```
struct date
{
  int year;
  int month;
  int day;
}
struct date hire_date, birthdate, review_date;
```

Structure Tag
```
struct name
    {
        char lastname[12];
        char initial;
        char firstname[10];
    };
```

The reserved word *struct* is used to define and access the data in a structure. This structure contains three items: lastname, initial, and firstname. The tag name is not a variable but merely a shorthand notation for the structure definition for use when declaring any variables to be of this type of structure.

A variable can be declared to be of this structure type as follows:

```
struct name employee;
```

Now there is a variable called `employee` of a structure type with the tag "name".

Structure Variables There may be multiple variables of a given structure type. These may be declared when the structure is defined or declared later in the program.

```
struct
{
    int year;
    int month;
    int day;
} hire_date, birthdate, review_date;
```

This example does not have a tag, so additional variables may not be designated as this structure type later without redefining the structure. The hire_date, birth-date, and the review_date are all variables that contain three integers each.

Size of a Structure The size of a structure is the sum of the size of all of its parts. The size can be found by adding up the size of each of the component fields, but this may change from one type of machine to another. Also, if any changes are made to the structure then the size will also change. A better way to determine the size is through the use of the *sizeof* operator. The *sizeof* may refer to the tag or the variable.

```
struct name
    {
        char lastname[12];
        char initial;
        char firstname[10];
    };
```

In this example

```
sizeof(name)
```

would yield a 23 with Quick C or Borland C++.

Referring to a Field within a Structure   To refer to the individual elements of a structure, the structure variable name is combined with the field name, separated by a period.

```
structurevariable.fieldname
```

This notation can be used anytime that a field within a structure is accessed, including printing, input, and calculations.

```
struct name
{
    char lastname[12];
    char initial;
    char firstname[10];
}employee;
```

To assign the first name "Steve" it is necessary to say:

```
strcpy(employee.firstname, "Steve");
```

Similarly, to input the initial the field will then be referred to as `employee.initial`.

```
scanf("%c",&employee.initial);
```

Variable name   field name

Self-Test

1. Declare a structure called inventory that will contain a 25 character description, a quantity (integer), the current unit_cost (float), and the last_order_date (9 characters).
2. Write a scanf( ) function to input the unit_cost from the inventory structure.
3. Write a printf( ) function that will print the description and the quantity from the inventory structure.

Answers

```
1. struct
   {
       char description[25];
       int quantity;
       float unit_cost;
       char last_order_date[9];
   } inventory;

2. scanf("%f", &inventory.unit_cost);
```

```
3. printf("%-30s %4d\n",inventory.description,
   inventory.quantity);
```

Structures within Structures   Structures may also be used as a data type within the definition of another structure. Name would be a common data type in many different applications.

```
struct name
      {
        char lastname[12];
        char initial;
        char firstname[10];
      };

struct date
      {
         int year;
         int month;
         int day;
      };

struct
      {
        struct name employee;
        char social_security[12];
        struct date hire_date;
      }  emp_rec;
```

Emp_rec is a variable name for a structure that contains two other structures as well as a character array.

```
gets(emp_rec.employee.firstname);
```

To enter data into the first name field, firstname will be used with a period behind employee. Employee is a component field of the structure variable emp_rec so another period notation is required.

Arrays of Structures   A structure may be declared to be an array allowing multiple records containing the same field types.

```
struct name
      {
        char lastname[12];
        char initial;
        char firstname[10];
      };
```

```
struct date
    {
        int year;
        int month;
        int day;
    };

struct
    {
      struct name employee;
      char social_security[12];
      struct date hire_date;
    }  emp_rec[25];
```

Note that emp_rec is an array of 25 structures.

Entering Data into a Structure Array   When referring to an array of structures, the subscript follows the structure identifier and prior to the individual field. The following program will allow the first name to be entered into the first emp_rec.

```
struct name
    {
      char lastname[12];
      char initial;
      char firstname[10];
    };

struct date
    {
        int year;
        int month;
        int day;
    };

struct
  {
    struct name employee;
    char date[8];
  } emp_rec[25];

void main( )
  {
    /*    prompt for the employee name    */
   puts("Employee:    ");
```

```
        /*   enter data into employees first name in
             the 0 element within the emp_rec[] array */

    gets(emp_rec[0].employee.firstname);

    printf("The employee's first name is %s",
        emp_rec[0].employee.firstname);
}
```

Normally it is necessary to put values into each position within the array. An input routine would obtain data for each of the component fields of the structure, continuing on to the next structure in the array, most likely with a *for* loop.

Placement of Array Brackets Consider the following two input functions.

```
gets(emp_rec[0].employee.firstname);
```

versus

```
gets(emp_rec.employee.firstname[0]);
```

The brackets[] are placed behind the array name. In the first situation, data is being entered into the emp_rec array. When placed behind the variable firstname, the array index is pointing to a character within firstname.

```
struct
{
    struct name studentname;
    float exam[3];
    float program[10];
} student[40];
```

To enter data into the first program grade within the structure for the fifth student, the input function would be:

```
scanf("%f",student[4].program[0]);
```

Naming Tags and Variables the Same There is not a problem if the same name is used as a structure tag and as a structure variable. The compiler will be able to determine which one is being referred to by the usage.

```
struct date
{
     int month;
     int day;
     int year;
} date;
```

The structure tag is the same name as the variable assigned to the structure. With the notation

```
date.month
```

it is obvious to the compiler that the reference is to the variable date. However, when declaring

```
struct date date_in;
```

date refers to the structure tag.

Replacing Multidimensional Arrays with an Array of Structures

When accessing data in a multidimensional array, all of the items within the array must be of the same type. A table that will contain sales for ten reporting periods for 25 salespeople makes sense as a multidimensional array because all items are sales.

This is not true, though, for much of the storage of information required in a business setting. Usually, there is an entire file of information, within which each record contains a multitude of different fields, each of which is of a different storage type. This characteristic of a structure lends itself easily to the situation where the field types are different within the record. An array of these structures can make up the file. (Storing these files on disk is covered in Chapter 10.)

Title	Author	Publisher	ISBN
Megatrends	Naisbitt, John	Warner Books	0-446-51251-6
Illusions	Bach, Richard	Delacorte Press	0-440-04318-2

```
struct
{
     char title[30];
     char author[30];
     char publisher[30];
     char ISBN[15];
} book[1000];
```

Self-Test

1. Declare a variable called date_of_hire to be of structure type date.
2. Create a structure that contains an address. The fields within the structure will be street, city, state, and zip. Each field will be of type char[].
3. How could the size of the address structure be determined?
4. Write a structure that contains the employee name, address, and date of hire.
5. What notation would be used to refer to the city for an employee?

Answers

```
1. struct date date_of_hire;
2. struct address
   {
        char street[15];
        char city[15];
        char state[3];
        char zipcode[10];
   };
3. sizeof(address);
4. struct
   {
        struct name employee_name;
        struct address employee_address;
        struct date date_of_hire;
   } employee;
5. employee.employee_address.city
```

Unions

A union definition appears the same as a structure but in a **union** it is not a combination of variables but rather a list of possible variables. In a union, the actual variable will contain only one of the defined types. This allows a great deal of flexibility where the specific situation may determine the actual form that a field will take.

union An aggregate data type in which the data may be one of multiple specified types.

```
union  [tag]
{
    field1;
    field2;
    ....field[n];
} [variablename1, variablename2,...];
```

A field for month may be spelled out or written as an integer number, but it will only be one or the other.

```
union month
     {
        char name[10];
        int number;
     };
```

The data can be accessed as follows:

```
month.name
```

or

```
month.number
```

Size of a Union   The size of the union is the size of the largest type within the union since all of the types will not exist at the same time. If a union is set up that contains the month in `char[10]` or integer form, the string would require more space. Remember that the month will be either a string or an integer, it will not be both at the same time.

```
union month
{
   char name[10];
   int number;
};
```

The union will be 10 characters long since that is the longer field of the two. The *sizeof* operator may be used to determine the size.

Structures and Unions   A structure could be a part of a union. Likewise, it would be possible to have a union as one of the component fields of a structure. And, of course, a union could contain another union. Whew, what a world of possibilities. Consider the following:

1. A structure that contains a union.

   ```
   struct date
   {
       int year;
       union months month;
       int day;
   };
   ```

2. A union that contains a union.

```
union discount
{
    float percent;
    float amount;
};

union
{
    union discount saleprice;
    float employee_price;
} saleamt;
```

3. A union that contains a structure.

```
union
{
    struct date today1;
    char today2[9];
} date;
```

Self-Test

1. Write a union for a test answer. The answer may be fill-in which would require a 10-character string, or it may be multiple choice of one character.
2. What is the size of the answer union?
3. Give an example of a union and structure combination.

Answers

```
1. union answer
   {
   char fill_in[10];
   char mult_choice;
   };
```

```
2. sizeof(answer), which will be 10, the length
   of fill_in.
```

Enum

Enum stands for enumerated data type. It is actually an integer variable that takes its value from a list of constants that are listed in the definition. The *enum* is not a

enum An integer data type that allows a word to be used to represent a numerical value.

new data type; rather, it is designed merely to improve the readability of the program code. The general format for defining an enumerated data type is

```
enum [tag] {name1,name2,...namen}[variable name];
```

As with *union* and *struct,* the tag or the variable name is optional, but you may need to use one depending on whether you are declaring your variable name now or later.

Each name within the definition is assigned an integer value. If no values are assigned when the enumerated variable is defined, the first name will be given a value of 0, the second a 1, etc. The ANSI standard calls for *enum* to represent integers but some compilers allow other numeric data types.

```
enum category {comedy, drama, sci-fi, western};
```

In this instance, the tag is `category`. The enumerated constants are inside of the braces. By default, `comedy` will be assigned the integer value of 0, `drama` is 1 etc. A variable can now be assigned to the *enum* type.

```
enum category video, book;
```

The variables video and book are both of type category and can be assigned the enumerated constants `comedy`, `drama`, `sci-fi`, and `western`.

Assigning Values to the Constant Names   The integer values of the constant may also be specified as in the following:

```
enum test{true = 1, false = 0};
```

There may be multiple *enum* constants with the same value. The previous example could be expanded to

```
enum test{true = 1, false = 0, yes = 1, no = 0};
```

In the last two examples, a tag has been declared with the *enum*. This could be followed by assigning a variable to the type `test`.

```
enum test answer = yes;
```

The variable `answer` has been declared with an initial value of `yes`.

```
#define CLS printf("\033[2J")

enum   {mon,tue,wed,thu,fri,sat,sun} day;

void main( )
{
 CLS;
 puts("0 Monday\n1 Tuesday\n2 Wednesday\n3 Thursday");
 puts("4 Friday\n5 Saturday\n6 Sunday");
 printf("Select the number for day of week   ");
 scanf("%d",&day);

 if (day == sun|| day == sat)
    puts("Weekend!!!");
 else
    puts("Weekday");

}
```

An integer number is entered into "day". When the "day" is used in the decision statement it is compared to the *enum* names which makes the decision easier to read.

The *if* above is actually equivalent to:

```
if(day == 5 || day == 6)
     puts("Weekend");
else
     puts("Weekday");
```

The *if* using an *enum* certainly makes more sense at a quick glance than comparing to the codes used for day. This technique may be used anytime a series of integer numbers is used as a code for a list of possible values.

Self-Test

    1. Write an enumerated data type for marital status given the following codes:

Single	1
Married	2
Divorced	3
Widowed	4

2. Use the default integers to assign an enumerated data type to the directions north, south, east, and west.
3. What is the integer value of east in your direction enum?

Answers

1. ```
   enum marital_status{Single = 1, Married,
       Divorced, Widowed};
   ```

   Notice that the 1 was assigned to single, the remaining values will automatically increment from 1. You could also explicitly state each integer value.

2. ```
   enum directions {north, south, east, west};
   ```

3. East has a value of 2. The default is for the first integer value to be 0 and for the others to increment by one.

Typedef

typedef Reserved word allowing a new name to be given to an existing data type or for a complex data type to be created.

The reserved word ***typedef*** is used to assign a new name to an existing data type or to create complex data types. Maybe you would prefer to call your *float* data REAL instead of *float*. The format of the type definition is

```
typedef  current-name new-name;
```

The current-name or the new-name can then be used for declaring variables. The *typedef* does not destroy the existence of the reserved words but merely provides a synonym. Complex data types may be created with *typedef*. To create a synonym for *float* called REAL use:

```
typedef float REAL;
```

A valid declaration would then be:

```
REAL amount = 5.00;
```

The result will be amount becoming a *float* variable. *typedef* can also be used with structures. The *typedef* name can then be used rather than the structure tag in declarations.

```
typedef struct name{
                char lastname[12];
                char initial;
                char firstname[10];
              } NAME;
```

The structure tag is name while NAME is a typedef of type struct name.

Assigning *typedef* to an Array When assigning an identifier to an array using `typedef`, the size of the array will follow the identifier.

```
typedef array_type identifier[size];
```

If the first name, last name, street, and city were all to be assigned to character arrays of 15 characters each, the following could be used:

8-3.c

```
/*   set up a typedef for an array   */
typedef char STRING[15];

/*   use the typedef identifier to declare variables   */
STRING lastname, firstname, street, city;

void main( )
{
  /*          example of use of string - still the same     */
  puts("Enter City");
  gets(city);
  printf("The city is %s",city);
}
```

The *typedef* may be used to make a program more readable or for consistency with terminology within a particular company environment. If a *typedef* is used frequently for applications, it should become part of the header file associated with the project.

Self-Test

1. Write a typedef to use the entire word integer for integer numbers.
2. What would the typedef be to assign a character array of 10 characters to the type WORD?
3. Where would the typedefs usually be declared?

Answers

1. `typedef int INTEGER;`
2. `typedef char WORD [10];`
3. The typedefs could be declared in the header file so that they could be included in multiple programs.

DATE AND TIME FUNCTIONS

The date functions are part of the `time.h` header file. In that file, there are some *typedefs* and structures that need to be understood in order to deal with the time functions.

```
struct tm
    {
       int tm_sec;
       int tm_min;
       int tm_hour;
       int tm_mday;        /* day of the month */
       int tm_mon;         /* month*/
       int tm_year;
       int tm_wday;        /* days since Sunday */
       int tm_yday;        /* Julian day */
       int tm_isdst;       /* daylight savings time flag*/
    };
```

This structure has been defined for you in the header file with a tag `tm`. You may assign this structure to any variable you wish in your program, and you then can access the individual fields within the structure.

Another definition that is provided in the header file is an alternate name for type *long* which will be used to hold a time value. The time as it is accessed from the system is the current time in seconds since January 1, 1970, Greenwich Mean Time. The integer number used to express this would be too long for a normal short integer and is, therefore, be given the type *long*. The header file contains the definition:

```
typedef long time_t;
```

In order to use these types it is necessary to include the `time.h` header file in your program. After that, you may declare your own variables of these data types. There are several functions that operate on these data items.

8-4.c

```
#include <time.h>
#include <stdio.h>

struct tm *currenttime;
time_t aclock;
```

```
void main( )
{
 time(&aclock);                        /*get time in seconds*/
 currenttime = localtime(&aclock);    /*converts to struct*/
 printf("The current date and time are %s\n",
          asctime(currenttime));
}
```

The time( ) function

The time( ) function is used in this program to get the time in seconds from the system. The seconds are stored in a variable of type time_t called aclock.

Converting time( ) Seconds to tm Structure

The seconds in the variable aclock can be converted to the structure format by using the localtime( ) function. This is assigned to a variable called currenttime in this example. The * is necessary in the declation to indicate that the return value is a pointer.

The asctime( ) Function

The value in the structure currenttime is then accessed with the asctime( ) function which converts the time to a 26 character string containing day of the week, month, time, a new line character, and a null character.

An Easier Way   In Microsoft C the date and time can be accessed directly from the system in the form of mm/dd/yy and hh:mm:ss using the _strdate( ) and _strtime( ) functions. These formats require the data to be entered into a character array of 9 characters, allowing for the trailing null character. Once the date has been accessed, the variable can be used over and over. To update the time, it is be necessary to call the _strtime( ) function again.

```
#include <time.h>

struct tm date;
time_t now;
char buffer[9];

void main( )
{
  printf("%s\n", _strdate(buffer));
  printf("%s\n", _strtime(buffer));
}
```

Since only one item was printed at a time, it was possible to use the same buffer for both function calls in this example.

Putting the Date in a Title

You may also wish to initialize the date in your initialization function and then use it when printing your titles and headings.

8-6.c

```c
#include <time.h>

void initialization( );
void titles( );

char today[9];
int linecount, pagecount;

void main( )
{
   initialization( );
   titles( );
   etc......
}

void initialization( )
{
   /*       This will work in Microsoft C   */
     _strdate(today);
}

void titles( )
{
   linecount = 0;
   pagecount++;
   printf("  %s                    Title              Page %d",
          today, pagecount);
}
```

Performing Date Arithmetic

The fields within the tm structure are defined as integer type and can be used in calculations. The following program will access today's date and determine what the date will be 30 days from now.

```
/*   ch8-7.c   This program will calculate the date 30 days from now   */

#include <time.h>

struct tm *dateinfo;
time_t seconds, datethen;

void main( )
{
  time(&seconds);
   dateinfo = localtime(&seconds);
   dateinfo->tm_mday +=30;
   datethen = mktime(dateinfo);

   printf("Thirty days from today it will be %s",
             asctime(localtime((&datethen))));
}
```

Summary of Date Functions

asctime( )	Converts the tm structure to a 26-character string of the format Mon Sep 10 16:00:00 1990\n\0.
localtime( )	Converts the long integer time_+ into a struct tm.
mktime( )	Converts localtime into a calendar value.
time( )	Gets the time in seconds since 1/1/70 in Greenwich. Mean Time from the system and adjusts according to the time zone.
_strtime( )	Returns the current time as hh:mm:ss.
_strdate( )	Returns the current date as mm/dd/yy.

Self-Test

1. Declare a variable that will store the date to be printed at the top of the page as part of the titles.
2. Write the statement to accept the date into the variable for the page title date.
3. Write a statement that would accept the date and print the title in one step.

Answers

1. `char date[9];`
   Can be any character variable that allows eight characters for the date and one for the null character.

2. `_strdate(date);`

3. `fprintf(stdprn,"      %s             Title              Page`
   `              %d",  _strdate(date), pagecount++);`

An Example Program

Write a program using structures and unions to contain employee information and print a report after the information is entered (see Figures 8-1 through 8-3).

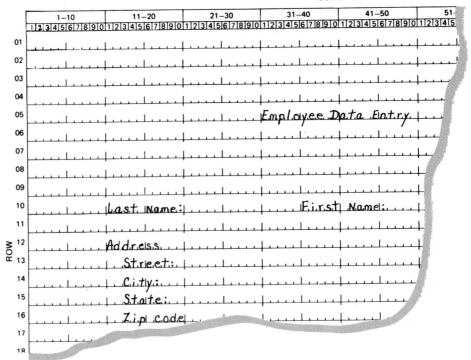

FIGURE 8-1
Screen Layout for Employee Data

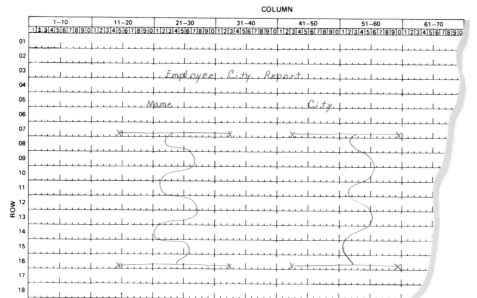

FIGURE 8-2
Report Layout for Employee Report

Display Screen Layout Sheet

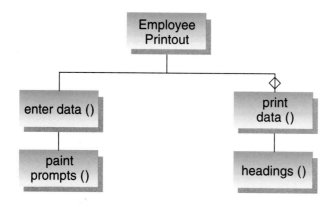

FIGURE 8-3
Hierarchy Chart for Employee Report

◇ if number_employees > 1

8-8.c

```c
#include <stdio.h>
#define MAX 500
#define CLS printf("\033[2J")
#define LOCATE(row, column) printf("\033[%d;%dH",row, column)
```

```c
int enter_data( )
void paint_prompts( );
void print_data(int);
void headings( );

struct name
{
   char last[15];
   char first[10];
};

struct address
{
   char street[20];
   char city[15];
   char state[3];
   char zip[10];
};

union date
{
    int year;
    int month;
    int day;
};

enum type
{
   salary = 0,
   hourly = 1
};

struct
{
   struct name name;
   struct address address;
   union date hiredate;
   union date birthdate;
   char social_security_num[12];
   enum type level;
} employee[MAX];
```

```
void main( )
{
    int number_employees;

    number_employees = enter_data();
    /*  test if any data was entered  and then print */
    if(number_employees > 0)
    {
      print_data(number_employees);
    }
}


/*-------------------------------------------------------
                enters data into the structure
-----------------------------------------------------*/
int enter_data( )
{
    int i = 0;

    paint_prompts( );
    while(strlen(gets(employee[i].name.last))!=0)
    {
      LOCATE(10,53);
      gets(employee[i].name.first);
      LOCATE(13,25);
      gets(employee[i].address.street);
      LOCATE(14,25);
      gets(employee[i].address.city);
      LOCATE(15,25);
      gets(employee[i].address.state);
      LOCATE(16,25);
      gets(employee[i++].address.zip);

          paint_prompts();
    }
  return(i);
}


/*-------------------------------------------------------
                creates data entry screen
-----------------------------------------------------*/
```

```c
void paint_prompts( )
{
  CLS;
  LOCATE(5,35);
  puts("Employee Data Entry");
  LOCATE(10,10);
  puts("Last Name:");
  LOCATE(10,40);
  puts("First Name:");
  LOCATE(12,10);
  puts("Address:");
  LOCATE(13,12);
  puts("Street");
  LOCATE(14,12);
  puts("City");
  LOCATE(15,12);
  puts("State:");
  LOCATE(16,12);
  puts("Zip Code");


  LOCATE(10,21);
}


/*-----------------------------------------------------------
                    prints out the structure
------------------------------------------------------------*/
void print_data(int maximum)
{
    int i, linecount;
    char name[30];

    headings();
    for(i = 0; i < maximum; i++)
    {
      if(linecount++ > 40)
      {
      fprintf(stdprn,"\f");   /*  advance to new page   */
      headings();
      }
```

```
        strcpy(name,employee[i].name.first);
        strcat(name," ");
        strcat(name,employee[i].name.last);
        fprintf(stdprn, "    %-30s %-20s\n\r",name,
          employee[i].address.city);
      }
   fprintf(stdprn,"\f");   /*  eject the paper  */
}


/*----------------------------------------------------
            prints out the page headings
-------------------------------------------------------*/
void headings( )
{
  fprintf(stdprn,"\n                    Employee City Report\n\r");
  fprintf(stdprn,"                Name                 City\n\n\r");
}
```

KEY TERMS

aggregate data types	enumerated variable	tag typedef
enum	structure	union

CHAPTER SUMMARY

Data types beyond the basic types can be created using *struct, union, enum,* and *typedef.* The structure represents a group of fields combined together as a unit, which is representative of a record. A data type that allows a variable to be one of a variety of types and associated names is *union. Enum* allows an integer to be assigned to a name for use in conditions. In order to use a different term for any data type in C, the *typedef* may be used.

REVIEW QUESTIONS

1. Differentiate between a structure and a union.
2. What is the purpose of a tag for an aggregate data type?

3. Differentiate between a tag name and a variable name being declared when an aggregate data type is declared.

4. Of what advantage is an enumerated data variable?

5. When would it be appropriate to use a typedef?

6. Give an example of a typedef that is used in the ANSI standard header files.

7. When the date is accessed from the system, what form is it in?

8. List five of the data elements from within the tm structure from the time.h header file.

9. How can the time be changed from a long integer into the tm structure?

10. Write the variable name to print the calendar Julian date, assuming that the variable *today* has been declared to be of type tm.

11. Give an example of a structure that contains another structure.

12. How can a union contain a structure?

13. Why is the enum not very programmer friendly?

14. Find an example of a typedef in the stdio.h file.

EXERCISES

1. Write a program that will request employee information until the user types "quit" or presses enter. The program must allow for a maximum of 25 employees. The output will be a detail report of the name and phone numbers. At the end of the report specify the number of salaried and the number of hourly employees. The employee information will contain the name, address, phone number, and status:

   The name will consist of a last name and first name (15 characters each).
   The address will consist of street and city (15 characters each), the state (2 characters), and the zip (10 characters to allow for a hyphen).
   The status field may contain either the value salary or hourly.
   Set up a typedef called STRING that contains a character array of length 15.
   Testing: Input at least five data elements to test the program.

2. Write a program that will track student progress for a karate studio. The program will utilize an array of structures containing information about each student. Enter at least 10 records into your array and create a report that prints the name, phone number, and current rank for each student.

   Input:
   Create a well-designed input screen that includes prompts for all of the information that belongs in the student structure.
   Structure:
   Each record will contain the following information:
       Name: Consisting of last name and first name
       Phone number:
       Dates array:
           Start date:
           White belt date:

Orange belt date:

Blue belt date:

Green belt date:

Brown belt date:

First degree black belt date:

Kata array: An array that can contain up to 20 katas, allow 25 characters for the name of each kata.

Weapons Array: Will contain a Y in the array for each weapon learned. The elements in the array will stand for:

Bo staff

Joto

Nunchaku

Samurai sword

PROCESSING

Detail:

Determine the current rank by finding the last date in the rank array and determining belt color by element number from the array.

Summary:

Calculate the number of students that know each weapon type. Print these at the end of the report. Also print the total number of students.

OUTPUT

Titles:

Include the page number.

Detail:

Name, phone, and belt ranking using the word from rank.

Summary:

Number knowing each weapon type. Number of students on record.

3. Using an array of structures, write a program to create a roster for a Little League team. For each player, include first name, last name, address (another structure), age, years participated, phone number, parent's name, and insurance company. Allow for a maximum of 15 players on a team. The program will produce two reports:

a. The first will contain the information about each player neatly formatted. If the output exceeds one page, include a title and page number on the consecutive pages.

b. The second will be a phone list that contains the players' names in column 1 (as last name, comma, then first name). The parents' names will be in column 2, and a third column will contain the phone numbers. This report should fit on one page.

4. Write a program to monitor tank levels for an oil refinery. There are seven tanks. For each tank, the program must have a structure to maintain the tank product type and barrel contents at three-hour intervals over a 24-hour period. Four tanks can vary at any given time, two will increase as oil is produced and two will decrease as oil is piped out. Use the structure to create a report that lists the following information for each tank:

a. Minimum level in number of barrels and time of day.

b. Maximum level in number of barrels and time of day.

c. Average level.

5. Use the time structure to calculate the number of days a loan is overdue.

> **Input:** Due date of loan.
> **Output:** Number of days overdue.
> **Processing:** Use the time structure to get the current date and find the number of days between the due date and the current date.

6. Create an array of structures for student information. Each student record will contain a name, address, phone, and an array of structures of classes completed. The address will be a structure of street, city, state, and zip code. The classes completed structure will contain the course title, prefix and course number, number of units, grade (may be a letter or an integer between 0 and 100), and date completed. Input data into the array for at least three students. Print a report with the name and phone number of each student. Print a second report that contains the name and total units completed for each student.

7. Modify Exercise 6 using an enumerated data type to represent student grades. (All grades will be letter grades: A, B, C, D, F.) Use the program to calculate GPA assuming that an A is 4 points. Don't forget to weight the GPA according to the unit value of the course.

8. Complete the disk program CH8-9.C so that the remaining data is entered. Modify the report to print the name, the hire date, and the social security number.

9. Modify Program 1 in Chapter 7, (see page 220), the Grocery Sales Receipts, so that the data about each product is stored in an array of structures. Each structure will contain the product code, the description, and the price.

HAYLEY OFFICE SUPPLIES

Create a structure for the inventory items. Each structure will contain the product number, product description, the aisle number, current cost, quantity on hand, minimum order quantity, and vendor.

Use the structure to create a program for sales transactions. The sale transaction screen will allow the user to enter the product number or, if not known (press Enter), the product description. The price will be calculated as a 35% markup. Assume all items are taxable. The results will be an invoice calculating the amount due, and an update to the structure quantity field.

For this example, make up sample data and enter it into the array of structures at the beginning of the program to simulate a data file.

CHAPTER

CHAPTER OBJECTIVES

By the end of this chapter you should be able to:

- Learn the pointer operators for declaring variables to store addresses and for referring to values stored at those addresses.

- Avoid indirection errors through an understanding of levels of indirection.

- Determine the types of calculations that are legitimate with pointers.

- Access arrays using pointers.

- Use pointers to access multidimensional arrays.

- Treat multidimensional arrays as single-dimensional arrays.

- Use pointers to return and pass addresses to a function.

❶ ❷ ❸ ❹ ❺ ❻ ❼ ❽ ❾ ❶ ❷ ❸ ❹ ❺ ❻

Pointers

- Utilize pointers and a function for validating data.

- Apply pointers to structures of data.

- Use pointers to allow a function to access a memory location by reference rather than by value.

CHAPTER OVERVIEW

The true power and flexibility of C comes through the use of pointers to access memory locations. This chapter will introduce the use of pointers to store addresses of variables and functions.

The relationship between pointers and array notations in C will improve an understanding of the various ways of dealing with data. Through pointers, a reference to an array—including a string—may be passed to or returned from a function.

Through the use of a function, data may be validated as the data is entered. The address of the "validated" data may then be returned to a function for storage.

POINTER VARIABLES

address A location in memory where data or a function is stored.
pointer A variable that contains an address of a variable, a function, or another pointer.

One of the greatest advantages of C is the ability to use pointers. A **pointer** is a variable that contains an **address,** a location in memory. The address may be of a variable, a function, or another pointer.

There are many reasons for using pointers. The primary ones are:

1. To pass arrays as parameters to a function.
2. To allow other functions to know the location of a local variable so that the actual value may be altered.
3. Efficiency.

The ability to pass arrays provides the capability of passing and "returning" strings. If a pointer variable contains the address where the string begins, that address may be referred to in other parts of the program.

Recall that local variables are defined within a function and are visible to that function only. If an argument is passed to a function, we have passed the value of the original variable but the receiving function does not know where that original variable is really located. Therefore, the value of the original variable cannot be changed. The function may return a value which is then assigned at the point where the function is called.

```c
void main( )
{
        int num = 5, square;

        square = square_it(num);
        printf("%d %d",num,square);
}


square_it(int number)
{
   return(number*number);
}
```

A few problems with this approach include the following:

1. Only one value can be returned from a function. If a pointer is used to store the address, then the functions can change the contents at that memory address, even though the original variable name is unknown to the called function. No other function can alter the memory location, the variable is not visible except to the original function. Several pointers may

be passed to a function and may thereby allow the function to change the value of multiple memory locations.

2. The original values cannot be changed by any other function. The variables could be changed to global and then the value could be changed. However, any and all functions would then have the ability to change the variable.

The concept of pointers and addresses has already been used. The `scanf( )` requests the address of a variable, such as `&number`. The declaration `char *result` was used with `bsearch( )` to hold an address.

Pointer Operators

Two symbols are used with pointers, the asterisk * and the ampersand &. The * is used when declaring a pointer. The **indirection operator(*)** is also used when referring to the contents(value) stored at the location being pointed to (the **indirect value** of the pointer). The & is the **address operator** and will be read as "the address of".

indirection operator The * used as a unary operator to denote a pointer at time of declaration or to dereference a pointer value.
indirect value The value stored at the address stored in a pointer variable.
address operator &, used to refer to an address in memory.

Declaring a Pointer

To declare a pointer, the * operator must be placed before the variable name, and it must be declared to be of the data type for the address which it will contain. This takes the format:

```
data_type *pointer_name;
```

Thus,

```
char *charptr;
```

declares a pointer that will contain the address of (point to) type character. The character it will have the address of has not yet been assigned but a pointer variable has been created. The pointer must be assigned a character variable or by a function returning a character pointer.

```
float *floatptr;
int *intptr;
```

The variable `floatptr` will contain the address of a floating point variable and `intptr` will contain the address of an integer variable.

```
char letter, *charptr;
```

Even though letter and the pointer to a character have been declared, there is nothing yet that associates the two of these together. If the intention is to have the pointer `charptr` hold the address of `letter` then it is necessary to assign the address of the variable to the pointer. This action may be performed with an assignment statement.

Assigning a Pointer the Address of a Variable

The assignment may be made by saying:

```
charptr = &letter;
```

This reads as the address of `letter` is assigned to the pointer `charptr`.

Address	Identifier	Value
1000	charptr	1002
1002	letter	?

Notice that when assigning an address to a pointer it is not necessary to use a pointer operand on `charptr`. At this point, `charptr` is a variable, which is being assigned the address of the variable `letter`.

Further, assign a value to `letter`:

```
letter = 'a';
```

Address	Identifier	Value
1000	charptr	1002
1002	letter	a

Therefore,

Value	Reference	Meaning
1002	charptr	Address of letter
a	*charptr	Indirect value (value at address indicated in charptr)
1002	&letter	Address of letter
1000	&charptr	Address of charptr
a	letter	Value of letter

Combining Declaration and Assignment of Pointers

The declaration and assignment may be made in one step by coding:

```
char letter, *charptr = &letter;
```

Note that the * was necessary in this case to designate that `charptr` is a pointer.

Now, what about declaring a variable of type character, initializing the variable, declaring a pointer to the variable and assigning the address at one time?

```
char letter = 'a', *charptr = &letter;
```

The result:

letter = 'a'	The contents of `letter` is 'a'.
*charptr = 'a'	The indirect value of `charptr` is 'a'.
charptr = &letter	The pointer variable contains the address of `letter`.

A Pointer Contains Memory Address

A pointer variable contains a memory address; however, the pointer must be declared as the type to which it will be pointing. This makes sense if you consider incrementing an address location to look at the next item in memory. The number of bytes of memory that are occupied by each value is determined by the type of data that it is. Therefore, if a pointer is used to reference character data that only occupies 1 byte, the address of the next character will only be 1 byte away. However, if the data being pointed to is of type *float*, each item occupies four bytes, and the beginning of the following data item address would be 4 bytes higher than the first one.

```
float *ptrnum1, *ptrnum2, num1, num2;
ptrnum1 = &num1;
ptrnum2 = &num2;
```

Address	Variable	Value
1000	ptrnum1	1004
1002	ptrnum2	1002
1004	num1	
1008	num2	

The address of `ptrnum2` is 2 bytes beyond `ptrnum1` assuming that an integer field is 2 bytes long. Each of the floating point variables occupies 4 bytes.

An Example with Pointers

Declare an integer variable called `num` and a pointer to integer called `numptr`. Assign the pointer to the variable. Print out the value of `num`, `*numptr`, `&num`, and `numptr`.

```
void main( )
{
        int num = 5;
        int *numptr;
        numptr = &num;

printf(" num = %d \n",num);
printf(" *numptr = %d \n",*numptr);
printf(" &num = %u \n",&num);
printf(" numptr = %u \n",numptr);
}
```

9 - 2 . c

Output

```
num = 5
*numptr = 5
&num = 12
numptr = 12
```

Remember that &num and the contents of numptr are addresses so the 12 will change with different executions of the program. The %u specifier for unsigned integers is used for printing addresses.

Self-Test

Complete the exercises given the following:

```
float amount, *ptramt;
```

1. Code the statement to assign the address of amount to the pointer ptramt.
2. Using the pointer, assign the value 10.24 to amount.
3. If #1 and #2 have been executed, what is the value of the following?

    a. amount
    b. *ptramt
    c. &amount
    d. &ptramt
    e. ptramt

Answers

1. ptramt = &amount;
   The asterisk is not required because we are assigning the address of amount to the variable called ptramt. The ptramt variable is expecting to contain an address because it was defined with an * making it a pointer.

2. `*ptramt = 10.24;`

   The indirection operator is used in this instance because we are assigning a value, not into ptramt but into the address location, which is indicated by the number stored in ptramt and which is actually the address of amount.

3. a. 10.24
   b. 10.24
   c. The address of amount.
   d. The address of ptramt.
   e. The address of amount, which has been stored in ptramt.

SUMMARY OF POINTER CHARACTERISTICS

From the discussion to this point, three characteristics about pointer variables have been referred to. Specifically, each pointer variable:

1. Is a location in memory.
2. Contains a value that is an address.
3. Can be used to obtain the indirect **(dereferenced)** value of the address that the pointer contains.

dereference Find a value associated with an address thereby reducing the level of indirection.

Given the following declaration,

```
int *pointer_variable;
```

&pointer_variable	Address of `pointer_variable`.
pointer_variable	Contents of `pointer—variable` (can be assigned an address)
*pointer_variable	Indirect value that tells the contents at the address contained in `pointer_variable`.

Therefore,

pointer_variable = pointer;	Assigns something to be the value of `pointer_variable`; this will be interpreted as an address (pointer should be the address of an integer value).
number = *pointer_variable;	Assigns the indirect value; finds the address in `pointer_variable`, goes to that address and gets the value and then assigns that value to `number` (number should be an integer variable).

```
int **p = &pointer_variable;
```
Assigns the address of `pointer_variable` to a variable being declared as a pointer to a pointer to an integer value.

POINTERS TO POINTERS AND LEVELS OF INDIRECTION

You may have encountered the error message that reads "different levels of indirection." Exactly what does that mean and how can it be solved?

The level of indirection is the "distance" from the value.

```
int *intptr;
```

Therefore, `*intptr`, would have zero levels of indirection because it refers directly to the value. On the other hand, `intptr` has a level of 1 because the address in `intptr` has to be accessed to reach the value.

Errors are caused when values are assigned that are at different levels of indirection. All addresses are above the zero level of indirection because they must be dereferenced to get to the indirect value.

```
int number, amount;
```

Legal: `number = amount;`
Number is at indirection level 0; amount is at indirection level 0.

Illegal: `number = &amount;`
`number` is at indirection level 0; `&amount` is at level one of indirection.

It would, of course, be illegal to assign the address of `amount` to `number` or vice versa because they are not pointer variables. The * and & operators, as well as the declaration, determine what level a variable is. The * operator decreases the value of indirection as it dereferences to get toward the value. When the & operator is used, the level of indirection increases because the address of something is being referred to which is another level away from the actual value.

```
int *ptr, **ptrptr;
```

`ptr` is at level 1 of indirection because the declaration is for a pointer that contains an address, not a value—must be dereferenced for the value; `ptrptr` is at level 2 by declaration because it contains an address that contains an address that contains a value.

```
int number, amount;
int *ptr, **ptrptr;
```

Legal: `ptr = &amount;`
       /* assigns an address to a pointer*/
       `ptr` is level 1

Legal: `*ptr = amount;`
       /* assigns a value to a value */
       `*ptr` is level 0; `amount` is level 0.

Illegal: `ptr = amount;`
       `ptr` is level 1; `amount` is level 0.

Legal: `ptrptr = &ptr;`
       `&ptr` is up one level from `ptr` (level 2); `ptrptr` is level 2.

Illegal: `ptrptr = ptr;`
       `ptr` is level 1; `ptrptr` is level 2.

Self-Test

Give the levels of indirection for the following assignments. Which are legal?

```
float amount = 5.0, *ptramt = &amount, **ptrptr = &ptramt;
```

```
1. *ptramt = amount;
2. amount = *ptramt;
3. ptramt = *ptrptr;
4. ptramt = &ptrptr;
5. amount = *ptrptr;
6. ptramt = ptrptr;
7. amount = &ptramt;
8. *ptramt = 10;
9. **ptrptr = 10;
10. amount = 10;
```

Answers

At declaration,

    `amount` is level 0
    `ptramt` is level 1
    `ptrptr` is level 2

    1. both level 0, legal   (* decreases level of ptramt)
    2. both level 0, legal   (* decreases level of ptramt)
    3. both level 1, legal   (* decreases level of ptrptr)
    4. illegal:
       `&ptrptr` is level 3   (& increases level of ptrptr)

5. illegal:
   ptrptr is level 1   (decreases level but it still refers to an address
                                  not a value)
6. illegal, different levels
7. illegal:
   &ptramt is level 2   (& increases the distance from the value)
8. both level 0, legal   (* decreases level of ptramt)
9. both level 0, legal   (** decreases level of ptrptr by 2)
10. both level 0, legal

POINTER CALCULATIONS

The address contained in a pointer variable may be incremented or decremented
to point to the next or previous value in memory.

```
*number + 2;
```

This expression means add 2 to the value whose address is &number. The
* operator has a higher precedence than the + operator.

```
*(number + 2);
```

This expression means add to the address and then get the value at that location in memory.

When working with pointers, it is important to consider the precedence compared to the other operators we have already been using.

The pointer * and the incrementer ++ have the same precedence from **right
to left.** Therefore, *intptr++ gets the indirect value and increments the pointer to the next address. If we use parentheses to read (*intptr)++, we have
an operation that says get the value and then increment the value.

9-3.c

```
int *intptr;
int intarray[] = {5,7,2,3,9,1}; /* an array is used because
                        consecutive addresses will be
                        assigned  */


void main( )
{
   intptr = &intarray;
   printf("%d contents of intptr\n\n", intptr);
        /*where does address start*/
```

```
/*                 *++intptr                    */
puts("Using *++intptr");
printf("%d %d\n",*++intptr, intptr);
printf("%d contents of intptr\n\n""", intptr);

/*                 *intptr++                     */
puts("Using *intptr++");
intptr = &intarray;
printf("%d %d\n",*intptr++, intptr);
printf("%d contents of intptr\n\n", intptr);

/*                 (*intptr)++                   */
intptr = &intarray;
puts("Using (*intptr)++");
printf("%d %d\n",(*intptr)++, intptr);
printf("%d contents of intptr\n\n", intptr);

/*                 *(++intptr)                   */
puts("Using *(++intptr)");
intptr = &intarray;
printf("%d %d\n",*(++intptr), intptr);
printf("%d contents of intptr\n", intptr);
}
```

Output

```
170 contents of intptr
Using *++intptr
7 170
172 contents of intptr

Using *intptr++
5 170
172 contents of intptr

Using (*intptr)++
5 170
170 contents of intptr

Using *(++intptr)
7 170
172 contents of intptr
```

In the following example

```
*charptr1++
```

increases the value of the address from -11 to -10.

```
*(charptr1++)
```

increases the value of the 'a' to a 'b'

9-4.c

```c
void main( )
{
        char *charptr1, *charptr2;
        char letter1 = 'a', letter2 = 'b';

        charptr1 = &letter1;
        charptr2 = &letter2;

        /*                    print original values                  */
        printf("The addresses of letter1 and letter2 are %d %d\n", charptr1,
                                        charptr2);
        printf("The indirect values are %c %c\n\n", *charptr1, *charptr2);

        *charptr1++;              /* increment the address   */

        printf("The addresses of letter1 and letter2 are %d %d\n", charptr1,
                                        charptr2);
        printf("The indirect values are  %c %c\n\n", *charptr1, *charptr2);

        charptr1 = &letter1;   /* reset the value */

        (*charptr1)++;            /* increment the contents */

        printf("The addresses of letter1 and letter2 are %d %d\n", charptr1,
                                        charptr2);
        printf("The indirect values are %c %c\n\n", *charptr1, *charptr2);
}
```

Output

```
The addresses of letter1 and letter2 are -11 -12
The indirect values are a b

The addresses of letter1 and letter2 are -10 -12
The indirect values are    b

The addresses of letter1 and letter 2 are -11 -
12
```

Determine what each of the following mean

```
++*ptr
*ptr++
*++ptr
```

The increment and the pointer * are at the same level and are associated from right to left. This can be used to interpret the previous examples with the following program, which deals with consecutive memory locations in an array.

9 - 5 . c

```
#include <stdio.h>
int p[]={2,4,6}, *ptr = p;  /* ptr is set to beginning of array */

void main( )
{
        fprintf(stdprn, "%d %d\n", ptr, &ptr);

        /*    print using pointers       */
        fprintf(stdprn,"%d %d %d\n", ++*ptr, *++ptr, *ptr++);

        /*    print new values in the array   */
        fprintf(stdprn,"%d %d %d\n",p[0],p[1],p[2]);
}
```

Output

```
168 174
7 6 2
2 4 7
```

Note: The output is affected because the calculations begin at the right. Split these calculations onto separate lines and the results will be more predictable.

Explanation

++*ptr—will reference the value that is being pointed to and then increment that value.

*++ptr—will increase the address and then find the value in that new address.

*ptr++—the ++ will bind to the ptr first so that we take the address and do a postfix increment.

POINTERS AND ARRAYS

The name of an array references an address. The array name contains the address of the first element of the array. This explains why the & notation was not used on the scanf( ) when accessing an array. Recall that with numbers, the function call is

```
scanf("%d",&num)
```

but with an array it is merely

```
scanf("%s",name).
```

Strings, as we already know, are arrays. What the variable name really refers to is &name[0]. So we could say that

```
name      is equivalent to      &name[0]
```

A pointer variable may be used as an lvalue or as an rvalue; a pointer constant (address of) may only be used as an rvalue. The address of the array is a constant not a variable. Since an array name is a pointer containing an address, it is possible to increment the pointer to access the elements in the array. The contents of the array can be obtained with the pointer rather than using subscripts. If

```
int number[] = {5,10,15}
```

then

```
number[0] = 5
*number = 5
number[1] = 10
*(number + 1) = 10
number[2] = 15
*(number + 2) = 15
```

The parentheses are required when incrementing the position in the array because we wish to add to the address itself and not to the contents of the address.

Self-Test

Given the following declarations and assignments, what operation will be performed according to the precedence of operators?

```
int intnum = 5, *intptr = &intnum;
int intarray[] = {5,7,2,3,9,1};
```

1. `intptr += 5`
2. `intarray + 5`
3. `*(intarray + 5)`
4. `*intarray + 5`
5. `intnum + 5`
6. `intptr++`
7. `*intptr++`
8. `intarray++`
9. `(*intptr)++`
10. `*++intptr`

Answers

1. Since intptr is a variable and not an array name, it can point to various items, such as a pointer variable. This statement changes the address stored in the pointer so that it contains an address 5 integer size fields beyond intnum.
2. Adds 5 to the address of the array and therefore points to intarray[5]. Remember that the name of an array is a pointer to the address of the array.
3. Adds 5 to the address and then gets the value of `intarray[5]`.
4. Gets the value of `intarray[0]` and adds 5 to the value.
5. Adds 5 to the value of the variable `intnum`, no pointers here.
6. Increases the pointer to point to the address following `intnum`, actually changing the pointer to point to a different location.
7. Increases the address stored in `intptr` and then gets the value at that new address.
8. Can't do this. We are trying to say change the pointer address for the array to point to one address higher. An array name cannot be changed. We could say `intarray + 1` which would not change `intarray` but would point to one position beyond the beginning of the array. The increment operator would attempt to actually change `intarray`, which cannot be done.

9. Increases the value of `intarray[0]` from a 5 to 6.
10. Increments intptr to the next address and then retrieves the value at that address. This value cannot be determined from information given.

Accessing a Single-Dimensional Array with Pointers

Since the name of the array is the address of the first element, it is possible to increment the address of the array thereby pointing to the next element within the array. The address will automatically increment by the correct number of bytes because of the pointer declaration.

An Example with Arrays

Since incrementing the pointer causes the address to point to the next location in memory, an array can be accessed by incrementing the pointer and then getting the indirect value.

9-6.c

```
int int_array[ ] = {10,20,30,40};

void main( )
{
   int *ptr;
   int count;
   ptr = int_array;   /*store the address of the first
                      element in ptr       */

   /*   loop through the array, changing the subscript and
                incrementing ptr to next array address   */

   for (count=0; count<4; count++, ptr++)
     printf("int_array[%d] = %d\n", count, *ptr);
}
```

Output

```
int_array[0] = 10
int_array[1] = 20
int_array[2] = 30
int_array[3] = 40
```

Caution: Because the name of an array contains an address it may be used similar to a pointer variable. However, it is not a variable and therefore cannot have an address assigned to the variable name or be incremented, decremented, etc.

With a single-dimensional array, the data could also be read from the array as follows:

```
int i, number[] = {5,10,15};

void main( )
{
  /* each time through the loop increment the
            address and print the element by
            subscript and by pointer  */

  for(i=0; i<3; i++)
    print f("%d        %d\n: number[i], *(number = i));
}
```

Output

```
5    5
10   10
15   15
```

Accessing a String Using Pointers

With a character array, the data can be accessed without a *for* loop. The end of the array is marked by a null character. Therefore, we can access a character array using a pointer and testing for a null character.

```
void main( )
{
  static char word[] = "pointer";
  char *wordptr = word;

  while(*wordptr)
    printf("*wordptr = %c\n", *wordptr++);

  /* this loop will exit when it points to a null */
}
```

Output

```
pointer
```

The *static* storage class is required on some compilers if a local array is initialized at the time that it is declared.

Self-Test

Will the following calculations increment the contents or the address given dates [3]?

1. dates + 2   *con   # date [2]*
2. *(dates + 2) *add*
3. *dates + 2
4. Write the loop using pointers that will find the average of the array grades.

```
int grades[10];
```

Answers

1. address, dates + 2 is equivalent to &dates[2].
2. address, adds to the address and then accesses—the value this means the contents of dates[2].
3. Contents, this will increase the contents of dates[0] by 2.

```
4. for(i = 0; i < 10; i++)
   {
        sum += *(grades + i);
   }
   average = sum/10;
```

Multidimensional Arrays and Pointers

Pointers can also be used with multidimensional arrays. This may require a pointer to a pointer.

Pointers to Pointers and Multidimensional Arrays   Consider the declaration of a two-dimensional array. The following array declares five arrays, each of which is a subarray containing 10 elements.

```
int number[5][10];
```

The `number` contains the address of the first element of the entire array. It is also the address of the first subarray of 10 elements.

```
number == &number[0]
```

and

```
&number[0] == &number[0][0];
```

Even though the address of the entire array, the subarray, and the address of the first element are all the same, there is a difference when doing pointer calculations.

Incrementing the address of the subarray should take us to the next subarray while incrementing the entire array, or the first element will take us to the address of the next element.

The difference between the levels is as follows:

number	The address of the entire array.
*number	The address of the first subarray.
**number	The value in the first element.

Incrementing the Pointers

Although *number and number will hold the same address, there will be a difference when they are incremented.

number	Is a pointer to an array of five elements, each one containing 10 integers. number + 1 points to the address of the next subarray. With our compilers, 20 would be added to the address, to account for 10 integers.
*number	Is a pointer to an integer. *number + 1 points to the address of the next integer element. With our compilers, 2 will be added to the address, to account for 1 integer.

As a result of precedence, the array can be incremented to either the first subscript or to the second subscript depending on the use of parentheses.

*(number + 1)	Yields number[1][0].
*(number + 2)	Yields number[2][0].
*number + 1	Yields number[0][1].
*number + 2	Yields number[0][2].

In summary, a multidimensional array can be accessed as follows:

By row	No parentheses.
By column	Use parentheses.

Summary of Relationships

```
number[0][0]  ==  *number[0]  ==  **number
number[1][0]  ==  *number[1]  ==  *(*(number + 1))
number[2][3]  ==  *(number[2] + 3)  ==  *(*(number + 2) + 3)
number[x][y]  ==  *(number[x] + y)  ==  *(*(number + x) + y)
&number[0][0]  ==  number[0]  ==  *number
&number[1][0]  ==  number[1]  ==  *(number + 1)
```

Accessing a Multidimensional Array with Pointers

Using the pointer notation, `*(*(number + x) + y)`, all of the elements in a two-dimensional array can be accessed using two loops. One loop will control the value of x and the second will control y. The x relates to the row and the y to the column of each element within the array.

```c
int quantity[5][4] = {{12,4,6,8},{1,3,5,7},
                {3,6,9,12},{0,1,2,3},
                {3,2,1,0}};


void main( )
{
   int row, col, total;

   /*     add up all elements in the array    */
   for(row = 0; row < 5; row++)
   {
     for(col = 0; col < 4; col++)
     {
       total += *(*(quantity + row) + col);
     }
   }
   printf("The total is %d\n", total);
}
```

Output

```
The total is 88
```

Accessing a Multidimensional Array as a Single Array

Since an array can be accessed with pointers, a multidimensional array can be accessed as though it were one long single-dimensional array. The following example really has two lists with three elements in each list. However, it may be treated as one list of six elements.

```
int i, number[2][3] = {
                          {2,4,6},
                          {8,1,2}
                      };

void main( )
{
  /*  access a 2 level array as a single level array */
  for(i=0; i<6; i++)
  {
    printf("%d   ",*(number[0] + i));
  }
}
```

Another way that this two-dimensional array could be perceived is as a single array of pointers. The first pointer will point to the first list of three elements and the second pointer holds the address of the second list.
Thus,

```
number[2][3]  ==  *number[6]
```

```
int i, *number[] = {2,4,6,8,1,2};

void main( )
{
    for(i=0; i<6; i++)
    {
      printf("%d   ",*(number+i));
    }
}
```

The relationship of arrays could also be visualized by printing the amount of memory occupied.

```
#include <stdio.h>
void main( );
{
    int number[2] [3];
    printf("%d %d %d", sizeof (number),
            sizeof(*number), sizeof(**number));
}
```

Output

```
24     8     2
```

Self-Test

1. Use pointer notation to add up the elements in the array:

   ```
   float sales[7]10];
   ```

Answers

1.
   ```
   for(i=0;  i < 70;  i++)
   {
   total +=    *(sales[0] + i);
   }
   ```

Pointers as Function Arguments

The two primary reasons for passing a pointer to a function are to allow a local variable to be modified by another function or to pass an array.

Function Call by Reference to a Local Variable Address   Let's take a look again at the `square_it( )` function using a pointer as the argument. This will eliminate the need for a return in the called function and an assignment in the calling function. In other words, we have eliminated the need for the variable `square`. The print statement asks for each item to be printed to clarify what is happening. The address will change when you execute the program because the location is determined at run time. If you run this program then the address may not be 5852.

```
void square_it(int * number);
void main( )
{
  int num = 5, *numptr;
  numptr = &num;
  square_it(numptr);
  printf("address:%d, contents of address:%d,%d",
            &numptr,*numptr,num);
}
void square_it(int *number)
{
      *number *= *number;  /* multiply number by itself*/
}
```

Output

```
address:5852, contents of address:25, 25
```

By using a pointer, the memory location has been passed rather than passing a value. The value of the variable "num" in the main function was altered by the action of square_it( ) upon the contents of the memory location *number.

The declaration of number in the square_it( ) function required the asterisk notation since we had actually passed a pointer. This function must also know that it is dealing with a pointer.

Passing an Array to a Function An array is not really passed to the function but rather the address of the first element of the array is passed as a parameter. This allows the function being called to manipulate the data within the array.

The receiving parameter for the address of the array may indicate that it is an array or not by using either notation:

```
compare(char arg1[ ],char arg2[ ])
compare(char *arg1, char *arg2)
```

The name of the array denotes the address of the first element of the array, but it is frequently desirable to let the receiving function know that the address points to an array. It is usually wise to also indicate the size of the array.

This can be denoted in two ways for a two-dimensional array.

```
int array[ROWS][COLUMNS];

arrayfunction(array, ROWS*COLUMNS); /* function call*/

/* function headers */
arrayfunction(int array[][COLUMNS], int numelements)
```

or

```
arrayfunction(int (*array)[COLUMNS], int numelements)
```

Example

Write a program that will find the totals by row and the totals by column for a table that has five rows, and four columns.

```
/*          a demo program for multidimension arrays and pointers    */
#define ROWS 5
#define COLUMNS 4

int find_total(int *qty, int num);
int find_coltotal(int (*qty)[COLUMNS], int num);

void main( )
{
    int subtotal, i;
    static int quantity[ROWS][COLUMNS] = {{12,4,6,8},{1,3,5,7},
                         {3,6,9,12},{0,1,2,3},
                         {3,2,1,0}};

    /*      find overall total   */
    printf("The total is %i\n", find_total(quantity, ROWS*COLUMNS));

    /*      find total by rows    */
    for(i=0; i < ROWS; i++)
    {
     printf("Total for row %i is %i\n", i, find_total(*(quantity + i),
        COLUMNS));
    }

    /*      find total by columns   */
    for(i=0; i < COLUMNS; i++)
    {
     printf("Total for column %i is %i\n",i, find_coltotal(*quantity+i,
        ROWS));
    }
}

/*-------------------------------------------------------------------
         treats the array as a single dimension, note address is
     received as parameter *qty
    --------------------------------------------------------------- */
int find_total(int *qty, int numelements)
{
    int total=0, i;
```

```
   for(i = 0; i < numelements; i++)
   {
     total += qty[i];
     printf("%d  ",qty[i]);
   }
   return(total);
}



/*-----------------------------------------------------------------
    treats array as multidimension, notice (*qty)[COLUMNS]
------------------------------------------------------------ */
int find_coltotal(int (*qty)[COLUMNS], int numelements)
{
  int i, total = 0;

  for (i=0; i < numelements; i++)
  {
    total += *qty[i];
    printf("%d  ",*qty[i]);
  }
  return(total);
}
```

The last function could be modified as follows:

```
/*         treats array as multidimension, notice qty[ ][COLUMNS]   */
int find_coltotal(int qty[][COLUMNS], int numelements)
{
  int i, total = 0;

  for (i=0; i < numelements; i++)
  {
    total += *qty[i];
    printf("%d  ",*qty[i]);
  }
  return(total);
}
```

An example where pointers were used to pass values to a function was the compare that was used with qsort( ) and bsearch( ). Let's take another look at the three compare functions from the array chapter.

Example 1 String Array

```
int compare(char arg1[],char arg2[])
{
        return(stricmp(arg1,arg2));
}
```

In this example, it may not have been obvious that pointers were used. Recall that the name of an array is an address. Therefore, `arg1[ ]` and `arg2[ ]` are pointers to the addresses of arrays. The notation `*arg1` and `*arg1` could also have been used in the arguments.

The `strcmp( )` performs a comparison on an array. It is not very obvious but consider that the array terminates with a null character, so if we send the address of the first character, the entire string will be used in the comparison.

Example 2 Comparing Two Integers

```
int compare( unsigned *elem1, unsigned *elem2 )
{
    if( *elem1 > *elem2 )
       return 1;
    else if( *elem1 < *elem2 )
       return -1;
    else
       return 0;
}
```

In this example it is much more obvious that pointers are being used. In the function header, it can be seen that `elem1` and `elem2` are pointers to unsigned integers. In the actual comparison, the indirect value of the pointer is accessed through the use of the * operator.

Example 3 Taking the Difference in Values of Integers

The third example of a compare declares two pointers to integer type, `num1` and `num2`. The *return* takes the difference in the indirect values of the two pointer variables.

```
int compare(int *num1, int *num2)
{
   return(*num1-*num2);
}
```

Self-Test

1. Code the function to find the average of the numbers in each column of the following array.

```
float item_cost[2][3] = {{1.45, 4.32, 7.24},
                         {1.64, 4.25, 7.01}}
```

2. Write a function to find the average for each row.
3. Write a function to find the average of the entire array.

Answers

```
1. float find_colavg(float (*item_cost)[COLUMNS], int numelements)
   {
       int i, total = 0;

       for (i=0; i < numelements; i++)
       {
           total += *item_cost[i];
       }
   return(total/ROWS);
   }
```

```
2. for(i=0; i < ROWS; i++)
   {
      printf("Average for row %i is %4.2f\n", i,
         find_average(*(quantity + i),COLUMNS));
   }

   float find_average(float *item_cost, int numelements)
   {
        int total=0, i;

        for(i = 0; i < numelements; i++)
        {
           total += item_cost[i];
        }
        return(total/COLUMNS);
   }
```

```
3. /*     find overall total    */
   printf("The average is %4.2f\n", find_average(quantity,
   ROWS*COLUMNS));

       float find_average(float *item_cost, int numelements)
       {
         int total=0, i;

         for(i = 0; i < numelements; i++)
         {
```

```
            total += item_cost[i];
        }
    return(total/COLUMNS*ROWS);
    }
```

POINTERS AND STRUCTURES

A structure can also use a pointer to access the members of the structure. A pointer to a structure is declared the same as other pointer variables. There is, though, a new operator for accessing the elements of a structure. The operator is ->, which is typed by following a hyphen with a greater than symbol.

```
struct name
{
    char first[15];
    char last[10];
}

struct person
{
    struct name name;
    char phone[15];
}

struct person *their;
```

*their points to a structure of type person. This variable does not yet contain the address of a particular item.

```
struct person friends[20] =  {
                        { {"Tricia", "Mills"},
                          "(714) 555-1111"}
                        { {"Mitzi", "Johnston"},
                          "(818) 555-2222"}
                        }
their = friends;   /* assign the array to the pointer */
```

Now

```
their          contains &friends[0]
their + 1               &friends[1]
```

To access individual elements of the structure:

```
their->phone
```

would access the phone number of the first structure within the array.

```
(their + 1)->phone
```

accesses the phone number for the second structure in the array. The parentheses are necessary to avoid having the 1 bind with the pointer, which would be meaningless, not to mention an error.

9-9.c

```
#define NUM 2
struct names
{
  char first[10];
  char last[15];
};

struct person
{
    struct names name;
    char phone[15];
};


struct person friends[NUM] ={
                "Tricia", "Mills","(714)555-1111",
                "Mitzi","Johnston","(818)555-2222" };

struct person *their = friends;


void main( )
{
   int i;
     for( i=0; i< NUM; i++)
     {
      printf("Name:  %s\n",(their+i)->name.last);
      printf("Phone: %s \n\n", (their+i)->phone);
     }
     puts(their->phone); /*  this will point to first structure */
}
```

1. Write a loop to print out the title and author of each of the books.

```
struct bibliography
{
    char title[30];
    char author[30];
    char publisher[30];
    char ISBN[15];
} book[1000];

struct bibliography *bib;
```

Answer

```
1. for(i = 0; i < 1000; i++)
   {
        printf("/t%-40s%-30s\n", (bib+i)->title,(bib+i)->author);
   }
```

Programming/ Debugging Hint

An application that lends itself to the use of pointers is the validation of data as it is entered.

Data Validation

Data validation is the process of checking data character by character as it is entered from the keyboard. In order to perform data validation we will have to accept one character from the keyboard at a time. As each character is entered it will be checked against a series of "valid characters."

In a numeric field, this data validation test can allow only numeric character or a period to be accepted. The keyboard will appear to be "locked" against other characters.

Inputting One Character at a Time In C, one character can be input at a time in ANSI code by using `getc( )`, `getchar( )`, or the `fgetc (stdin)`. The `getc( )` function and `fgetc( )` act the same, the difference being that the `getc( )` is implemented as a macro, while the `fgetc( )` is a function.

The data validation routine we will be using is testing data as it is entered from the keyboard. If the character that is entered is a valid character it must be printed on the screen and added to a **buffer** that we will set up for valid data.

buffer Temporary storage.

The data will be echoed to the screen if it is a "good" character. This means that we want a C function that does not echo automatically to the screen. Only the valid characters will be printed. We must also allow for the user to make changes so we will test for the back arrow or backspace to indicate a change. If a backspace is encountered it will be necessary to erase the previous character from both the screen and the valid data buffer.

You may prefer to have different functions to test for valid characters for different types of fields. For example, a name field will contain letters and spaces, but it may also contain an apostrophe or a hyphen. A phone number field may allow parentheses and the hyphen as well as numbers. A field that will be used for numeric data only cannot contain anything but numbers or a period. (Technically we should allow for a sign in the first position only. Some may also wish to test that there is not more than one period.)

The following example uses one function to enter all of the types of fields but uses a code to determine which test will be applied to the particular field that is being entered. This `input_rtn( )` function sends two parameters, the maximum length of the field and the type of test that is to be performed.

```
/*      An input routine that returns a pointer to type char
        The parameters call for the field length and a type
        to determine what characters should be checked for */

char *input_rtn(int fieldlen, char type)
{
  char c, buffer[30];
  int i=0;

  strcpy(buffer, "");

  while((c = getch( )) != 13)
    {
      /*            check to see if alphabetic test needed  */
      if(type == 'a')
      {
      c = toupper(c);
      if(c>='A' && c<='Z' || c==' ' || c=='.' || c=='-'|| c=='\'')
      {
        buffer[i++] = c;  /* if good add to buffer*/
        putchar(c);        /* print good character on screen */
      }
    }
```

```
       /*        check to see if numeric test needed            */
    if(type == 'n')
      if(c >= '0' && c <= '9')
      {
       buffer[i++] = c;
       putchar(c);
       if( i == fieldlen)
         break;            /* leave if number of characters filled */
     }
   /*    check for a backspace or left arrow            */
       if(c == 8 || c == 29)
          if(buffer[0] != NULL)
      {
       BACKSPACE;     /* can't do a backspace if no characters */
       i-;
      }
     }
   buffer[i] = NULL;
   return (buffer);
}
```

Default Values

Another item to be considered when writing data validation routines is the usefulness of a default answer. If the answer will be one value most of the time, a **default** answer may save the data entry person a lot of time. Consider, for example, the state where a person lives. If a company deals almost exclusively with clients from one state the value can be set as the automatic answer unless the data entry clerk selects to alter the entry.

```
     /*                    check for a default value            */
    if(strlen(areacode) == 0)
      strcpy(emp.phone,"714");
    else
      strcpy(emp.phone, areacode);
   LOCATE(12,24);
     /*       ask for 3 numeric characters                */
    strcat(emp.phone, input_rtn(3,'n'));
```

The example uses a default value for the area code for the phone number. If an enter key is pressed an area code of 714 will be stored in the emp.phone field, otherwise the value that was typed will be placed in emp.phone.

Converting String to Numeric Types

Data can be converted from string into numeric, either an integer type or a float. The functions that will be necessary to perform the function are `atoi( )` and `atof( )`. These functions are located in different header files. The `atoi( )` function is located in `stdlib.h` while the `atof( )` is in `math.h`.

```
#include <stdlib.h>
..........
/*        ask for numeric data and then convert to alpha */
          emp.num = atoi(input_rtn(3,'n'));
```

The example uses the `atoi( )` function to convert the employee number from the string buffer which was returned from the input routine into an integer field.

Suppose it was necessary to have a field for hourly pay rate. This field would need to be of type float to allow for the cents positions. The same `input_rtn( )` function could be used with a slight modification. For the float field, it would be necessary to allow for a decimal point. To be perfectly correct, it would probably be best to check to assure that only one decimal could be entered for each number.

Example

Write a program that validates data being entered into a structure. The structure contains an employee name, phone number, and an integer number. The phone number will contain a default area code of (714).

```
                                                        9 - 1 1 . c
/*                        data validation by character       */


#include <stdio.h>
#include <conio.h>
#include <ctype.h>
#include <stdlib.h>
#define LOCATE(r,c) printf("\033[%d;%dH",r,c)
#define CLS printf("\033[2J");
#define PAUSE LOCATE(23,30);puts("Press Any Key to
                                        Continue");getche( );
#define BACKSPACE putchar(8);putchar('_');putchar(8);

void paint_screen( );
void dataentry( );
char *input_rtn(int fieldlen, char type);
```

```
struct
{
 char name[20];
 char phone[14];
 int num;
}emp;


void main( )
{
    paint_screen( );
    while(strlen(emp.name)!=0)
    {
      dataentry( );
      PAUSE;
      paint_screen( );
    }
}




/*        creates a prompt screen and enters the name field  */
void paint_screen( )
{
  CLS;
  LOCATE(10,10);
  puts("Name: ");
  LOCATE(10,18);
  puts("_____");
  LOCATE(12,10);
  puts("Phone:");
  LOCATE(12,18);
  puts("(714) ____-_____");
  LOCATE(14,10);
  puts("Rate:");
  LOCATE(14,18);
  puts("_____");
  LOCATE (10,18);
  /*  calls the data validation routine and copies the value into
         the structure field for name. The field length is passed
```

```
              as 20 and 'a' is the type of validation to perform
              (for alphabetic)                                */
    strcpy(emp.name, input_rtn(20,'a'));
}



/*      enters the remaining fields using the same data validation
            routine, using a default value for the area code and the
            atoi( ) function for the integer number.   */

void dataentry( )
{
  char areacode[4];

  LOCATE(12,19);
  strcpy(areacode,input_rtn(3,'n'));
  /*                    check for a default value          */
  if(strlen(areacode) == 0)
    strcpy(emp.phone,"714");
  else
    strcpy(emp.phone, areacode);
  LOCATE(12,24);
   /*        ask for 3 numeric characters              */
  strcat(emp.phone, input_rtn(3,'n'));
  LOCATE(12,28);
  strcat(emp.phone, input_rtn(4,'n'));

  LOCATE(14,18);
  /*        ask for numeric data and then convert to alpha */
  emp.num = atoi(input_rtn(3,'n'));
}

/*      An input routine that returns a pointer to type char
        The parameters call for the field length and a type
        to determine what characters should be checked for */

char *input_rtn(int fieldlen, char type)
{
  char c, buffer[30];
  int i=0;
```

```
strcpy(buffer, "");

while((c = getch( )) != 13)
  {
    /*              check to see if alphabetic test needed   */
    if(type == 'a')
    {
     c = toupper(c);
     if(c>='A' && c<='Z' || c==' '|| c=='.' || c=='-'|| c=='\'')
     {
       buffer[i++] = c;   /* if good add to buffer*/
       putchar(c);           /* print good character on screen */
     }
    }

     /*         check to see if numeric test needed              */
    if(type == 'n')
      if(c >= '0' && c <= '9')
      {
        buffer[i++] = c;
        putchar(c);
        if( i == fieldlen)
         break;          /* leave if number of characters filled */
      }
    /*     check for a backspace or left arrow            */
    if(c == 8 || c == 29)
      if(buffer[0] != NULL)
      {
       BACKSPACE;    /* can't do a backspace if no characters */
       i--;
      }
    }
    buffer[i] = NULL;
    return (buffer);
}
```

These data entry routines could be enhanced to allow the user more control over the screen. These do not allow for full-screen editing.

Self-Test

1. Write the call to the input function, to enter in a product description:

```
char prod_desc[25];
char *input_rtn(int fieldlen, char type)
```

2. Why is it necessary to check for ASCII codes 8 and 29?
3. What action must be taken if a backspace key is pressed?
4. What is wrong with the following?

```
#include <stdlib.h>
float amount;
amount = atof(input_rtn(3,'n'));
```

Answers

1. `strcpy(prod_desc, input_rtn(24,'a'));`
2. To allow data entry corrections, ASCII codes 8 and 29 check for the backspace and left arrow keys respectively.
3. The backspace requires that we check to see if there are characters in the buffer; if there are characters, remove the last character from the buffer and from the screen.
4. The atof( ) function, unlike the atoi( ) function, requires the inclusion of the math.h file.

KEY TERMS

address	default	indirect value
address operator	dereference	pointer
buffer	indirection operator	

CHAPTER SUMMARY

A pointer variable stores the address of a variable or a function. Pointer variables may be used in limited types of calculations—incrementing or decrementing.

The declaration for a pointer variable indicates the type of data to which the pointer will be pointing. When a pointer variable is incremented by 1, the new address will increase by the size of the type of pointer. Thus, a float pointer when incremented will have the address increased by 4 bytes since each float data item occupies 4 bytes.

Pointers are especially useful for returning multiple values from a function or for allowing a function access to "private" data. A pointer to an array will allow the beginning address of the array to be returned by the function.

When working with pointers, it is important to understand the levels of indirection to keep track of multiple layers of pointers. This will eliminate many common errors. Another common error to be watchful for is a null pointer assignment, where a pointer does not really point to anything.

Data entry should check the validity of each character as it is entered. When the character is acceptable it will be concatenated to a "good data" buffer. Using a data validation routine, it is also possible to set up a default value for a field. The purpose of data validation is to help ensure that the information being entered is as accurate as possible and to save time for the data entry person.

REVIEW QUESTIONS

1. What is a pointer?
2. When a pointer variable is incremented, how many bytes is it increased by?
3. What is the relationship between arrays and pointers?
4. Why use pointers? Give an example of a situation where a certain action could not be accomplished without pointers.
5. When we pass an array as a function argument, what are we really passing to the function?
6. How can a pointer be used to change the value of a variable that is local to a different function?
7. Why must a pointer variable be defined as the same data type as the variable to which it will point?
8. Why is the * operator not necessary when assigning an address to a pointer that has already been declared?
9. What is meant by the phrase "levels of indirection"?
10. What are some of the factors that must be checked for in validating numeric data? Nonnumeric data?
11. What is meant by a default value for a field in data validation?

EXERCISES

1. Modify the following quarterly sales program to:
   a. Contain two functions: one for the yearly totals and yearly average and one for the quarterly totals.
   b. Pass the array address to the function.
   c. Use pointer notation to access the array.

```
#include <stdio.h>

#define QTR   4     /* number of quarters in a year */
#define YRS   3     /* number of years data         */

void main( )
{
     static int sales[YRS][QTR] = {
                         {5000,5025,6800,3750},
                         {5555,5050,7000,4590},
                         {6000,6000,6700,7000}
                          };
     int quarter, year;
     long subtot, total;

     fprintf(stdout,"                      YEAR   SALES            \n");
     for ( year = 0, total = 0; year < YRS; year++)
       {
        /* for each year, sum sales for each quarter*/
        for (quarter = 0 , subtot = 0; quarter < QTR; quarter++)
          subtot += sales[year][quarter];
        fprintf(stdout,"            %5d %10d\n",
                     1990 + year, subtot);
        total += subtot;        /* total for all years */
        }
        fprintf(stdout,"\nThe yearly average is $%5d \n\n",
                     total/YRS);
        fprintf(stdout,"                           Quarterly");
        fprintf(stdout," Averages:\n\n");
        fprintf(stdout,"    1st Qtr  2nd Qtr  3rd Qtr  4th Qtr\n ");

        for (quarter = 0; quarter < QTR; quarter++)
          {
          for (year = 0, subtot = 0; year < YRS; year++)
                subtot += sales[year][quarter];
          fprintf(stdout,"%9d", subtot/YRS);
          }
          fprintf(stdin,"\n");
   }
```

2. Using pointers to pass local variable values, write a program to calculate sales commissions.

Input:	Enter salesperson's name, commission level (1 or 2), and amount of sales.
Processing:	For commission level 1 the commission rate is 6%, for level 2 the commission rate is 8%.
OUTPUT	
Titles:	Print appropriate titles and headings. The title must include a page number.

Detail:	Each detail line should include the salesperson's name, sales, and commission amount.
Total:	Print a report total for the sales and commissions totals.
Variables:	Page count—static local variable in titles module. Salesperson's name, level, and sales local to detail, passed as needed.

3. Write the following program, using a data validation routine that works for numeric, as well as character data. Calculate a grade average for a student. The input will ask for the student name and will prompt for two test scores and three program grades. The tests are worth 50% of the grade and the programs are worth 50% of the grade.

Input:	Student name:
	Two test scores:
	Three program grades:
Processing:	Find the average by taking 50% of the sum of the tests, divided by 2, and add that to 50% of the sum of the programs divided by 3. Find the name and average of the student with the highest average. Find the overall average grade for all students.
OUTPUT	
Heading:	Course title and appropriate headings.
Detail:	Student name, test scores, program grades, and average.
Summary:	Highest name and student average. Average grade for all students.

4. Write a program to find the area of a rectangle. Use pointers to return the values from the calculation module.

Input:	Length and width.
Output:	The area of the rectangle.
Processing:	Multiply the length by the width.

5. Write or modify the following program from Chapter 7 using pointer notation for accessing the arrays. Write a program that tallies total calendar sales for each girl in a Girl Scout troop.

Array:	Create an array that contains the girls' names and an array to accumulate the total sales.
Input:	Enter the girl's name and the quantity sold.
Output:	Produce a report that lists the total sales by girl.
	The report should contain appropriate titles and column headings. Each detail line will print a girl's name and the total number sold by that girl. Print a summary line containing the total sold for all girls.
Processing:	Add the quantity sold to the proper element in the total sales array for the girl making the sale.
TEST DATA	
Girls:	Laurie, Julie, Christine, Heather, Lisa
Sales:	Laurie, 5
	Julie, 5
	Heather, 4
	Lisa, 10
	Christine, 7

HAYLEY OFFICE SUPPLIES

Use the inventory structure array from Chapter 8. Find the cost value of the inventory on hand, by multiplying the cost by the quantity for each product in the array. Print a summary report that gives the inventory value on hand at cost and at retail.

CHAPTER OBJECTIVES

By the end of this chapter, you should be able to:

- Read from and write data to sequential data files.

- Demonstrate the use of structures in data files.

- Utilize the fwrite( ), fread( ), and fseek( ) functions.

- Create and access a random file.

- Use file functions to update a random file including add a record, delete a record, and edit.

- Develop hashing algorithms for use in C.

File Input/Output with Structures

CHAPTER OVERVIEW

In order to access a data file it must be opened as a stream and the mode in which it will be accessed must be specified. Files in C may be produced using familiar input/output operations, such as `fprintf( )` *or* `fscanf( )` *similar to* `scanf( )`.

Files can also be created using data structures. The structure data type provides a convenient way to deal with data as a unit or record. With the file commands that deal with structures, it is possible to read or write an entire array of structures with a single function call.

This chapter will also include a file update, including adding records, deleting records, and editing records. The update program will be menu driven and will include options for listing the data.

Disk files in C are handled the same as other methods of input or output. Disk files can use the same functions to read and write data as were used for the keyboard and the monitor. Specifically `fprintf( )` may be used to write to a file. Since `scanf( )` defaults to accepting input from the keyboard, `fscanf( )` may be used instead for reading from the disk file.

Opening a File

stream Sequence of data for input/output.

Before a disk file can be accessed, it must be opened. By opening the file a name will be assigned to the file that is used as the stream name. A **stream** is the term used in C input/output to refer to a sequence of data. Sometimes the term stream is used synonymously with file. Both `stdprn` and `stdout`, though, are streams declared in the `stdio.h` file.

The opening of a file refers to a special data type called `FILE` that has been described by a type definition in the `stdio.h` file. This data type is a structure and has two parts, a file name and a pointer to the file buffer.

Declaring a Stream Name   In the global declarations, `FILE` is used as the data type followed by the stream name we wish to use for our files. The format of this declaration is:

```
FILE *logicalfilename;
```

The asterisk is necessary because of the way `FILE` has been defined in the header file. The data type is a pointer to a structure defined in the `stdio.h` file. The * is critical when declaring a name to be of "type" `FILE`.

physical file name Name of data file on disk.

logical file name Name of data file when referred to in a program.

Each disk file that is to be accessed must have its own stream name. This is not the name of the file on the disk, the **physical file name,** but rather a name that will be referred to in the program when we want to access that specific file, the **logical file name.** The logical file name is internal to the program code and will follow the guidelines for naming identifiers in C. The physical file name must follow DOS naming constraints, including an extension if desired.

A file that will be referenced as `clientfile` would be declared as:

```
FILE *clientfile;
```

The physical file name that is on the disk will be associated with the logical name with the `fopen( )` function.

The fopen( ) Function   The function that opens the file will specify the file mode in which the file will be accessed and associate the physical file name with a stream. The `fopen( )` function format is assigned to a stream as follows:

```
stream = fopen("physical file name", "file mode");
```

As the file is opened we must specify the **file mode** in which the file will be accessed. The modes available are as follows:

file mode Determines whether a file will be used for input or output.

"r"   Open for read will cause error if no such file exists.

"w"   Opens an existing file and sets ready to write new data at the beginning of the file. If it does not exist the file will be created.

"a"   Opens the file for write; new data will be added at the end of an existing file. If the file does not exist it will be created.

The preceding modes will allow the file to be accessed only for read (input) or only for write (output). However, we also have the option of opening the file with a plus sign (+) which will open it for both read and write, making updates to a file easier.

"r+"   Opens existing file for update, read as well as write. If the file does not exist, an error message will be generated.

"w+"   Opens an existing file and truncates length of file to 0. If no file exists, one will be created for update—both read and write.

"a+"   Opens a file for appending. If no such file exists, one will be created for both read and write.

In addition to these ANSI C file modes, sometimes text modes are available. These would contain a t with the mode name, such as at—append in text mode. The text mode gives an end of record mark as well as an end of file mark.

If a file is being used to change existing names and addresses, the "r+" will work. If a file is being generated to serve as an audit trail where a notation for every transaction will get written, it would be appropriate to use the mode of "a".

Examples

```
FILE *clienttfile;
FILE *clientreportfile;

clientreportfile = fopen("datafile","a");
/* a file with a specific path */
clientfile = fopen("c:\123\data","r");
```

Two declarations specify that streams called `clientfile` and `clientreportfile` are of type `FILE`. The first statement opens a physical file on the disk called "datafile" for append mode and assigns the file to the name `clientreportfile`. The `clientreportfile` may now be referenced as the stream name in the read and write functions.

The second statement opens a file for a mode of read only. Notice that the entire path is used. The file name may contain any required path notation.

Testing if the File Exists Even though some file modes will create a file if one does not exist, there are some occasions where we need to see if the file is on the disk. If the file is not there to open it may indicate that the user has the wrong disk or that the wrong file name was given. When a file is not successfully opened, the fopen( ) function returns a NULL. The NULL can be tested for when an attempt is made to open the file with an option for some alternative to be taken if the fopen( ) was not successful.

```c
#include <stdio.h>
#include "my.h"

FILE *outfile;

void main( )
{
   /* open the file if possible, exit in the event of
         an error in accessing the file */

    if(outfile = fopen("hospital","w")== NULL)
    {
        puts("Unable to open file");
        PAUSE;
        exit(1);
    }
```
. . . . .

When opening the file for a read mode, either "r" or "r+", a test for the existence of the file should be performed.

Self-Test

1. Write the FILE declaration and the open statement to assign the device name of inv_file to the disk file INVEN.DAT in an append mode that can be used for read and write.

2. What is wrong with the following?

```c
FILE *pay;
pay = fopen("Payroll.Dat","r");
....
fprintf(pay,"%s %d",name,hours);
```
write (handwritten annotation)

3. What is wrong with the following?

```c
FILE *sales;
sales = fopen("Sales.dat","r+");
...
fprintf(sales.dat,"%s",name);
```

4. What is wrong with the following?

```
FILE *count;
number = fopen("Count.Dat","w");
...
fprintf(number,"%d",count);
```

Answers

1.
```
FILE *inv_file;
inv_file = fopen("Inven.Dat","a+");
```

2. The file mode of r can only be used for reading from a file, not for writing to it.
3. The fprintf( ) must contain the device name not the disk file name. In this case the device name is sales.
4. The stream name on the FILE declaration was count but in the remaining statements it is number.

Writing to the File

To write to the disk file, `fprintf( )` is used with the appropriate stream name.

```
fprintf(stream,"format specifier string",variables);
```

The format string and the variable list portions of the `fprintf( )` function work the same as always. The only thing that has changed is that, instead of writing to the printer or screen, it will now write to the disk file assigned to the stream.

```
FILE *outfile;
outfile = fopen("Hospital", "a");


write_to_file( )
{
  fprintf(outfile,"%s %c %d", name, room, days);
}
```

The format specifier may be set up with sizes or any format notation that is used for the `fprintf( )`. If a report is to be stored to disk, the formats for actual printed output may be used. This, however, does take more disk, space than just writing the data to the file.

Closing a File

After the access to the data file is complete it must be closed by using `fclose( )` or `fcloseall( )`. The `fclose( )` function will close a specified file while `fcloseall( )` will close any file besides the header defined files, such as `stdprn` or `stdout`. The format for these statements are:

```
fclose(stream);
fcloseall( );
```

The function to close all of the files, `fcloseall( )`, does not accept any arguments.

It would be possible to close the file named earlier as `outfile` using the `fclose( )` function. Any other files that may have been open at the time will not be affected. This will appear as:

```
fclose(outfile);
```

Self-Test

1. Code a statement to write one record to disk, using the stream name of inventory_file that contains the following fields:

   ```
   char description[15];
   int quantity;
   float cost;
   ```

2. Assume that two files, clientfile and clientreport file, are currently open. Write the statement to close only the clientfile stream.

Answers

1. `fprintf(inv_file,"%s %d %f", description, quantity, cost);`
2. `fclose(clientfile);`

Example Creating a File

Create a data file called testfile on the disk that will contain a hospital patient's names, the type of room, and the number of days hospitalized (see Figure 10.1).

The input screen will be printed and the data entered from the keyboard in the same manner as we have been doing. After the information about one person has been entered, the data will be written to disk.

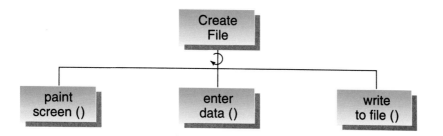

FIGURE 10-1
**Hierarchy Chart for
Creating a Disk File**

Input (screen)	Processing	Output (disk)
Name	None	Name
Room type		Room type
Number of days		Number of days

Pseudocode
Open the file
Paint input screen
Do until no more data
   Enter data
   Write to disk
   Paint input screen
End of loop
Close data file

`10-1.c`

```
/*------------------------------------------------------------
          create a disk file containing a patient name,
          type of room, and number of days
-----------------------------------------------------------*/
#include <stdio.h>
#define CLS printf("\033[2J")
#define LOCATE(r,c) printf("\033[%d;%dH",r,c)


FILE *out;

void paint_screen( )
void enter_data( )
void write_to_file( )
```

```c
char room, name[10];
int days;

void main( )
{
  out = fopen("testfile","a+");

  paint_screen( );
  fflush(stdin);
  while((strlen(gets(name)) != 0)
    {
      enter_data( );
      write_to_file( );
      paint_screen( );
    }
  fclose(out);
  CLS;
}

/*---------------------------------------------------------------
      data entry screen
----------------------------------------------------------------*/
void paint_screen( )
{
 CLS;
 LOCATE(10,10);
 printf("Enter a name or press enter to quit     ");
 LOCATE(12,10);
 printf("Type of room: (p) private (s) semiprivate ");
 LOCATE(14,10);
 printf("Number of days of stay            ");
 LOCATE (10,52);
 fflush(stdin);
}

/*---------------------------------------------------------------
                  input from the keyboard
----------------------------------------------------------------*/
void enter_data( )
{
    LOCATE (12,52);
```

```
      scanf("%c",&room);
      LOCATE (14,52);
      scanf("%d",&days);
}


/*-----------------------------------------------------------------
          write to disk
-----------------------------------------------------------------*/
void write_to_file( )
{
   fprintf(out,"%s %c %d", name, room, days);
}
```

Reading Data from a Disk File

The fscanf( ) function may be used to read data from a file. This function operates the same as scanf( ) but allows for a stream name to be specified. The format for the function is:

```
fscanf(stream name, "format specifier(s)", variable list)
```

Assuming that a stream has been declared and the file opened, we may have a read from that file such as:

```
char name[30];
.....
fscanf(input_file,"%s",name);
```

THE FIELDS WILL BE READ FROM THE FILE IN THE SAME ORDER AS THEY WERE WRITTEN. THE SPACING MUST ALSO BE THE SAME.

If the file was created to print three fields such as description, quantity, and cost, the fprintf( ) might appear as:

```
fprintf(inv_file,"%s %d %f",description, quantity, cost);
```

In that case, an appropriate fscanf( ) would look the same:

```
fscanf(inv_file,"%s %d %f",description, quantity, cost);
```

Testing for the End of the File

When reading the data back from a file, the read operation must be continued until the end of the file is reached. The termination of the processing loop will be dependent upon the length of the file. The stdio.h header file has defined a preprocessor constant for the end of a file as EOF. Using EOF in the loop will make the code easier to read than testing for a bad return from the fscanf( ) function.

In effect, we will loop through the file as long as fscanf( ) does not return a value equal to EOF. This test can be placed as the condition within a while loop:

```
while(fscanf(in,"%s %c %d",name,&room,&days)!=EOF)
```

This statement reads a record from the file each time through the loop. If it is not the end of the file, the loop condition is satisfied and the loop will be processed. When EOF is returned the loop will be exited.

Programming Example

Read the data file that was created in the example on page 305 and print the data to the screen.

Input (from disk)	Output (screen)
Name	Name
Room	Room
Days	Days

    Pseudocode
    Open the file
    While not end of file get a record
      Print the record
    End of loop
    Close the file

```
*/-----------------------------------------------------
     read data from a disk file and output to the screen
------------------------------------------------------*/
#include <stdio.h>
#define CLS printf("\033[2J")
#define LOCATE(r,c) printf("\033[%d;%dH",r,c)


FILE *in;
```

```
char room, name[10];
int days;

void main( )
{
   if((in = fopen("testfile","r+")) ==NULL)
      {
            puts("Cannot open file\n");
            exit(1);
      }
   CLS;

   while(fscanf(in,"%s %c %d",name,&room,&days)!=EOF)
   {
     printf("name: %s\nroom: %c\n days: %d\n",name,room,days);
   }
   fclose(in);
}
```

The loop will read all of the records sequentially from the file until the end of file marker is reached. The read starts from the beginning of the file because the file was opened in mode "r". Each time a read operation is performed the data will be read from where the last read left off until EOF is returned.

Self-Test

Complete the exercises given the following open statement:

```
inventory = fopen("invtry.dat","a+");
```

1. Can the file be used for input or output?
2. What is the physical name of the file on the disk?
3. Write the appropriate close statement for this file.
4. What is EOF and when is it used?

Answers

1. The file is both input and output because of the + after the mode type. This particular file is opened for append, which means that the record pointer will be set to point to the end of the file. Any new records will be added to the end but to read we must set the pointer back further in the file.
2. The physical name on the disk is invtry.dat on the default drive.

3. `fclose(inventory);`

4. An EOF is a test for the end of file marker and would be used when reading from the file.

SEQUENTIAL vs. RANDOM FILE ACCESS

sequential file Every record is read in order.

random file Records may be accessed in any sequence.

Data files may be accessed for update either randomly or sequentially. A **sequential** file requires that every record be read in order to access data later in the file. With a **random file** a record towards the end of the file may be accessed directly.

To illustrate the difference between sequential and random access consider media for audio. Access on a cassette tape for music is normally sequential while a compact disc can be accessed randomly by specifying the track and the song number.

The `fscanf( )` function and the `fprint( )` function can only be accessed as **sequential files** where the data is read starting from the beginning of the file and accessing every record. Because the size of each record may vary, it is impossible to go directly to a specific record.

In order randomly to select a record, the size of each record must be known. Although the record size could be specified using the format specifiers with `fprintf( )`, fixed length records can be created with a structure.

Using Structures in Data Files

The use of structures can greatly ease file access. With a structure defined to contain all of the information for one record, an entire record or file can be accessed with a single read or write. We accessed a complete record with `fscanf( )` and `fprintf( )` but the format had to be given for each field. With the structure, we needn't worry about what constitutes a record at the time we are reading or writing to the file because the declaration of the fields is specified at the time the structure is declared.

Random File Access

It is possible to access the records randomly if structures are used because the length of each record becomes a set size. The *sizeof* operator gives the size of a data type. With a random file it is not necessary to access each record in sequence. If we know the record number we can go directly to the appropriate record. The beginning byte of the record within the file will be the record number times the size of one record (structure).

As usual, we can read and write to the file without closing it if the appropriate mode is set. The `fopen( )` function will operate the same as it did in earlier file programs.

The fwrite( ) Function

The `fwrite( )` function causes up to a specified number of items of a specified size to be written from a buffer to an output stream specified by the stream name. The stream name will still be the file pointer to the structure `FILE`. The format of the function is

```
fwrite(buffer, size, count, stream);
```

The buffer refers to the address of your structure, the size is the size of the structure, and the count could be one record at a time. Therefore, the completed statement may be

```
fwrite(&patient_record,sizeof(patient_record),1,fileptr);
```

count

where

buffer	address of the structure patient_record
size	size of one patient record
count	one record will be written at a time
fileptr	device name from the fopen( )

Writing an Array of Structures When using an array of structures multiple records may be written at one time using the count option of `fwrite( )`. When doing `fprintf( )` one record was entered and then written to disk. This requires a disk I/O operation for every record. With `fwrite( )` all of the data may be input into the array and then a single `fwrite( )` function will write all of the data to the buffer. The limitation here is the size of the array which may be restricted by memory size of the machine or of the compiler model size.

The `fwrite( )` function returns the number of records that were successfully written and maintains the current position within the stream. This feature may be used to create a file larger than the array size.

Creating a File The steps to creating a file include the following:

Input data from keyboard
Write to the data file

```
/*------------------------------------------------
          create a file using structures
---------------------------------------------------*/
#include <stdio.h>

void create( );
void paint_screen( );
void enter_data( );
```

```
FILE *file_out;
struct patient
      {
            char name[25];
            char room;
            int days;
      }patient_record[25];

int i;

void main( )
{
  file_out = fopen("hospital","w");
  create( );
  fclose(file_out);
}
/*-------------------------------------------------
            loop until all data entered into the
            array and then do a write to the file
----------------------------------------------*/
void create( )
{
  paint_screen();
  while( strlen(gets(patient_record[i].name))!=0)
     {
      enter_data( );
      paint_screen( );
     }
     fwrite(&patient_record, sizeof(struct patient),--i,
               file_out);
}


/*-------------------------------------------------
            data entry screen
----------------------------------------------*/
void paint_screen( )
{
  BLUEBK;
  WHITE;
  CLS;
  LOCATE(7,35);
```

```
    puts("Data Entry Screen");
    LOCATE(10,10);
    puts("Name:");
    LOCATE(12,10);
    puts("Room Type(p private, s semiprivate):");
    LOCATE(14,10);
    puts("# days");
    LOCATE(10,50);
    fflush(stdin);
}


/*------------------------------------------------
            enter data from the keyboard
-----------------------------------------------*/
void enter_data( )
{
    LOCATE(12,50);
    scanf("%c", &patient_record[i].room);
    LOCATE(14,50);
    scanf("%d", &patient_record[i++].days);
}
```

Self-Test

1. Write the statement to write 10 records of the following structure type to a file opened with the device name of data_file.

```
struct inventory
{
      char description[20];
      float unit_price;
      int qty_on_hand;
      struct date last_order_date;
      int min_order_qty;
}    inventorty_rec;
```

2. Why does the use of structures in a data file allow us to do random updates to the file?

Answers

```
1. fwrite(&inventory_rec, sizeof(struct inventory),
      10, data_file);
```

2. When using a structure there is a fixed length record, making it possible to determine the beginning byte of each record.

Reading a File

The function used to read a structure from a file is the fread( ), which can read multiple records at a time. The format is as follows:

```
fread(buffer, size, count, stream name);
```

The arguments for the function call are the same as the ones used with the fwrite( ). The number of records that have been read are returned when the function is called. In addition, the current position within the stream will be maintained automatically.

If the count of records to be read exceeds the file size, fread( ) will successfully terminate when the end of file is reached. If the count is less than the file size, a pointer will be maintained by the system so that the next call to fread( ) will continue reading from the file where the previous read left off.

The fread( ) function returns an integer value indicating the number of records that were successfully read from the file that can be used in a loop to print or process the records that are accessed from the file. In order to take advantage of this return value, use an assignment statement when fread( ) is called.

```
int maxrecs;
maxrecs = fread(&my_record, sizeof(myrecord), NUM, file_in);
```

After the assignment statement is executed the array of records will be filled with up to NUM records. To process these records use a *for* loop.

```
for(i=0; i < maxrecs; i++)
{
      /* processing to be performed on records */
}
```

Advantage of Reading Multiple Records at a Time   One of the main advantages of reading several records is that since input/output operations are much slower than processing, we can reduce the number of times that the program accesses the disk. Another advantage is that if the file is small enough to fit in memory at one time, the array of structures can be used to perform a sort or search of the file information. Also, with buffers and/or cache, processing time is much faster.

Example Using fread( )   Write a program that will read an array of patient structures from a data file called hospital.

Pseudocode
Read the file
In a loop, print the records up to the size of the file

```c
/*-------------------------------------------------
            read structures from a disk file
-------------------------------------------------*/
#include <stdio.h>
#define MAX 200

void retrieve( );

FILE *file_ptr;
struct patient
      {
         char name[25];
         char room[1];
         int days;
      }patient_record[MAX];

int i, maxrecs;

void main( )
{
     file_ptr= fopen("hospital","a+");

     retrieve( );
     fclose(file_ptr);
}


/*-------------------------------------------------
     load array and return number of records read,
     then loop and print until that number is reached
-------------------------------------------------*/
void retrieve( )
{
   maxrecs = fread(&patient_record,sizeof(struct patient),
          MAX, file_ptr);
   while( i < maxrecs)
      {
         printf("%s\n",patient_record[i++].name);
      }
}
```

The fseek( ) Function

The `fseek( )` function can be used to control the location of the next record to be accessed. Using `fseek( )`, the file pointer may be set to the beginning of the data, to the end, or to any point in between.

```
fseek(device name, offset, location constant);
```

The available constants for the location of the pointer are:

SEEK_SET	Beginning of the file(0).
SEEK_CUR	Current location in the file(1).
SEEK_END	End of the file(2).

The offset is a long integer that indicates the number of bytes; the pointer should be set from the location constant. Normally we will offset by 0 bytes. To indicate this as a data type of long integer, use 0L.

```
fseek(data_file, 0L, SEEK_SET);
```

This function call will set the file pointer to the beginning of a file that has been opened with a stream name of `data_file`. This may be necessary to do if we are working on a file and then decide we want to list the records or search the file from the beginning of the file. If the file were to be closed and reopened, this might also be accomplished but `fseek( )` can change the pointer position without closing the file.

Perhaps a file is being edited and a record needs to be added to the end of the file. Once again, it will be possible to reposition the pointer without closing the file.

```
fseek(data_file, 0L, SEEK_END);
```

The previous function call will set the pointer immediately behind the last record in the file.

Self-Test

1. How many records are read when an fread( ) is executed?
2. What does the fread( ) function return when it is called?
3. Code the statement(s) to print the fifth record in the file.

Answers

1. Depends on the third argument of the function call. If the structure is an array you may wish to read several records at a time.

2. The fread( ) returns the number of records successfully read from the file.

3.
```
fseek(file_ptr, 4*sizeof(struct patient), SEEK_SET);
fread(&patient_record[0],sizeof(struct patient), 1, file_ptr);
printf(....);
```

UPDATING A RANDOM FILE

A **file update** needs to provide the user with the ability to add records to the file, to delete records, and to edit existing records (see Figure 10-2). In addition, it is handy to have an option to list the records to the screen or to the printer. The easiest way to present this program in a useful manner is to use a menu program. The last item on the menu will be an option to exit the update.

At the beginning of the program the file will be opened to a mode of "a+". The file will remain open until just before the program is terminated. While the file is open we will position the cursor to the desired location using fseek( ). Because of the append mode being used, it would be desirable to display a message if there are no records in the file. We can do this in each of the modules.

file update Ability to add, delete, or edit records in a file.

Update Menu

1. Add a record.
2. Delete a record.
3. Edit/Change a record.
4. List records.
0. Exit.

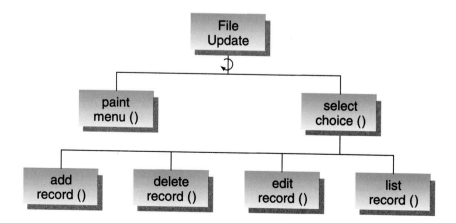

FIGURE 10-2
Updating a Random File

```
██ ██ - ██ . ██
```

```
/*------------------------------------------------------------
                    Updating a Random File
------------------------------------------------------------*/
#include <stdio.h>
#include <stdlib.h>

#define MAX 200
#define SPACES "                "
#define CLS printf("\033[2J")
#define LOCATE(r,c) printf("\033[%d;%dH",r,c)
#define BLUEBK printf("\033[44m")
#define WHITE printf("\033[37m")
#define PAUSE LOCATE(23,25); puts("Press any key to continue");getche( )

FILE *file_ptr;

void paint_menu( );
void select_choice( );
void add_record( );
void delete_record( );
void edit_record( );
void list_record( );

struct patient
     {
      char name[25];
      char room;
      int days;
     }patient_record[MAX];

int i, option, maxrecs;

void main( )
{
   /*-------------open the file -------------*/
  if((file_ptr = fopen("b:hospital","r++")) == NULL)
    {
     CLS;
```

```
      LOCATE(10,20)L
      puts("File does not exist");
      puts(" - You must add records or insert proper disk");
      file_ptr = fopen("b:hospital", "a++");
      PAUSE;
      /* exit(EXIT_FAILURE); */
    }

  /*  paint menu and loop until exit is chosen */
  paint_menu( );
  do
  {
    select_choice( );
    paint_menu( );
   }
  while(option != 0);

  fclose(file_ptr);
}


/* ------------------------------------------------------------
                              Menu
------------------------------------------------------------*/
void paint_menu( )
{
  BLUEBK;
  WHITE;
  CLS;
  LOCATE(7,30);
  puts("Hospital Update Menu");
  LOCATE(10,10);
  puts("1. Add a patient record");
  LOCATE(12,10);
  puts("2. Delete a patient record");
  LOCATE(14,10);
  puts("3. Edit/Change patient information");
  LOCATE(16,10);
  puts("4. List all patient records");
  LOCATE(18,10);
  puts("0. QUIT");
```

```
  LOCATE(20,10);
  puts("Enter the option number");
  LOCATE(20,50);
  scanf("%d", &option);
}


/*-------------------------------------------------------
                 get menu option and select
                    appropriate function
----------------------------------------------------*/
void select_choice( )
{
  switch (option)
  {
    case 1:
      add_record( );
      break;
    case 2:
      delete_record( );
      break;
    case 3:
      edit_record( );
      break;
    case 4:
      list_record( );
      break;
    default:
     LOCATE(22,15);
     puts("Invalid option - Please select again");
     PAUSE;
    }
}
```

Adding Records to the File

append Add records to end of file.

To add a record to the file, we will move the file pointer to the end of the file. Adding records is the same as originally creating the file. It is not necessary to have two separate programs, one to create and one to add a record. If the file is opened in **append** mode, records are added to the end of the file. If the file is being created for the first time, the end of the file is the beginning of the file and that is where the records will be placed.

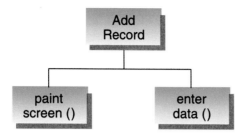

FIGURE 10-3
Adding a Record

The steps to add a record (see Figure 10-3) are:

1. Position the pointer to the end of the file.
2. Get data from the keyboard until no more records.
3. Write to the file.

```c
void add_record( )
{
 /* place file pointer to the end of the file */
 fseek(file_ptr, 0L, SEEK_END);

 paint_screen( );
 while( strlen(gets(patient_record[i].name))!=0)
     {
      enter_data( );
      paint_screen( );
     }
     fwrite(&patient_record, sizeof(struct patient),i, file_ptr);
}

/*-------------------------------------------------------
                data entry screen
-----------------------------------------------------------*/
void paint_screen( )
{
  CLS;
  LOCATE(7,35);
  puts("Data Screen");
  LOCATE(10,10);
  puts("Name:");
  LOCATE(12,10);
  puts("Room Type(p private, s semiprivate):");
  LOCATE(14,10);
```

```
    puts("# days");
    LOCATE(10,50);
    fflush(stdin);
}


/*-------------------------------------------------------------
            input data from the keyboard
---------------------------------------------------------*/
void enter_data( )
{
    LOCATE(12,50);
    scanf("%c",&patient_record[i].room);
    LOCATE(14,50);
    scanf("%d",&patient_record[i++].days);
}
```

Deleting or Editing a Record

To delete or edit an existing record we must begin by finding out which record is to be deleted/processed. If the user knows the record number of the record to be deleted, we could go directly to that position in the file. If not, we will have to ask for a field in the record. We will then search for this record in the file. Recall from Chapter 7 (see page 205) that the field being searched for is called the key. If the data was sorted in the array by the key field, we could use `bsearch( )`.

After the record is located we should display the information from the record and verify that this is the proper record. If the answer is yes, the record will then be processed.

Delete

So how do we delete this record? One way would be to rewrite the file and to not write this record back in. This method is slow and it also changes the record number for all of the records following it. Another alternative would be to use a **delete flag** to mark the record as deleted or inactive.

delete flag Marks a record as deleted or inactive.

Flagging a Record for Delete   There are two common ways to flag a record for delete. If you've worked with DOS you are probably aware that files are not really deleted from the disk immediately but, instead, the first letter of the file name is deleted in the directory table. Next time a file is saved, this space will appear as available.

A second method is to set up an extra field that will contain a code to determine if the record is active or inactive. This method is especially desirable when there is a good chance that records will need to be "undeleted."

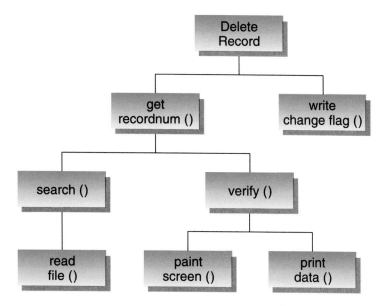

FIGURE 10-4
Deleting a Random
Record

Steps in deleting a record (see Figure 10-4):

1. Get the record number or a key field of the record to be deleted.
2. Find the record.
3. Verify that the record that is found is the one the user wishes to delete.
4. Flag the record as deleted.

```c
/*                Delete Routine          */


void delete_record( )
{
  int delete_ok;

  CLS;
  LOCATE(7,30);
  puts("Delete Option");
  delete_ok = getrecordnum( );
  if(delete_ok >= 0)
   {
     strcpy(patient_record[delete_ok].name,"*");
     LOCATE(21,30);
     printf("Record deleted");
     write_change(delete_ok);
   }
```

```
      else
          {
         LOCATE(21,30);
         puts("Record not found");
            }
      PAUSE;
}

/*        Shared routines for Delete and Edit */
/*        getrecordnum( )
          search( )
          verify( )
          write_change( )
          print_data( )          */


/*----------------------------------------------------------
          asks for the record number, if unknown
          a search is performed
------------------------------------------------------------*/
int getrecordnum( )
{
   int recordnum;
   char key[15], answer;

   LOCATE(10,5);
   puts("Enter Record Number(if known) or type -1");
   LOCATE(10,47);
   scanf("%d",&recordnum);

   if(recordnum == -1)
     {
       /* get the key of record to be deleted */

       fflush(stdin);
       LOCATE(10,5);
       puts("Enter name of patient to be found      ");
       LOCATE(10,45);
       gets(key);
       recordnum = search(key);
     }
     if(recordnum!=1)
```

```
    {
     answer = verify(recordnum);
          /* was it the correct record  */
     if(toupper(answer) == 'Y')
         return recordnum;
     else
        return -1;
    {
      else
          return -1;
    }

int search(char key[])
{
              /*          find the record   */
   int i;

   read_file();
   for(i = 0; i < maxrecs; i++)
      if(strncmp(patient_record[i].name, key, strlen(key)) == 0)
       {
          return(i);
       }
     return -1;
       }
}

char verify(int recnum)
{
    char answer;

    /*  make sure we have the correct record */
    paint_screen();
    print_data(recnum);
    LOCATE(20,20);
    puts("Is this the correct record (Y/N)");
    LOCATE(20,60);
    scanf("%c", &answer);
    return(answer);
}
```

```
void print_data(int i)
{
      /*   fills in data from record to data screen   */
    LOCATE(10,50);
    printf("%s",patient_record[i].name);
    LOCATE(12,50);
    printf("%c",patient_record[i].room);
    LOCATE(14,50);
    printf("%d",patient_record[i].days);
}


void write_change(int recnum)
{
  int currentpos;

  currentpos = sizeof(struct patient) * recnum;
  fseek(file_ptr, currentpos, SEEK_SET);
  fwrite(&patient_record[recnum], sizeof(struct patient), 1,
  file_ptr);
}


/*      reads file for list and search   */
void read_file( )
{
  fseek(file_ptr,0L, SEEK_SET);
  if(maxrecs = fread(&patient_record, sizeof(struct
          patient),MAX, file_ptr)==0)
  printf("The file is empty\n");
}
```

Editing Records

To edit a record, we must first locate it just as we did with the delete option (see Figure 10-5). After the record is found, we then need to know which changes the user wishes to make. Once again, there are different approaches to this problem. Some programs simply treat an edit like an add and all fields must be reentered. However, this does not seem very user friendly.

    Another approach would be to give users a menu and then permit them to

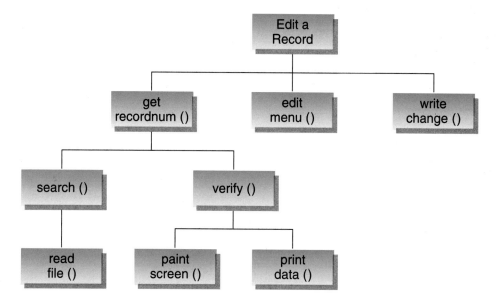

FIGURE 10-5
Editing a Record

select the field to be changed. This would be placed in a loop that would terminate when the users chose an option for "No More Changes."

The menu screen will use two previous functions: `paint_screen( )` from the add and delete functions and `print_data( )` from the delete function. Once the fields and the data from the record are displayed on the screen, we can then place menu numbers in front of the field names.

```
/*              Edit Routine          */

void edit_record( )
{
  int edit_ok;

  CLS;
  LOCATE(7,30);
  puts("Edit Option");
  edit_ok = getrecordnum( );
  if(edit_ok >= 0)
   {
     edit_menu(edit_ok);
     write_change(edit_ok);
   }
  else
```

```
          {
      LOCATE(21,30);
      puts("Record not found");
      PAUSE;
          }
}
/*----------------------------------------------------
          Give options of which field to edit
--------------------------------------------------*/

void edit_menu(int i)
{
 char option;

 do
   {
    LOCATE(10,7);
    puts("1.");
    LOCATE(12,7);
    puts("2.");
    LOCATE(14,7);
    puts("3.");
    LOCATE(16,7);
    puts("0. No more changes");
    LOCATE(20,15);
    puts("Select option =============>                ");
    LOCATE(20,50);
    fflush(stdin);
    scanf("%c", &option);

    /*----------------------------------------------
                input new data for appropriate field
    --------------------------------------------*/
    switch(option)
    {
      case '1':
      LOCATE(10,50);
      puts(SPACES);
      LOCATE(10,50);
      fflush(stdin);
      gets(patient_record[i].name);
```

```
        break;
        case '2':
        LOCATE(12,50);
        puts(SPACES);
        LOCATE(12,50);
        fflush(stdin);
        scanf("%c", &patient_record[i].room);
        break;
        case '3':
        LOCATE(14,50);
        puts(SPACES);
        LOCATE(14,50);
        scanf("%d", &patient_record[i].days);
        case '4':
        break;
        default:
        LOCATE(20,15);
        puts("Please enter an appropriate letter or number ");
        LOCATE(17,40);
        fflush(stdin);
        scanf("%c", &option);
        }
    }while(option != '0');
}
```

Listing Records from the File

When we are listing records we will only want to display or print the active records, which will necessitate checking for the delete code. The file pointer must be set to the beginning of the file.

Printing to the Screen   When printing to the screen the program must count lines to determine when the screen is full. When the screen is filled, the screen should pause until the user is ready to continue. At that point the screen will be cleared and the titles reprinted. This will continue until all records have been printed.

Printing to the Printer   A printed listing of records should contain the logic for multipage output (covered in more detail in Chapter 11, see page 346; see Figure 10-6). This routine will differ from the screen in the number of lines per page and also in using a form feed rather than a clear screen.

FIGURE 10-6
Listing Records to Printer or Screen

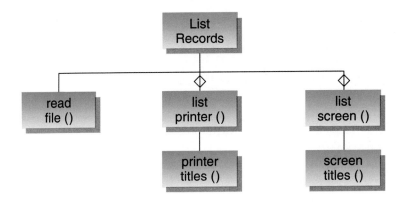

```
/*-------------------------------------------------
          a menu selection for options
          to print to the screen or
          to the printer
-----------------------------------------------*/
void list_record( )
{
     int i = 0;
     char option;

     read_file();
     CLS;
     LOCATE(7,35);
     puts("Listing Option");
     LOCATE(10,20);
     puts("1. Send to the printer");
     LOCATE(12,20);
     puts("2. Display on the screen");
     LOCATE(15,18);
     puts("Enter your Choice (1 or 2)");
     LOCATE(15,48);
     fflush(stdin);
     scanf("%c", &option);


     switch (option)
     {
      case '1':
      case 'P':
      case 'p':
     list_printer( );
```

```
             break;
             case '2':
             case 'S':
             case 's':
             list_screen( );
             break;
             default:
          LOCATE(20,15);
          puts("Please enter an appropriate letter or number ");
               LOCATE(15,48);
          fflush(stdin);
          scanf("%c", &option);
             }
       }

/*-------------------------------------------------------
            creates a printed report of patient names
-------------------------------------------------------*/
void list_printer( )
{
       int linecount = 0;

       titles( );
       for(i = 0; i < maxrecs; i++)
         {
            if(linecount > 48)
               {
               linecount = 0;
               titles( );
               }
            if(strcmp(patient_record[i].name, "*") != 0)
            {
               linecount++;
               /* add to linecount only if a line is printed */
               fprintf(stdprn,"     %s\n\n",patient_record[i].name);
            }
         }
}

/*-------------------------------------------------
                    Titles for the printed report
-------------------------------------------------*/
void titles( )
{
    static int pagecount;
```

```c
        pagecount++;
        fprintf(stdprn,"\f                  Patient Listing     Page
                                     %d\n\n", pagecount);
}


/*----------------------------------------------------------------
            Creates a screen display of patient names
--------------------------------------------------------------*/
void list_screen( )
{
        int linecount = 0;

        screen_titles();
        for(i = 0; i < maxrecs; i++)
          {
          if(linecount++ > 7)
            {
              PAUSE;
              linecount = 0;
              screen_titles( );
            }
          if(strcmp(patient_record[i].name, "*") != 0)
             {
                linecount++;
                /* add to linecount only if a line is printed */
                printf("    %d      %s\n\n",i, patient_record[i].name);
             }
         }
       PAUSE;
}


/*----------------------------------------------------------------
            Titles for the Screen Report
--------------------------------------------------------------*/
void screen_titles( )
{
  CLS;
  LOCATE(7,35);
  puts("Patient List\n\n");
}
```

Replacing Deleted Record Positions During Add

If the possibility of undeleting records is not going to be used a record that is being added could be placed in a record position that contains a deleted record marked by an *.

To replace deleted records when adding a record a loop will be used to find the first record location that contains an * in the appropriate field. If no records have been deleted the new record will be placed at the end of the file.

Using a Delete Code

Sometimes it is desirable to maintain the information in a deleted record. An example may be a file in which records are active or inactive, as indicated earlier. In order to do this an extra field, a **delete code,** will be added to each record that contains the status of the record.

delete code A separate field used to mark a record as deleted or inactive.

```
struct patient
    {
      char name[25];
      char room[1];
      int days;
      enum {A,I} delete_code;
    }patient_record[MAX];
```

In order to delete the record the delete code would be changed to inactive, rather than using the * flag. To give the menu option to undelete records all records that contain a delete code of inactive would be listed.

PROGRAMMING/DEBUGGING TIP

Another method used to access records directly is by using an algorithm to derive the record key.

Hash Addressing

Hash addressing is the programming technique in which the key field is used to generate a record number for a random file. The field, such as name, has an algorithm applied to it to determine a record number within the file size. This record number, sometimes called a *hash key,* can then be used for direct access to a random file using `fseek( )`.

An overflow area for records with duplicate keys is required because it cannot be guaranteed that all key fields will produce a unique record number. When a key generates a record number that has already been assigned, a **collision**

hash addressing An algorithm used to determine an address key for a random file.

collision Two values resulting in the same key using a hashing algorithm.

occurs. The same hashing function may yield a different rate of collisions depending on the type of data used for the key field (string or numeric). In general, the steps in hash addressing are:

1. Change the key to a record number.
2. Get the record.
3. If the record is blank, write the data if not blank, chain to next available record number in the overflow area.

Hashing Algorithm

The algorithm used should not be too complicated and must minimize collisions. The following method starts by entering the key field, converting each of the characters to ASCII code, and finding the sum of the ASCII codes. A prime number close to the file size is used in finding the record number.

Example

Use a sum of the ASCII codes and a modulus assuming a file size of 100 to determine a hash key for the following fields:

```
Jones
Johnson
Johnston
Jensen
Johns
```

10-6.c

```c
/*-------------------------------------------------------
      implement hashing algorithms to find a record number
-----------------------------------------------------*/
#include <stdio.h>

char name[5][9] = {"Jones",
          "Johnson",
          "Johnston",
          "Jensen",
          "Johns"};

int asciisum(char name[ ]);

void main( )
```

```
{
   int i, key, sum;

   fprintf(stdprn," Name    ASCII sum  key\n\r");
   for(i =0; i < 5; i++)
   {
      sum = (int)asciisum(name[i]);
      key = sum % 101;  /* uses modulus and a prime number */
      fprintf(stdprn,"%-15s%4i    %i\n\r",name[i],sum,key);
   }
}
/*------------------------------------------------
   finds the sum of the ASCII code for
   each letter in a name
-------------------------------------------------*/
int asciisum(char name[])
{
   int i, sum;

   for(i=0; name[i] != NULL; i++)
   {
      sum += (int)(name[i]);  /*type cast each letter to integer */
   }
   return sum;
}
```

Output

```
Name       ASCII sum   key
Jones      517         12
Johnson    1252        40
Johnston   2103        83
Jensen     2714        88
Johns      3228        97
```

USING fscanf( ) WITH STRING ARRAYS

The fscanf( ) function will have its usual problems when reading string data from an array. The input for a string array will be terminated when a white space is encountered. The white space could be entered into the file as a special character.

There are ways to search for a specific character. An example that is common is a comma between fields in a text file. The fscanf( ) function, as well as scanf( ), can indicate the character to be "read up to" by using the [bracket. Only certain characters may be accepted or, by using the ^, all characters will be input up to the specified character. Therefore, [^, means read everything before the comma.

```c
#include <stdio.h>
#define CLS printf("\033[2J")

void print_to_scrn( )
char fname[10], lname[10];
float pay;
FILE *paydata;

void main( )
{
   int i;
   char comma;
   paydata = fopen("Payroll","r");

   CLS;
   while(++i<4)
   {
      fscanf(paydata,"%[^,]s",fname); /* reads up to comma */
      fscanf(paydata,"%c",comma);    /* gets the comma */
      fscanf(paydata,"%[^,]s",lname);
      fscanf(paydata,"%c",comma);    /* gets the comma */
      fscanf(paydata,"%f",&pay);
      print_to_scrn( );
   }
}

void print_to_scrn( )
{
   printf("%s %s %f\n",fname,lname,pay);
}


/*------------------------------------------------------------
      incorporate the check for comma in a single fscanf( )
---------------------------------------------------------------*/
```

```
#include <stdio.h>
#define CLS printf("\033[2J")
void print_to_scrn( );
char fname[10], lname[10];
float pay;
FILE *paydata;

void main( )
{
  int i;
  char comma;
  paydata = fopen("Payroll","r");

  CLS;

while(fscanf(paydata,"%[^,]s%c%[^,]s%c%f",fname,comma,lname,comma,&pay)
  !=EOF)
    print_to_scrn( );
}

void print_to_scrn( )
{
   printf("%s %s %f\n",fname,lname,pay);
}
```

KEY TERMS

append   file mode   physical file name
collision   file update   random access
delete code   hash address   sequential access
delete flag   logical file name   stream

Summary of file commands:

`FILE *stream`   Declares file name for program.

`stream = fopen("diskfile name","mode")` Opens the file in
the desired mode and assigns the physical disk name to the streamname that
will be used in the program.

```
fprintf(stream,....)          Write to a file.
fscanf(stream,"format".)      Read from a file.
fclose(stream)                Close the file buffer.
fcloseall()                   Close all open files.
```

CHAPTER SUMMARY

Files can be input or output from disk using the same commands that are available for the standard devices, `fscanf( )` and `fprintf( )`. The hardware-dependent items are handled within the library functions for the programmer. Before the disk may be used for input/output operations it must be assigned a stream name using `fopen( )`. When the processing of the file is complete the file must be closed using `fclose( )` or `fcloseall( )`.

There are many different ways to access data from a disk file. One of the most efficient is through the use of structures. An array of structures may be accessed in block form by using the `fread( )` and the `fwrite( )` functions. Both of these functions return the number of items processed and they will maintain the current position within the stream for further processing.

A file update provides the capability of adding, deleting, and changing records within a file. These operations are most conveniently tied together through the use of a menu program.

REVIEW QUESTIONS

1. What statement is used to read a file using structures?
2. List the four arguments necessary to do an fwrite( ).
3. When accessing a file of structures, how can you find out how many records to read?
4. If the array size is set at 100 and the file contains 4253 records, how can all of the records be processed?
5. What are the advantages of using a delete code rather than just changing an existing field?
6. In the example program why does the list file check for an * before printing?
7. What are the steps necessary to do an edit to an existing record?
8. What is meant by an index?
9. What is the purpose of hashing?
10. What is meant by the phrase "hashing algorithm"?
11. Give an example of a hashing algorithm.
12. What is a "collision"?

1. Write a program to create a disk file using the employee structure from Exercise 1 in Chapter 8 (see page 252). After the file has been created write a second program that will access the employee file and create the report as indicated in the Chapter 8 exercise.

2. Write a program that will input data from the keyboard and create a file of inventory records using the following structure:

```
struct inventory
{
    char description[20];
    float unit_price;
    int qty_on_hand;
    struct date last_order_date;
    int min_order_qty;
    inventory_rec;
}
```

3. Write a program that will produce a report to the screen or to the printer listing the records from the inventory file created in Exercise 2.

4. Write a program that will create a sequential data file for a used car dealership. Each inventory record will consist of the manufacturer, model name, year, vehicle number, and market value. The vehicle number is a 15-character string field and the market value will be float.

   OUTPUT

   Read the records from the data file and produce a list of the data with appropriate titles and column headings.

   Data:
   ```
   Chevrolet, Blazer, 87, AND042049, 12000
   Chevrolet, Camaro, 69, TOM022765, 5000
   Dodge, Ramcharger,79, CAB070480, 6000
   Ford, Mustang, 69, ERI032075, 5000
   Ford, 150-Pickup, 90, ART062137, 19000
   Ford, Thunderbird, 89, WEN984567, 12500
   Honda, LXI, 88, GEN092330, 4500
   Honda, Civic,91,LES11234,5500
   Honda, Civic,92,MES21334,6500
   Jeep, Scout, 75, ALP122720, 1000
   Jeep, Scout, 85, ABB432189,3000
   Mazda, 323, 90, GOG123456, 6000
   Mazda, 626, 84, TRI082573, 4000
   Peugeot, 505S, 84, ANI081650, 4000
   ```

5. Create a random file using the data from the used car dealership in Exercise 4. Each structure will consist of the manufacturer, model name, year, vehicle number, and market value. The vehicle number is a 15-character string field and the market value will be float.

OUTPUT

Read the records from the data file and produce a list of the data with appropriate titles and column headings.

6. Create a data file for a bowling league. Each record will contain the team name, the bowler name, the number of games played this season, the total pins, and the high series. Records for females will contain an asterisk.

Data:

```
Team Supreme   Al Argus       18  3135  572
Team Supreme   Mary Menace    15  2024  420  *
Team Supreme   Bob Menace     18  3004  550
Team Supreme   Karin Dee      18  3030  525  *
Alley Gators   Chris Carson   18  2788  479  *
Alley Gators   Audy Carson    18  3011  590
Alley Gators   Eddie Tomas    15  2275  455
Alley Gators   Cindy Tomas    15  1788  395  *
Lucky Strikes  Andy Marvin    18  3055  602
Lucky Strikes  Ann Marvin     18  2020  398  *
Lucky Strikes  Linda Noon     18  2550  456  *
Lucky Strikes  Scott Noon     18  2888  522
Sub            Lou Garcia      6  2088  488  *
```

7. Write a program that will create and update an employee file. For each employee, you must use a structure to store the information. Each record will include the following:

Last name:
First name:
Middle initial:
Social security number:
Date hired:
Vanpool (yes or no):
Salary code (S for salaried, H for hourly):
Salary level (may be an hourly rate or an annual salary):
Year-to-date income:
Year-to-date federal income taxes:
Year-to-date state income taxes:

The update program must be menu driven and must include options for adding a record, deleting a record, editing a record, and for listing the records to the screen or to the printer. The list option should print the employees in order by last name.

8. Write a program to create a payroll report from the employee file created in Exercise 7.

INPUT

Design an input screen that will print the employee name and social security number on the screen from the file. Prompt the user to enter the number of hours worked, if hourly. If the individual is salaried, ask for number, if any, of sick or personal leave days.

OUTPUT
Title:

The title will include a page number and the report date. Create column headings for name.

Detail Line: The detail line will include the following:

1. Employee name.
2. Regular pay.

3. Overtime hours.
4. Overtime pay.
5. Deductions.
6. Gross pay.

Summary:

The summary line should contain totals for overtime hours, overtime pay, and gross pay.

PROCESSING
Overtime:

For hourly employees, calculate overtime at a rate of time and one-half for all hours over 40.

Deductions:

Vanpool; if yes, deduct 14.50.
Federal taxes, use 15%.
State taxes, use 8%.
FICA.

9. Create a program that will input a last name and then print the address calculated by using four different hashing algorithms. Test the program for 20 different last names and print a summary of the number of collisions created by each method.

HAYLEY OFFICE SUPPLIES

Use the structure created in Chapter 8 (see page 254) for the inventory items to create a file. Each structure will contain the product number, product description, aisle number, current cost, quantity on hand, minimum order quantity, and vendor.

Use the file to create a program for sales transactions. The sales transaction screen will allow the user to enter the product number or, if not known (press enter), the product description. The price will be calculated as a 35% markup. Assume all items are taxable. The results will be an invoice calculating the amount due and an update to the structure quantity field.

For this example, make up sample data and enter it into the array of structures at the beginning of the program to simulate a data file.

CHAPTER

11

CHAPTER OBJECTIVES

By the end of this chapter, you should be able to:

- Produce reports that contain multiple pages and print page numbers and headings on each page.

- Create reports that will include subtotals and multiple pages of output.

- Understand the use of a control variable to test when to "break" the logic.

- Use multiple control variables for the generation of multiple levels of subtotals.

Creating Multipage Reports with Subtotals

CHAPTER OVERVIEW

To print a multiple page report it is necessary to count the lines printed and then advance to the next page at the appropriate time. After allowing for advancement to the top of a page, titles and headings may be printed or just the column headings. In order to include the page number in the heading an additional calculation field will be required.

Control break logic will be introduced in this chapter and then used to generate subtotals within the detail portion of the report. The subtotals will be accumulated into the report totals. Subtotals may be calculated on a field at one level of a control variable or subtotals may be found for multiple levels.

Many reports exceed a single page. It is critical that the output does not continue over a perforation or beyond the end of the page. Headings on subsequent pages may also be desired.

Multipage Output

When a report will exceed the length of one page, we must plan for advancing to the next page in our code. A normal 8.5" x 11" page has 66 lines (6 lines per inch). If allowance is made for a 1" margin at the top and bottom of the page, there are 54 lines remaining for printing the report. This area must hold titles, as well as column headings and detail lines.

Most printers will not automatically advance to the next page; it is up to the programmer to count the lines that have been printed and then decide when to advance to the next page. If the titles and headings are a set number of lines, these can be subtracted from 54 and then only the detail lines will need to be counted. Each time through the detail loop we will increment the detail line counter. The line counter will be an integer variable, defined as

```
int line_counter;
```

We can then program a decision that, if the detail line counter has exceeded the maximum number of lines per page, it is time to advance to the top of a new page.

```
if(++line_counter > 48)
{
        heading( );
 }
```

This line of code increments the line counter and checks to see, in this particular example, if we have reached 48 lines. If so, the heading( ) function will be performed. The maximum number of lines could be defined by a preprocessor constant. This would make it very easy to change the number of lines per page without searching a lot of code.

```
#define MAXLINES 48
.........
if(++line_counter > MAXLINES)
  {
     heading( );
  }
```

Placement of the Line Counter Decision

The decision that tests the line counter should be placed *before* the detail print to assure that there will be at least one detail line on the page. If we were to place this decision statement at the end of the detail print module, the titles would be printed after the detail line was printed as soon as the page is full. It is possible that this could have also been the last detail line which would cause headings to appear alone on the last page.

If the line count has been exceeded it is only necessary to go to a new page if we need one. If there is another detail line to print the detail print function would be called again the next time through the loop. The first thing that should happen then in that detail print module is to check to see if we need a new page. Detail print module must:

1. Test the linecount for new page.
2. Print a detail line.

Changes to the `heading( )` Function

The `heading( )` function must be modified to do some additional instructions. The paper must be advanced to the next page. It will be necessary to reset the line counter to 0 each time we start a new page.

If the line counter is not reset, it will still be too large the next time through the loop. This will cause the first page to work fine, but each subsequent page would have the headings and one detail line. After the one detail line, the `heading( )` function would be called again.

Form Feed

To advance to the next page, a **form feed** can be sent to the printer as an escape sequence or as an ASCII code. The escape sequence for a form feed is `\f`. The form feed escape sequence may be combined with the print line that prints the title.

form feed Advances the paper on the printer.

```
fprintf(stdprn,"\f......)
```

A second choice would be to print an ASCII code 12, the form feed character. This will look like

```
fprintf(stdprn,"%c",12);
```

As you can tell the ASCII character is printed by using the character specifier and printing the number 12.

Summary of Steps for Multipage Output   Detail processing:

1. Increment the line count for any printer lines during the detail loop.
2. Test the line count variable to see if it exceeds the maximum number of lines desired. If so, perform the titles function.

Titles:

1. Print a form feed.
2. Set the line count to 0 for a new page.
3. Add 1 to the page count, if one is desired.

Because we are calling the title function from the detail print module, it will be necessary to indicate this function by placing a box coming out from detail print in the hierarchy chart (see Figure 11-1). However, this is really the same titles module from the mainline. To indicate that this is the same module, color in the corner of the box.

Programming Example

To illustrate a multipage output report, we will create a program that produces a hospital billing report based on the file that was created in Chapter 10. The billing rate will be determined by the type of room that the patient occupies, private or semiprivate, and the number of days of hospitalization (see Figure 11-2).

Input:

For each patient, input the patient name, the number of days, and the type of room.

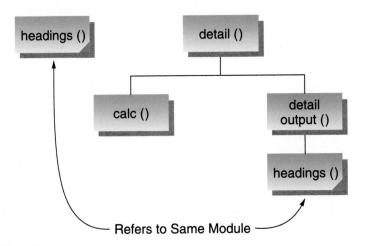

FIGURE 11-1
Indicating a Function
Called from Two Places

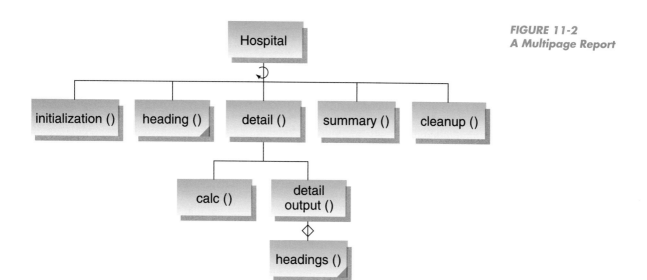

FIGURE 11-2
A Multipage Report

Calculations:

Find the appropriate rate based on the type of room and
calculate the billing amount by multiplying the rate by the
number of days. It will also be necessary to accumulate the
total billing for the end of the report.

Output:

Titles and column headings. Detail lines to include name,
days, and amount of billing. Summary line contains total
billing amount.

1 1 - 1 . c

```
/*---------------------------------------------------
                A Multipage Report
-----------------------------------------------------*/
#include <stdio.h>
#define CLS printf("\033[2J")
#define LOCATE(r,c) printf("\033[%d;%dH",r,c)

float calc(char *room, int *days);
void initialization( ), heading( ), detail( ), summary( );
void detail_output(char name[25], char room, int days, float amt);
```

```c
void cleanup( );
FILE *patient;
int linecount, totdays;
float totamt;

void main( )
{
  initialization( );
  heading( );
  detail( );
  summary( );
  cleanup( );
}



/*------------------------------------------------------------
             open the data file
-----------------------------------------------------------*/
void initialization( )
{
  if((patient = fopen("testfile", "r+"))==NULL)
  {
    printf("Unable to open the file");
    exit(1);
  }
}



/*------------------------------------------------------------
             Print page titles including a page number
-----------------------------------------------------------*/
void heading( )
{
  static int pagecount = 1;        /* pagecount must retain value */
  linecount = 0;
  fprintf(stdout,"%c\n",12);
  fprintf(stdout,"\t\t\t Hospital Billing Report  Page %d\n\n",
     pagecount++);
  fprintf(stdout,"    Name          Room Type    Days  Amount\n\n");
}
```

```
/*-----------------------------------------------------------
        Read and process the detail records
-----------------------------------------------------------*/
void detail( )
{
  char room, name[25];
  int days;
   float amount;

  while(fscanf(patient,"%s %c %d", name, &room, &days) != EOF)
  {
     amount = calc(&room, &days);
     detail_output(name, room, days, amount);
  }
}




/*-----------------------------------------------------------
     Calculate the amount for the detail line and
     add to the totals
-----------------------------------------------------------*/
float calc(char *room, int *days)
{
  float rate, amt;
  switch (tolower(room))    /* determine the room rate */
     {
     case 'p':
       rate = 500.;
       break;
     case 's':
         rate = 375.;
         break;
     default:
     break;
     }
   amt =(*days * rate);
   totamt+=amt;
   totdays+= *days;
   return amt;
  }
```

```
/*------------------------------------------------------------
            Prints a line on the detail report
--------------------------------------------------------*/
void detail_output(char name[25], char room, int days, float amt)
{
   if(++linecount > 48)
       heading( );
   fprintf(stdout,"%15s \t\t %c\t    %d\t   %5.2f\n",
       name,room,days,amt);
}


/*------------------------------------------------------------
              Prints the totals at the end of the report
------------------------------------------------------*/
void summary( )
{
fprintf(stdout,"\n%15s \t\t   \t  %d\t   %5.2f",
     "Total",totdays,totamt);
}


/*------------------------------------------------------------
              Close the data file
------------------------------------------------------*/
void cleanup( )
{
   fclose(patient);
}
```

Self-Test

1. Write the pseudocode for a titles module of a multipage report that will advance to the next page and print the page count as part of the title.
2. Code the C statement to cause the printer to advance to the next page and print the title and page count.
3. Why should the test for the line count be before the print in the detail output module?

Answers

1. Add 1 to page count.
   Print title with a form feed.
   Print column headings.
   Set line count to 0 for new page.

2. `fprintf(stdprn,"\f    Title    Page %d",pgcount);`
3. If the test for the line count was performed after the detail line was printed, a new page would be created with no detail lines.

CONTROL BREAKS

A **control break** tests a control field to determine when a break should be made in the routine processing to perform a particular function. The most common use of control break logic is to produce subtotals in a report.

A subtotal is printed within the detail portion of the report whenever the control variable changes. The control variable is determined by the particular application. All data will be in order according to the field that forms the grouping for the subtotals. Since the subtotals will be printed as that field changes, the field that changes is called the **control field.**

If we were creating a payroll report that included the name, department number, and pay information, it may be necessary to find subtotals for each department. To make this work, the data must be in order by department number. The subtotal would be printed whenever the department number changed.

control break Causes a function to be performed when the value of a control variable changes.

control field Variable used to determine when a break occurs.

ABC Company
Payroll Report

Name	Department	Hours	Gross Pay
Jones, A.	5	40	650.00
Smyt, J.	5	27	347.00
Subtotal for Department 5			997.00
Mills, T.	8	20	450.00
Erim, E.	8	40	625.00
Sherr, B.	8	30	500.00
Subtotal for Department 8			1575.00
Report Total			$2572.00

In order to determine if the department number has changed, the control variable contains the previous department number. As each record is read, the control variable will be compared with the department number. If they are the same, the department number has not changed, processing will continue normally, and the pay information for this individual will be added to the subtotal as part of the detail calculation module (see Figure 11.3).

FIGURE 11-3
Detail Processing with
Subtotals

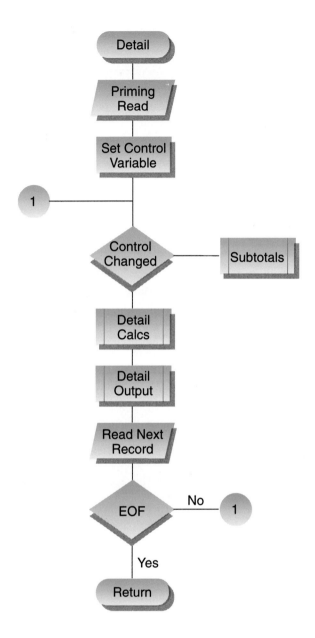

However, if the control variable is not equal to the department number on the new record then the department number has changed and it is time to do a subtotal. Therefore, we will take a "break" from the normal processing to do an extra module and then return to process this new record. This extra module is the subtotal module.

The Subtotal Function

It is obvious that the subtotal function must print the subtotals but there are several other actions that must also be taken. The subtotal(s) must be added to the report total(s) if report totals are to be printed. After this calculation, the subtotal(s) will be reset to 0 to prepare to process the next group of records. The control variable must also be changed to the new department number.

Example

Using the hospital data file produce a fee report with subtotals for the type of room. This means that the room will become the control variable (see Figure 11.4).

Input:

Read name, room type code, number of days from file. At priming read, assign room type to control variable.

Processing:

Determine the appropriate rate according to room type. Calculate the billing amount. Add to the subtotals for charges and for days. Compare to control variable, if not equal do subtotals.

Subtotals:

Print the subtotals line. Add the subtotals to the report total. Reset the subtotals to 0. Reset the control variable to the new room type. Add to the line count.

Output:

Titles:

Print a form feed. Print titles and column headings. Add to the page count. Reset the line count to 0.

Detail:

Detail line:

Print the name, room type, days, and charge.

Subtotal line:

Print the subtotal of charges

Summary:

Print the total of all charges.

FIGURE 11-4
A Report with Subtotals

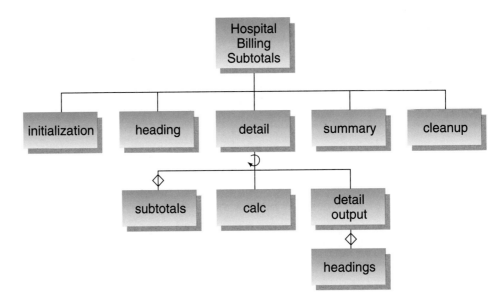

FIGURE 11-4
A Report with Subtotals

```
11-2.c
```

```c
/*-------------------------------------------------------
              Produces a report for hospital billing
              including subtotals by room type
----------------------------------------------------*/
#include <stdio.h>
#define CLS printf("\033[2J")
#define LOCATE(r,c) printf("\033[%d;%dH",r,c)

void initialization( );
void heading( );
void detail( );
void calc( );
void detail_output( );
void subtotals( );
void summary( );
void cleanup( );

FILE *patient;
char room, name[10], roomcontrol;
int days, linecount, totdays,subtotdays;
float amt, rate, totamt, subtotamt;
```

```
void main( )
{
  initialization( );
  heading( );
  detail( );
  summary( );
  cleanup( );
}

/*------------------------------------------------------------
                  Opens the data file
-----------------------------------------------------------*/
void initialization( )
{
  if((patient = fopen("testfile", "r+"))==NULL)
  {
    printf("Unable to open the data file");
    exit(1);
  }
}

/*------------------------------------------------------------
           Prints the titles at the top of each page
-----------------------------------------------------------*/
void heading( )
{
  linecount = 0;
  fprintf(stdout,"%c\n",12);
  fprintf(stdout,"\t\t\t Hospital Billing Report \n\n");
  fprintf(stdout,
    "    Name           Room Type    Days  Amount\n\n");
}



/*------------------------------------------------------------
           Accesses and processes each detail record
-----------------------------------------------------------*/
void detail( )
{
  fscanf(patient,"%s %c %d", name, &room, &days);
    /* priming read */
```

```
   roomcontrol = room;        /* assigns control variable */
   do
   {
     if (roomcontrol != room)    /* tests if subtotals needed */
       subtotals( );
    calc( );
    detail_output( );
   }
   while(fscanf(patient,"%s %c %d", name, &room, &days)!= EOF);
   subtotals( );     /* do subtotals for last group*/
}


/*------------------------------------------------------------
                       Calculate the room rate
                       accumulates subtotals
-----------------------------------------------------------*/
void calc( )
{
   switch (room)        /*  determine room rate */
      {
      case 'p':
        rate = 500.;
        break;
      case 's':
        rate = 375.;
        break;
      default:
      break;
      }
    amt = days * rate;
    subtotamt+=amt;
    subtotdays+=days;
   }


/*------------------------------------------------------------
                   Prints the detail lines
-----------------------------------------------------------*/
void detail_output( )
{
   if(++linecount > 48)
        heading( );
```

```
        fprintf(stdout,"%15s \t\t  %c\t   %2d\t   %7.2f\n",
           name,room,days,amt);
}


/*------------------------------------------------------------
               Control Break Processing to be performed
               when the room changes
----------------------------------------------------------*/
void subtotals( )
{
   fprintf(stdout,"\n%15s \t\t  \t   %2d\t   %7.2f\n",
           "Subtotal",subtotdays,subtotamt);
   totamt += subtotamt;
   totdays += subtotdays;
   roomcontrol = room;
   linecount++;
   subtotdays = 0;
   subtotamt = 0;
}


/*------------------------------------------------------------
                      Prints report totals
----------------------------------------------------------*/
void summary( )
{
fprintf(stdout,"\n%15s \t\t  \t   %2d\t   %7.2f",
        "Total",totdays,totamt);
}


/*------------------------------------------------------------
                      Closes the disk file
----------------------------------------------------------*/
void cleanup( )
{
   fclose(patient);
}
```

Self-Test

1. If we were doing a report on sales by each salesperson's number, what
   field should be used for the control variable if each input record contains
   the salesperson's name, number, and amount of sales?

2. What order must the data be in for the sales report in #1 to be able to produce a report with subtotals for each salesperson?
3. In what function would it be necessary to add to the subtotal?
4. In what function would it be necessary to add to the report total?

Answers

1. Salesman number.
2. Must be sorted in order by salesman number.
3. Add to the subtotal in the detail calculation function.
4. Add the subtotal to the report total in the subtotal function.

MULTILEVEL CONTROL BREAKS

Occasionally it will be necessary to have multiple levels of subtotals requiring multiple control variables. There may be different groupings or levels within an organization or product in which subtotals are needed for each.

A sales report may be divided into subtotals by client, salesperson, department, store, region, and so on. For each subtotal, an individual control variable will be required.

The control variables on a multilevel control break program are tested by the most major grouping first.

```
if(region_control != region)
{
    client_subtotals( );
    salesperson_subtotals( );
    department_subtotals( );
    store_subtotals( );
    region_subtotals( );
}
else if(store_control != store)
    {
        client_subtotals( );
        salesperson_subtotals( );
        department_subtotals( );
        store_subtotals( );
    }
else   if(department_control != department)
    {
        client_subtotals( );
        salesperson_subtotals( );
        department_subtotals( );
    }
```

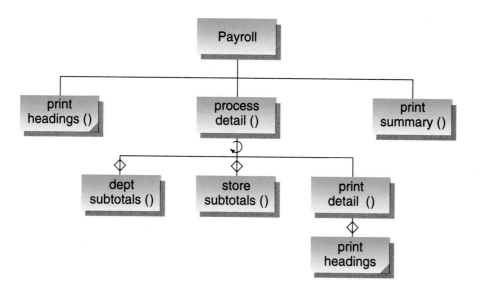

FIGURE 11-5
A Multilevel Control
Break

```
else   if(salesman_control != salesperson_control)
       {
           client_subtotals( );
           salesperson_subtotals( );
       }
else   if(client_control != client)
       {
           client_subtotals( );
       };
```

Example

Code a control break program for a payroll report for a company (see Figure 11.5). Subtotals should be printed for the store and for the department.

```
/*-------------------------------------------------
        a multilevel control break program
-------------------------------------------------*/
#include <stdio.h>
#define MAXLINES 48

void print_headings( );
void process_detail( );
```

```
void print_detail( );
void store_subtotals(float, int);
void dept_subtotals(float, int);
void print_summary( )

struct
{
   char name[25];
   int store;
   int dept;
   float hours;
   float pay;
} employee;
int linecount;
float report_tot;
FILE *infile;

void main( )
{
   if((infile = fopen("Payroll.dat", "r"))==NULL)
   {
     printf("Cannot open file");
     exit(1);
   }

    print_headings( );
    process_detail( );
    print_summary( );
    fclose(infile);
}

/*-------------------------------------------------------------
            print title and headings on each page
----------------------------------------------------------*/
void print_headings( )
{
    static int pagecount;
    fprintf(stdprn,"\t\t\t\t\tABC Company    Page %d\n\r",
pagecount++);
    fprintf(stdprn,"\t\t\t\tPayroll Report\n\n\r");
```

```
      fprintf(stdprn,"  Name    Store   Department");
      fprintf(stdprn,"   Hours    Gross Pay\n\n\r");
      linecount = 0;
}


/*-------------------------------------------------------------
                   produce detail portion of the report
----------------------------------------------------------*/
void process_detail( )
{
   int store_control, dept_control;
   float dept_subtot=0,store_subtot = 0;

   fread(&employee, sizeof(employee), 1, infile); /*get 1st record */
   store_control = employee.store;          /*set up controls*/
   dept_control = employee.dept;

   do
   {
     if(store_control != employee.store)
       /* check for control break */
       {
     dept_subtotals(&store_subtot, &dept_subtot,&dept_control);
     store_subtotals(&store_subtot,&store_control);
      }
     else if(dept_control != employee.dept)
       {
          dept_subtotals(&store_subtot,&dept_subtot,&dept_control);
       }
     dept_subtot += employee.pay;
     print_detail( );
   } while(fread(&employee, sizeof(employee), 1, infile));
   dept_subtotals(&store_subtot,&dept_subtot,&dept_control);
   store_subtotals(&store_subtot, &dept_subtot,&dept_control);
         /* force subtotals for last group */
}

void print_detail( )
{
   if(++linecount > MAXLINES)
```

```
        {
           fprintf(stdprn,"\f");
           print_headings( );
        }
        fprintf(stdprn," %-12s %3i %3i %15.2f %16.2f\n\r",
                       employee.name,
                       employee.store, employee.dept,
                       employee.hours, employee.pay);
}


void store_subtotals(float *store_subtot, int *store_control)
{
     report_tot += *store_subtot;
     fprintf(stdprn,"\n\t\tStore Subtotal    %7.2f\n\n\r",
                    *store_subtot);
     *store_subtot = 0;
     *store_control = employee.store;
     linecount+=2;
}


void dept_subtotals(float *store_subtot, float *dept_subtot, int
                   *dept_control)
{
     *store_subtot += *dept_subtot;
     fprintf(stdprn,"\n\t\tDepartment Subtotal %7.2f\n\n\r",
                    *dept_subtot);
     *dept_subtot = 0;
     *dept_control = employee.dept;
     linecount+=2;
}


void print_summary( )
{
     fprintf(stdprn,"\n\t\tReport Total    %7.2f\f", report_tot);
}
```

ABC Company Payroll Report

Name		Store	Department	Hours	Gross Pay
Jones, A.		1	5	40	650.00
Smyt, J.		1	5	27	347.00
Department Subtotal	997.00				
Mills, T.		1	8	20	450.00
Department Subtotal	450.00				
Store Subtotal	1447.00				
Erim, E.		2	8	40	625.00
Sherr, B.		2	8	30	500.00
Department Subtotal	1125.00				
Store Subtotal	1125.00				
Report Total					$2572.00

KEY TERMS

control break   control field   form feed

CHAPTER SUMMARY

To produce multipage reports a form feed will be issued whenever the count of the lines exceeds a determined number. Every time a line is printed, the line count should be adjusted.

Sometimes it is necessary to produce a report with subtotals within the detail lines. The field that changes when subtotals are needed is assigned to a control variable. The control variable will be checked to determine when it changes, and then the subtotal function can be executed.

Multiple levels of subtotals can be generated through the use of multiple control variables. The data must be sorted in order using the different control fields as primary and secondary keys prior to the control break processing.

EXERCISES

1. Write a multipage report of the car dealership inventory. The data will be read from the file created in Exercise 4, Chapter 10 (see page 339). The report will contain appropriate titles and headings including a page number. Each detail line in the report will contain the model name and the market value. Do not print the vehicle number. There will be a maximum of 20, double-spaced lines per page,

which includes the titles and the headings. At the end of the report, print out the number of vehicles in stock and the total market value.

2. Write a program that creates a report containing subtotals and report totals for the inventory at the car dealership ("Data File" created in Chapter 10, see page 339). The subtotal will contain the model, vehicle number and market value by manufacturer. This program will read data from a disk file. The report will contain 20 lines, double spaced, per page.

3. Create a multipage report with subtotals for the bowling league file created in Exercise 6, Chapter 10 (see page 340).

Input:

The team name, bowler name, number of games, total pins, and high series will be read from the data file.

Processing:

To calculate the handicap, subtract the average from 200 and take 80%. Also calculate the team total pins and total team handicap. At the end of the report indicate which team has the highest number of pins and both the female and male high series.

Output:

The title line will contain the page number. Each detail line will include the bowler name, average, handicap, number games, total pins, and high series. The team name will be included on the first detail line for each group.

Summary:

Will contain the average pins; men's high series, name, and amount; the womens's high series, name, and amount; and the team with the most pins.

4. Modify the multipage report program for the bowling league to contain subtotals. The subtotals will be printed for each team. Each detail line will include the bowler name, average, handicap, number of games, total pins, and high series. The team name will be included on the first detail line for each group and on the subtotal line.

HAYLEY OFFICE SUPPLIES

Use the inventory file to create a report by vendor. Place each vendor on a separate page with a listing of the product description, the product number, and the price. Place a count of the number of different products for that vendor at the end of the page.

CHAPTER 12

CHAPTER OBJECTIVES

By the end of this chapter, you should be able to:

■ Use the `malloc( )` and `calloc( )` functions for allocating memory.

■ Release or adjust the size of allocated memory using `realloc( )` or `free( )`.

■ Analyze alternatives for accessing data using single- and double linked lists

■ Create a double-linked list in sorted sequence from a disk file.

■ Delete elements from a linked list

■ Traverse the list while searching or printing the records.

Linked Lists

CHAPTER OVERVIEW

Memory management may be handled from within the program in C to avoid allocating memory until runtime. The allocation and deallocation functions will be covered.

This chapter will investigate linked lists, which is another method for accessing data. The linked list also allows a way to print data in a particular sequence or order while maintaining the disk file in the original sequence. The declaration of a linked list introduces the concept of recursion.

Access to the linked list will cover creating the list, deleting elements from the list, printing records in list order, and searching through the list.

ALLOCATING MEMORY

The operating system of a computer or a utility program normally handles the management of memory as programs are loaded and executed. Many modern languages also provide the ability to request memory at run time, including C.

Without the capability of requesting memory as it is needed, the programmer must anticipate the largest amount needed. For example, arrays are frequently set to a large size to accommodate whatever might come their way. This is not very efficient. Another memory management technique is to allocate and release memory as it is needed.

Two functions for allocating memory are `calloc( )` and `malloc( )`. In addition, `realloc( )` and `free( )` can be used to manage memory, by releasing it or adjusting the size. All four of these functions are part of `stdlib.h`.

`calloc( )`	initializes memory for an array of elements
`malloc( )`	reserves a specified number of bytes
`realloc( )`	changes the size (+ or -) of allocated memory
`free( )`	frees memory allocated with `calloc( )`, `malloc( )`, or `realloc( )`

When memory is allocated, the address of the block of memory is returned as a pointer of type void to the statement requesting it. If no memory is available, a NULL will be returned to indicate that the allocation was not successful. Therefore, when allocating memory:

1. Assign a pointer of the appropriate data type for which the memory is to be used to provide for proper access of the data.
2. Always test for the NULL to be certain that memory was indeed allocated.

Formats include the following:

```
calloc(number of elements, size of each element)
malloc(size in bytes)
realloc(pointer to old block, new size)
```

calloc( )

The `calloc( )` function is especially useful when assigning memory for an array. Normally an array size is specified at the time the array is declared and is made large enough to handle any application. This usually wastes memory. With the `calloc( )` function, the memory is allocated as it is needed in terms of the number of elements. This will work on a single array or even on an array of structures since the size of the structure can be determined. The pointer for assigning the address that is returned from the calloc( ) function may be an array of pointers.

```
struct info
{
    char name[25];
    int age;
} *infopointer[10];

if( (infopointer[i] =
    (struct info *)calloc( 1,sizeof(struct info) )) == NULL )
        printf("Cannot allocate for structure\n");
```

The (struct info *) casts the allocated memory to hold data of type structure info. The two arguments for the calloc( ) are 1 element of the size of struct info.

malloc( )

Only the size argument is required for the malloc( ) function, which can easily be specified with a *sizeof* operator. This allows more flexibility for program portability.

```
char *wordpointer[50];
if( (wordpointer[i++] =
    (char *)malloc(strlen(word)+1)) ==
                            NULL)
        printf("Cannot allocate memory for
wordpointer\n");
```

In this case, the pointer to the allocated memory is cast to hold *char* data. The number of bytes allocated will depend upon the length of a word. The 1 is added to the length of the word to allow for NULL.

realloc( )

If the size is overestimated or underestimated or changes as the program is run, it may be altered through the use of the realloc( ) function. Any elements that are stored in the block of memory at the time of the realloc( ) are guaranteed to remain intact up to the size of the original memory block, but the information does not necessarily remain at the same memory location.

```
if( (wordpointer[0] = (char *)realloc(wordpointer[0], 15)) ==
                            NULL)
    printf("Cannot be increased\n");
```

The arguments to `realloc( )` specify that the size of the memory block starting at `wordpointer[0]` is to be changed to 15 bytes.

free( )

The `free( )` function releases the memory once it is no longer required by the program. The only parameter required is the name of the pointer containing the address of the memory block.

```
free(wordpointer[i]);
```

Example

```
/* -----------------------------------------------------
      demonstrates the use of the memory allocation
   and management functions
                calloc( )
                malloc( )
                realloc( )
                free( )
------------------------------------------------------*/
#include <stdlib.h>
#include <stdio.h>

void use_calloc( );
void use_malloc( );

void main( )
{
     use_calloc( );
     use_malloc( );
}

/*-----------------------------------------------------
   calloc( ) specifies the number of elements needed,
                and the size of each element
------------------------------------------------------*/
void use_calloc( )
{
     int i=0;                  /* count for structures */
     struct info
```

```
        {
            char name[25];
            int age;
        } *infopointer[10];

        do
        {
        if( (infopointer[i] = (struct info *)calloc( 1,
                        sizeof(struct info) )) == NULL )
    printf("Cannot allocate for structure\n");
  else
        {
        puts("Enter Name");
        fflush(stdin);
        gets(infopointer[i]->name);
        if(strlen(infopointer[i]->name)==0)
            break;
        puts("Age");
        scanf("%d",&infopointer[i]->age);
        }
    }
    while((strlen(infopointer[i++]->name))!=0);
}


/*-----------------------------------------------------------
        malloc( ) specifies the number of bytes needed
------------------------------------------------------------*/
void use_malloc( )
{
        int i = 0;          /* index for array */
        int max;            /* actual number of words entered */
        char word[25];      /* holds each word as input */
        char *wordpointer[50]; /* pointers to 50 words */

        do
        {
        puts("Enter a word or press enter to quit");
        gets(word);
        if( (wordpointer[i++] = (char *)malloc(strlen(word)+1)) == NULL)
            printf("Cannot allocate memory for wordpointer\n");
        }
```

```
        while((strlen(word))!=0);
        max = -i;
/*-------------------------------------------------
            use realloc( )
    realloc( ) increases or decreases the size of an
            already allocated memory location
--------------------------------------------------*/
        if( (wordpointer[0] = (char *)realloc(wordpointer[0], 15)) ==
                            NULL)
        printf("Cannot be increased\n");
        else
            printf("realloc( ) Allocation Successful\n");



/* -------------------------------------------------
                use free( )
        free( ) releases the memory at a specified address
--------------------------------------------------*/
        for(i = 0; i < max; i++)
        {
            free(wordpointer[i]);
        }
        printf("Buffers freed\n");
}
```

Self-Test

1. Declare the pointer and code the statement to allocate space for a float variable called amount.
2. Declare the pointer array and code the statement to allocate space for an array of 10 float variables called amount.
3. Code the statement to expand the size of the amount array to add 10 more elements.
4. Code the statement to free the memory block allocated for the amount array.

Answers

```
1. float *amount; amount =
        (float *)malloc(sizeof(float));
2. float *amount[10]; amount =
        (float *)calloc(10,sizeof(float));
```

3. `amount = (float *)realloc(amount,20*sizeof(float));`
4. `free(amount);`

LINKED LISTS

A **linked list** is a list of structures in which each structure contains a data item that points to the next structure (see Figure 12.1). Unlike an array that uses contiguous memory locations, a linked list may have items in the list stored anywhere in memory. A linked list may be either single linked or double linked.

In a **single-linked** list each structure will point to the structure that follows it. The list can then be traversed in forward order. The last item will point to a NULL to indicate the end of the list or to the first item if we wish to make a **circular list**.

By traversing the links the data may be accessed in a particular order. The following data is linked alphabetically by fruit name. The root record is record 4 which then links to record 6, Bananas; which, in turn, links to record 10.

linked list A method of storing multiple values by allocating memory as it is needed; each element contains the address of the next element in the list.

single linked A linked list that can only be traversed in a forward direction—each structure contains only a pointer to the next element in the list.
circular list Last element in a linked list that points to the first element.

Root Record # 4 Apples

Record #	Key	Link
1	Cherries	2
2	Dates	3
3	Oranges	5
4	Apples	6
5	Peaches	8
6	Bananas	10
7	Watermelons	NULL
8	Strawberries	7
9	Boysenberries	1
10	Blueberries	9

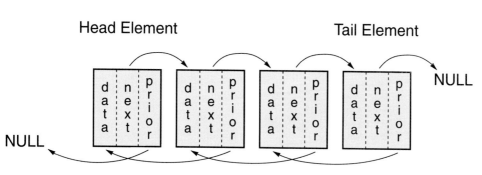

FIGURE 12-1
A Linked List

To be circular, the "last" record should chain to the "first" record. Therefore, record 7, which is Watermelons, would have a link of 4 to send it back to the root record.

The appropriate sorted order is:

Record #		Link
4	Apples	6
6	Bananas	10
10	Blueberries	9
9	Boysenberries	1
1	Cherries	2
2	Dates	3
3	Oranges	5
5	Peaches	8
8	Strawberries	7
7	Watermelons	NULL

Notice that the link on each record points to the next record in alphabetic order.

In a linked list file all records remain in the original order. Each record contains a field that is used to chain (link) to the next record in the file. The first record for the link must be stored as a "root" record. (The record number must be known to start the retrieval of records in the linked order.)

A file may need to be retrieved in different sequences for different applications. There could be multiple links for each sequence in which the data will be accessed, with different fields being used as the key field.

The **double-linked** list contains two addresses, one pointing to the previous structure and one to the structure that follows itself in the list. This will allow the list to be searched in either a forward or a backward direction, from one structure to the next.

double linked A list that can be traversed to the next record or to the prior record.

Root Record # 4

Record #	Key	Forward Link	Backward Link
1	Cherries	2	9
2	Dates	3	1
3	Oranges	5	2
4	Apples	6	NULL
5	Peaches	8	3
6	Bananas	10	4
7	Watermelons	NULL	8
8	Strawberries	7	5
9	Boysenberries	1	10
10	Blueberries	9	6

With a linked list, the number of elements does not need to be known in advance. An element (sometimes called a **node**) can be added to the list or deleted from it whenever necessary. The memory can be allocated as it is needed.

node An element in a linked list.

Coding a Linked List

Each element in the linked list will have one or more data variables and a pointer to the next element.

```
struct linkelement
{
    struct linkrecord      /* for the data */
    struct linkelement *nextlink /* pts to next */
    struct linkelement *priorlink /* if double link */
}
```

Notice that in this structure for an element in the linked list there is a pointer that points back to its own structure type. This is an example of **recursion.**

The first element in a linked list is known as the **head** or **root** element. The last element in the list will frequently be referred to as the **tail** or **trailing** element.

recursion A declaration that includes a reference to its own data type.
tail element The last element in a linked list—pointer to next will contain a NULL.

Adding an Element to a Linked List

In order to add records to a linked list, it is necessary to determine pointers to the next record location and the prior record location. These pointers will depend upon the value of the key field, compared to the other records.

The steps to add an element to the list include:

1. Allocating memory for a record structure.
2. Reading a record from the file.
3. Comparing the key field with keys in the linked list.
4. Building the appropriate links.

The possibilities that exist for comparisons of the key fields and for establishing appropriate links are the list is empty, the new record goes at the beginning of an existing list, the new element goes in the middle of the list, or the new element belongs at the end of the existing list.

1. Linklist is empty (see Figure 12-2):
   a. Headelement will be NULL
   b. New record becomes head element.
   c. New record becomes tail element.
   d. Next and prior links are NULL.

2. Insert at the beginning (see Figure 12-3):
   a. New record becomes head element.
   b. Next pointer will be old head element.
   c. Prior pointer will be tail element.
   d. Former head element has prior of new element.

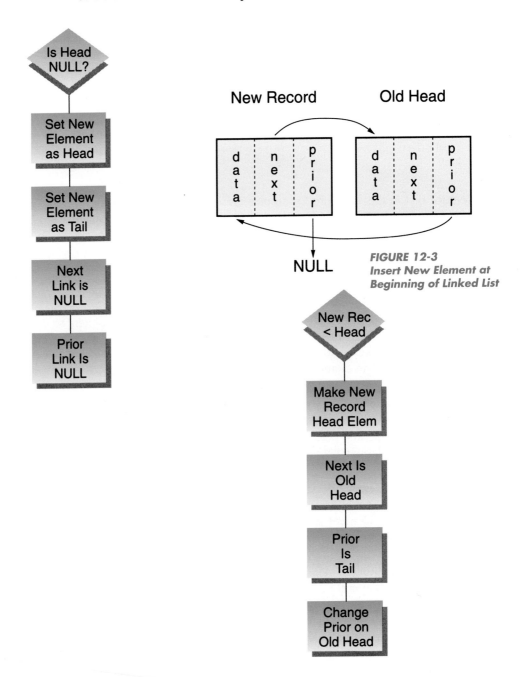

FIGURE 12-2
Linklist Is Empty

FIGURE 12-3
Insert New Element at
Beginning of Linked List

3. Insert in the middle (determine where the record belongs; see Figure 12-4):
   a. New element next will point to prior's former next.
   b. New element prior will be previous element.
   c. Change next on previous to point to new element.
   d. Change prior on the element following new element.

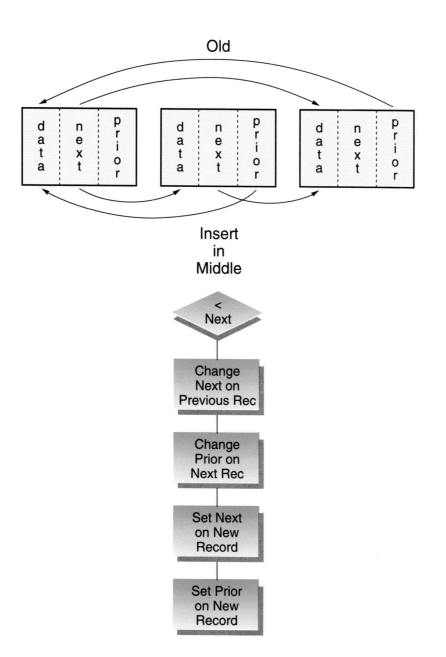

FIGURE 12-4
Insert in Middle of Linked List

4. Insert at end (see Figure 12-5):
   a. New record becomes tail element.
   b. Old tail has next of new record.
   c. Prior of new element is old tail.
   d. Next of new element is NULL.

FIGURE 12-5
Insert New Element at
End of Linked List

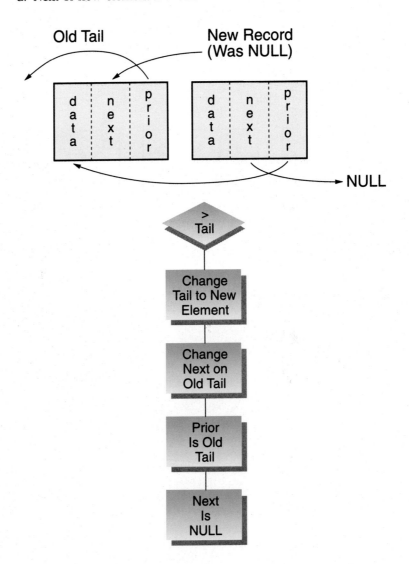

Consider a file that contains records with the following structure:

```
struct productinfo
{
int   code;
```

```
char description[25];
float cost;
};
```

The link structure could then be declared as:

```
struct link
{
struct productinfo *product;
struct link *next;
struct link *prior;
}element;
```

To create the list, there will need to be pointers for the beginning of the list, the end of the list, and the current position within the list during a search for the proper location.

```
struct link *headelement = NULL, *tailelement = NULL,
*currentelement = NULL;
```

The following code uses these declarations to build a linked list from a data file. Space is allocated for each record and the data is input from the disk file. Two additional functions are called findlink( ) and add( ). The findlink( ) determines the address of the elements next to which the new record will be placed according to the key field in the new record. The add( ) function actually sets the pointers within the list.

```
/*-------------------------------------------------------------
    buildlink creates the linked list or pushes a new element
    onto the list
--------------------------------------------------------------*/
void buildlink( )
{
   struct productinfo *recptr;        /* for malloc( ) */
   CLS;
   /* allocate memory for one record from the file */
   if((recptr = (struct productinfo *) malloc(sizeof(struct
                    productinfo)))== NULL)
      {
       printf("Not enough memory \n");
       exit(2);
      }
   while(fread(recptr,sizeof(struct productinfo),1,infile)!=0)
```

```
    {
        printf("%5i %-25s %4.2f\n",recptr->code,
             recptr->description, recptr->cost); /*display file data*/
        currentelement = findlink(recptr->code); /*find where to insert*/
        currentelement = add(currentelement);   /*build links*/
        currentelement->product = recptr;     /* point to data */

        /* allocate memory as needed for next record from the file */
        if((recptr = (struct productinfo *) malloc(sizeof(struct
                            productinfo)))== NULL)
{
        printf("Not enough memory");
        exit(2);
    }
    }
    PAUSE;
    fclose(infile);
}


/*-----------------------------------------------------------------
    returns a pointer to the new link, determines if new element
    is first element, goes before first element, after last element, or
    gets inserted in the middle
    ------------------------------------------------------------*/
struct link *add(struct link *currentelement)
{
    struct link *temp;

    if((temp = (struct link *) malloc(sizeof(struct link)))==NULL)
      {
       printf("Not enough memory \n");
       exit(3);
      }

    if ( !headelement )        /* first entry in chain */
      {
      temp->next = NULL;          /* assign pointers for link */
      temp->prior = NULL;
      headelement = temp;
```

```
            tailelement  = temp;
            return temp;           /* return address of new link */
            }

    if ( !currentelement )     /* adding to end of chain */
        {
        tailelement->next = temp;
        temp->next = NULL;
        temp->prior = tailelement;
        tailelement = temp;
        return temp;
        }

    if ( !currentelement->prior ) /* adding to beginning of chain */
        {
        headelement->prior = temp;
        temp->next = headelement;
        temp->prior = NULL;
        headelement = temp;
        return temp;
        }


    currentelement->prior->next = temp;        /* insert into chain */
    temp->prior = currentelement->prior;
    currentelement->prior = temp;
    temp->next = currentelement;
    return temp;
}

/*-------------------------------------------------------------------
     searches through the product codes to determine where new element
     fits in
-------------------------------------------------------------------*/
struct link *findlink(int code_key)
{
    if ( !(currentelement=headelement) )
    {
    return currentelement; /* check for empty chain */
    }
```

```
  do
  {
    if (currentelement->product->code > code_key)
      {
    return currentelement;
    }
      }
  while (currentelement = currentelement->next); /* check for NULL
next*/

    return currentelement;  /* end of chain, return NULL */


}
```

Self-Test

1. What line of code determines where the record belongs according to some type of "sort"?
2. List and explain the lines of code that set the links for a record that is inserted into the middle of the list.

Answers

1. if (currentelement->product->code > code_key)
2.
```
    currentelement->prior->next = temp;    /*
    insert into chain */
      temp->prior = currentelement->prior;
      currentelement->prior = temp;
      temp->next = currentelement;
      return temp;
```
insert in the middle (determine where the record belongs):
   a. New element next will point to prior's former next.
   b. New element prior will be previous element.
   c. Change next on previous to point to new element.
   d. Change prior on the element following new element.

Deleting an Element from a Linked List

The pointers in an element to be deleted must be reassigned around the deleted element. Once again, the pointer assignments depend upon the position of the element being deleted: a head element, a tail element, or a middle element.

Old Pointers

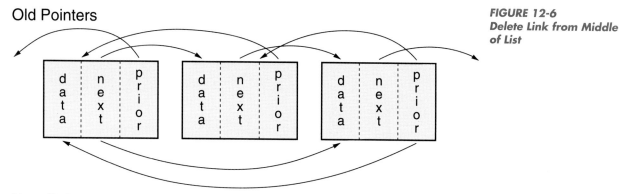

FIGURE 12-6
*Delete Link from Middle
of List*

New Pointers

Let's consider the middle element. The prior record must have the "pointer to next" which is from the deleted element, while the record following the deleted one must have its "pointer to prior" reassigned to the "prior pointer" from the deleted record (see Figure 12-6).

```
/*---------------------------------------------------------------
      deletelink removes an element (pops) from the list
------------------------------------------------------------*/
void deletelink( )
{
  int code;
  char answer;
  struct link *deleteptr;
  CLS;
  LOCATE(5,25);
  puts("Delete a record from the list");
  LOCATE(10,15);
  puts("Enter the product code to be deleted");
  LOCATE(10,55);
  scanf("%i", &code);
  deleteptr = findlink(code);
  /* since findlink returns next, must go to prior */
  if(deleteptr == NULL)
     deleteptr = tailelement;
  else
     if(deleteptr != headelement)
        deleteptr = deleteptr->prior;
```

```
LOCATE(12,15);
printf("%s", deleteptr->product->description);
LOCATE(14,15);
puts("Delete this product (Y/N)");
LOCATE(14,50);
fflush(stdin);
answer = getc(stdin);
if(toupper(answer) == 'Y')
{
    /* rebuild links */

    if(headelement == deleteptr) /* if first element */
    {
      headelement = deleteptr->next;
      if(headelement)        /* check if more than 1 element */
          headelement->prior = NULL;
      else
          tailelement = NULL;
    }
    else
    {
      deleteptr->prior->next = deleteptr->next;
      if(deleteptr != tailelement) /* deleting in the middle */
      deleteptr->next->prior = deleteptr->prior;
      else
      tailelement = deleteptr->prior; /* last element deleted */
    }
    free(deleteptr->product);   /* releases data */
    free(deleteptr);              /* releases link */
    LOCATE(15,35);
    printf("Deleted");
    PAUSE;
  }
}
```

Printing Data from a Linked List

In printing the elements from a linked list in sorted order the links may be traversed in forward sequence or in backward sequence. For a forward list, the first element will be the head element and then will progress through the list by accessing the record being pointed to by the pointer to next element.

The opposite will occur for a backward list. The first element will be the tail element and then the link for the prior record will be accessed. Both lists will terminate when a pointer to NULL is found, assuming that the list is not circular.

```c
/*------------------------------------------------------------
      list traverses the linked list and prints out the records
         using forward link and then backward link
---------------------------------------------------------*/
void list( )
{
    CLS;
    printf("\n\n linked list in forward sequence...\n\n");
    printf("      Code Description    Cost  \n\n");

    for (currentelement=headelement; currentelement;
                currentelement=currentelement->next)
    {
      printf("    %4d %-20s %5.2f \n",currentelement->product->code,
              currentelement->product->description,
              currentelement->product->cost);
    }
    PAUSE;

    CLS;
    /* now print the table information in reverse sequence */

    printf("\n\n linked list in backward sequence...\n\n");
    printf("      Code Description    Cost \n\n");

    for (currentelement=tailelement; currentelement;
          currentelement=currentelement->prior)
    {
      printf("    %4d %-20s %5.2f \n",
              currentelement->product->code,
              currentelement->product->description,
               currentelement->product->cost);
    }
    PAUSE;
}
```

1. What does the following code do?

```
if(headelement == deleteptr) /* if first element */
  {
   headelement = deleteptr->next;
   if(headelement)       /* check if more than 1
element */
        headelement->prior = NULL;
   else
        tailelement = NULL;
  }
```

2. Write the code to create a linked list for the fruit example.

Answers

1.

`12-2.c`

```c
#include <stdio.h>
#define CLS printf("\033[2J")
#define LOCATE(r,c) printf("\033[%d;%dH",r,c)
#define PAUSE LOCATE(23,30); puts("Press Any Key to Continue");
getche( )

    struct link
      {
       char (*fruit)[15];
       struct link *next;
       struct link *prior;
      }*element;

    struct link *headelement = NULL, *tailelement = NULL,
*currentelement = NULL;

    struct link *add(struct link *ptr);
    struct link *findlink(char fruit[15]);

void main( )
{
```

```
    prompt_screen( );
    while(strlen(gets(*element->fruit))!=0)
    {
      currentelement = findlink(element->fruit); /*find where to
                                                    insert*/
      currentelement = add(currentelement);    /*build links*/
      currentelement->fruit = element->fruit;  /* point to data */
      prompt_screen( );
    }
    list( );
}

prompt_screen( )
{
    CLS;
    LOCATE (10,15);
    puts("Type of fruit");
    LOCATE(10,30);
    fflush(stdin);
    /* allocate memory as needed for next record */
    if((clement->fruit = (char *) malloc(15)) == NULL)
      {
        printf("Not enough memory");
        exit(2);
      }
}


/*-----------------------------------------------------------------
   returns a pointer to the new link, determines if new element
   is first element, goes before first element, after last element, or
   gets inserted in the middle
   ---------------------------------------------------------------*/
struct link *add(struct link *currentelement)
{
    struct link *temp;

    if((temp = (struct link *) malloc(sizeof(struct link)))==NULL)
      {
        printf("Not enough memory \n");
         exit(3);
      }
```

```
  if ( !headelement )        /* first entry in chain */
    {
    temp->next = NULL;       /* assign pointers for link */
    temp->prior = NULL;
    headelement = temp;
    tailelement = temp;
    return temp;             /* return address of new link */
    }

  if ( !currentelement )            /* adding to end of chain */
    {
    tailelement->next = temp;
    temp->next = NULL;
    temp->prior = tailelement;
    tailelement = temp;
    return temp;
    }

  if ( !currentelement->prior )     /* adding to beginning of chain */
    {
    headelement->prior = temp;
    temp->next = headelement;
    temp->prior = NULL;
    headelement = temp;
    return temp;
    }


  currentelement->prior->next = temp;        /* insert into chain */
  temp->prior = currentelement->prior;
  currentelement->prior = temp;
  temp->next = currentelement;
  return temp;
}



/*-------------------------------------------------------------------
     searches through the fruit to determine where new element
     fits in
                                                                  -*/
struct link *findlink(char fruit[15])
```

```c
{
    if ( !(currentelement=headelement) )
    {
     return currentelement; /* check for empty chain */
    }

    do
    {
      if (strcmp(currentelement->fruit,fruit)>0)
    {
      return currentelement;
        }
    }
    while (currentelement = currentelement->next); /* check for NULL
                                                     next*/
    return currentelement;   /* end of chain, return NULL */

}

void list( )
{
    CLS;
    fprintf(stdout,"\n\n linked list in forward sequence...\n\n\r");
    fprintf(stdout," Description    \n\n\r");

    for (currentelement=headelement;
              currentelement; currentelement=currentelement->next)
      fprintf(stdout," %-20s \n\r", currentelement->fruit);
    PAUSE;

    CLS;
    /* now print the table information in reverse sequence */

    fprintf(stdout,"\n\n linked list in backward sequence...\n\n\r");
    fprintf(stdout," Description  \n\n\r");

    for (currentelement=tailelement; currentelement;
              currentelement=currentelement->prior)
    fprintf(stdout," %-20s \n\r", currentelement->fruit);
    PAUSE;
}
```

2. A comparison is made to determine if the address of the element to be deleted is the same as the head element. If the head element is deleted, the new head element will be whatever address is in the "pointer link to next" that was in the head element. A test is made to see if the "pointer to next" was a NULL, in which case the head element was the only element in the list and was also the tail element which must now become NULL to indicate an empty list.

Complete Link List Example

Create a double-linked list for product information. Each product record will contain the product code, the product description, and the product cost. The data is contained in the product.dat file and is to be read into memory through dynamic allocation to avoid the necessity of a large array.

The program will be menu driven and will provide options for building the links, deleting an element from the linked list, and for listing the elements in forward and backward sequence (see Figure 12.7).

12-3.c

```
#include <stdio.h>
#define CLS printf("\033[2J")
#define LOCATE(r,c) printf("\033[%d;%dH",r,c)
#define PAUSE LOCATE(23,30); puts("Press Any Key to Continue"); getche( )
```

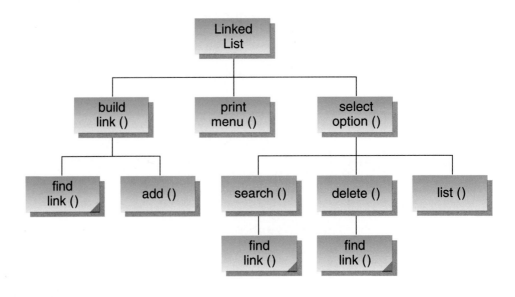

FIGURE 12-7
Creating, Deleting, and Accessing a Linked List

```c
void printmenu( );
void selectoption( );
void buildlink( );
void search( );
void delete_link( );
void list( );


    struct productinfo
    {
        int   code;
        char description[25];
        float cost;
    };

      struct link
     {
       struct productinfo *product;
       struct link *next;
       struct link *prior;
     }element;
    struct link *headelement = NULL, *tailelement = NULL,
                *currentelement = NULL;

    char option;      /* for menu selection */
    FILE *infile;
    struct link *add(struct link *ptr);
    struct link *findlink(int code);

void main( )
{
    /*---------------------------
         get file, if it exists
    ---------------------------*/
    if((infile = fopen("product.dat","r+"))== NULL)
    {
       puts("Error in opening file");
       exit( );
    }
    buildlink( );       /* set up linked list from file */
```

```c
      do
      {
         printmenu( );
         selectoption( );
      }while(option != '4');
}


/*------------------------------------------------------
         prints options for working with linked list
----------------------------------------------------*/
void printmenu( )
{
   CLS;
   LOCATE(5,30);
   puts("Linked List Menu");
   LOCATE(8,20);
   puts("1. Find a Record from list ");
   LOCATE(10,20);
   puts("2. Delete a record ");
   LOCATE(12, 20);
   puts("3. List all records ");
   LOCATE(14,20);
   puts("4. Exit");
   fflush(stdin);
   LOCATE(17,20);
   puts("Enter your option =====>");
   LOCATE(17,44);
   option = getc(stdin);
}


/*-------------------------------------------------------
         send to appropriate function for menu option
----------------------------------------------------*/
void selectoption( )
{
   switch(option)
   {
      case '1':
      search( );
      break;
```

```
      case '2':
      deletelink( );
      break;
      case '3':
      list( );
      break;
      case '4':
      CLS;
      break;
      default:
      LOCATE(20,25);
      puts("Please enter a number (1-4) only");
      PAUSE;
   }
}


/*-----------------------------------------------------------------
      buildlink creates the linked list or pushes a new element
         onto the list
-------------------------------------------------------------*/
void buildlink( )
{
   struct productinfo *recptr;                 /* for malloc( ) */
   CLS;
   /* allocate memory for one record from the file */
   if((recptr = (struct productinfo *) malloc(sizeof(struct
         productinfo))) == NULL)
      {
       printf("Not enough memory \n");
       exit(2);
      }
   while(fread(recptr,sizeof(struct productinfo),1,infile)!=0)
   {
     currentelement = findlink(recptr->code); /*find where to
        insert*/
     currentelement = add(currentelement);  /*build links*/
     currentelement->product = recptr;    /* point to data */

     /* allocate memory as needed for next record from the file */
     if((recptr = (struct productinfo *) malloc(sizeof(struct
         productinfo)))  == NULL)
```

```
      {
        printf("Not enough memory");
        exit(2);
      }
    }
  }
  fclose(infile);
}




/*-------------------------------------------------------------------
   returns a pointer to the new link, determines if new element
   is first element, goes before first element, after last element, or
   gets inserted in the middle
--------------------------------------------------------------------*/
struct link *add(struct link *currentelement)
{
    struct link *temp;

    if((temp = (struct link *) malloc(sizeof(struct link)))==NULL)
      {
       printf("Not enough memory \n");
       exit(3);
      }

    if ( !headelement )      /* first entry in chain */
      {
       temp->next = NULL;     /* assign pointers for link */
       temp->prior = NULL;
       headelement = temp;
       tailelement  = temp;
       return temp;            /* return address of new link */
      }

     if ( !currentelement )    /* adding to end of chain */
      {
       tailelement->next = temp;
       temp->next = NULL;
       temp->prior = tailelement;
       tailelement = temp;
       return temp;
      }
```

```
    if ( !currentelement->prior )  /* adding to beginning of chain */
       {
       headelement->prior = temp;
       temp->next = headelement;
       temp->prior = NULL;
       headelement = temp;
       return temp;
       }


    currentelement->prior->next = temp;   /* insert into chain */
    temp->prior = currentelement->prior;
    currentelement->prior = temp;
    temp->next = currentelement;
    return temp;
}

/*-------------------------------------------------------------------
    searches through the product codes to determine where new element
    fits in
-------------------------------------------------------------------*/
struct link *findlink(int code_key)
{
    if ( !(currentelement=headelement) )
    {
     return currentelement; /* check for empty chain */
    }

    do
    {
     if (currentelement->product->code > code_key)
        {
            return currentelement;
        }
    }
    while (currentelement = currentelement->next);
             /* loop until NULL next*/

    return currentelement;  /* end of chain, return NULL */

}
```

```
void search( )
{
   int code;
   char answer;
   struct link *findptr;
   CLS;
   LOCATE(5,25);
   puts("Find a record from the list");
   LOCATE(10,15);
   puts("Enter the product code to be found");
   LOCATE(10,55);
   scanf("%i", &code);
   findptr = findlink(code);
   /* since findlink returns next, must go to prior */
   if(findptr == NULL)
      findptr = tailelement;
   else
      if(findptr != headelement)
    findptr = findptr->prior;
   LOCATE(12,15);
   printf("Description: %s", findptr->product->description);
   LOCATE(14,15);
   printf("Cost:   %6.2f", findptr->product->cost);
   PAUSE;
}

/*-----------------------------------------------------------
      deletelink removes an element (pops) from the list
------------------------------------------------------------*/
void deletelink( )
{
   int code;
   char answer;
   struct link *deleteptr;
   CLS;
   LOCATE(5,25);
   puts("Delete a record from the list");
   LOCATE(10,15);
   puts("Enter the product code to be deleted");
   LOCATE(10,55);
   scanf("%i", &code);
```

```
deleteptr = findlink(code);
/* since findlink returns next, must go to prior */
if(deleteptr == NULL)
    deleteptr = tailelement;
else
    if(deleteptr != headelement)
        deleteptr = deleteptr->prior;
LOCATE(12,15);
printf("%s", deleteptr->product->description);
LOCATE(14,15);
puts("Delete this product (Y/N)");
LOCATE(14,50);
fflush(stdin);
answer = getc(stdin);
if(toupper(answer) == 'Y')
{
    /* rebuild links */

    if(headelement == deleteptr) /* if first element */
    {
     headelement = deleteptr->next;
     if(headelement)       /* check if more than 1 element */
         headelement->prior = NULL;
     else
         tailelement = NULL;
    }
    else
    {
     deleteptr->prior->next = deleteptr->next;
     if(deleteptr != tailelement) /* deleting in the middle */
     deleteptr->next->prior = deleteptr->prior;
     else
     tailelement = deleteptr->prior; /* last element deleted */
    }
     free(deleteptr->product);    /* releases data */
     free(deleteptr);    /* releases link */
     LOCATE(15,35);
     printf("Deleted");
     PAUSE;
    }
}
```

```
/*-------------------------------------------------------------
     list traverses the linked list and prints out the records
        using forward link and then backward link
-----------------------------------------------------------*/
void list( )
{
     CLS;
     fprintf(stdout,"\n\n linked list in forward sequence...\n\n\r");
     fprintf(stdout," Code Description    Cost  \n\n\r");

     for (currentelement=headelement; currentelement;
          currentelement=currentelement->next)
     {
     fprintf(stdout,"    %4d %-20s %5.2f \n\r",
               currentelement->product->code,
               currentelement->product->description,
               currentelement->product->cost);
     }
     PAUSE;

     CLS;
     /* now print the table information in reverse sequence */

     fprintf(stdout,"\n\n linked list in backward sequence...\n\n\r");
     fprintf(stdout,"    Code Description    Cost \n\n\r");

     for (currentelement=tailelement; currentelement;
          currentelement=currentelement->prior)
     {
       fprintf(stdout,"      %4d %-20s %5.2f \n\r",
               currentelement->product->code,
               currentelement->product->description,
               currentelement->product->cost);
     }
     PAUSE;
}
```

circular list   linked list   root element
double-linked list   node   single-linked list
head element   recursion   tail element

CHAPTER SUMMARY

A more efficient use of memory than an array if the number of elements is unknown is a linked list with memory allocated as it is needed. Memory may be allocated with the `malloc( )` or `calloc( )` functions and is released with the `free( )` function.

Recursion refers to an item that refers to itself and usually calls itself. In a linked-list structure there are recursive pointers that point to a link-list structure.

A linked list uses pointers within the record structure to point to the next element in the list. A double-linked list contains two pointers, one to the next record and one to the previous record.

The first element in a list is the head or root element and the last element is the tail or trailing element. Some refer to each element within the list as a node.

REVIEW QUESTIONS

1. How is a linked list circular?
2. Differentiate between an array and a linked list.
3. Why would a double linked-list be more advantageous than a single-linked list?
4. Give an example of recursion.
5. When would it be appropriate to use calloc( ) rather than malloc( )?
6. What steps are necessary to insert a link in the middle of a list?
7. Give the general prototype for a function that will return a pointer to a link structure.

EXERCISES

1. Use a single-linked list to store 10 employee records. Each structure contains:
   > Last name
   > First name
   > Hire date

Link the records by last name. The trailing element should contain a NULL as the pointer. Enter in sample data and then print the list in linked order.

2. Modify Exercise 1 to create a circular linked list so that the last record points back to the first.

3. Create a search routine to find a record in the linked list of employee records. Prompt for the record to be found by last name and then print the hire date when the record is found or an appropriate message if the record is not found.

4. Modify the employee linked list to produce a double-linked list. Prompt the user if they would like to see the next record or the previous record and display the records to the screen.

5. Create a double-linked list for the vehicle file from Chapter 10 (see page 339). Use the vehicle number as the key field and print the list in both forward and backward sequence.

6. Write a program that will input names (last name and first name) from the keyboard and will print the list in sorted order using a linked list.

HAYLEY OFFICE SUPPLIES

Read the inventory file into a double-linked list using the product number as the key field. Use malloc( ) for allocation of memory; do not use an array.

Output options include the following:

1. Print out a list to the printer of the products in forward and reverse sequence.

2. Provide a search option that will display a requested record on the screen.

3. Create an option that will allow the user to page forward from one product to the next. Each product will be displayed to the screen one at a time.

13

CHAPTER OBJECTIVES

By the end of this chapter, you should be able to:

■ Examine non-ANSI graphics functions for text in Borland and Microsoft compilers.

■ Understand the various video modes available and the associated coordinates.

■ Draw pixels, lines, rectangles, circles, and arcs.

■ Use graphic functions to produce business graphs and pie charts.

■ Demonstrate a light bar menu using the graphics functions.

❶   ❷   ❸   ❹   ❺   ❻   ❼   ❽   ❾   ❶   ❷   ❸   ❹   ❺   ❻

Using Graphics in C

CHAPTER OVERVIEW

This chapter will introduce the nonstandard functions that may be used for clearing the screen, positioning text, and using colors for text. In addition, the video mode will be used to allow access to functions for drawing lines, rectangles, and circles. The figures may be filled through the function that creates it or with a function to paint objects.

The graphics functions will be applied to graphing and creating menus appropriate to a business application. The business graphing includes creating pie charts and bar charts.

THE GRAPHIC LIBRARY

The graphics functions are not part of the ANSI standard for C code. Both Borland and Microsoft provide functions for doing graphics. However, these functions are not portable from one system to the other. If a program is created in executable form, it is not important what code was used to generate the graphics. The EXE file can be run from any compatible system. The source code, though, may not be recompiled from one compiler to the other.

To use graphics it will be necessary to access a header file graph.h or graphics.h and the graphics library. On some systems, this will require a special process to make the graphics library available to the compiler (see the programming tip about a program list that must be set in early versions of Microsoft QuickC).

You will notice that when you work with graphics functions, most of the function names begin with an underscore. This underscore symbol is actually part of the function name and must be included. If you get an undefined function error, check the inclusion of this underscore.

CLEARING THE SCREEN AND POSITIONING THE CURSOR

Previously, we have been using escape sequences to CLS and LOCATE. Although not a part of the ANSI standard for C, many libraries include functions for these.

Microsoft

There are graphics functions available in C to perform the clearscreen and position text commands. The commands to do this are `_clearscreen( )` and `_settextposition( )`. To perform any graphics functions the graph.h header file must be included in the program.

The format of the `_clearscreen( )` is

```
_clearscreen(constant);
```

where the constant may be

_GCLEARSCREEN	clears entire screen
_GWINDOW	clears a text window
_GVIEWPORT	clears a "view port"

The `_settexposition( )` function requires two arguments: the first for the row and the second for the column. The use of this statement is the same as the escape sequence constant that we have used for LOCATE. Format:

```
_settextposition(row, col);
```

Example

```
#include <graph.h>
#define PHRASE "Howdy!!"

void main( )
{
    _clearscreen(_GCLEARSCREEN);
    _settextposition(10,10);
    printf(" Hi %s",PHRASE);
}
```

Borland

Borland has a clear screen function called clrscr( ) that requires conio.h and will work on only IBM or compatible systems. The format of this function is

```
clrscr( )
```

with no arguments.

In addition, Borland compilers have graphic screen clear functions in the graphics.h header file. These are used to clear a graphics screen as opposed to a text screen.

The function used to position the cursor is the gotoxy( ) function. The format of this function is similar to the escape sequence constants for positioning text. It has two arguments: one for row and one for column. The format is:

```
gotoxy(col, row);
```

```
#include <conio.h>
#define PHRASE "Howdy!!"

void main( )
{
  clrscr( );
  gotoxy(10,10);
  printf("%s", PHRASE);
}
```

Note that in the Borland products, the cursor position arguments are the x direction across the screen, and then the y direction down the screen. This can be stated as column and then row, as opposed to the ANSI escape codes and the Microsoft _settextposition( ) which are row and then column. The x, y order is the sequence that will be used in the graphics commands when positioning a point on the screen.

SETTING TEXT COLORS

In order to set the color for printing text, two functions will be necessary. The _settextcolor( ) will change the color of the characters while the _setbkcolor( ) affects the background color. The required argument to these functions is the number for the desired color. The format for these functions is:

```
_settextcolor( color number);
_setbkcolor( color number);
```

where the color numbers are:

Black	0
Blue	1
Green	2
Cyan	3
Red	4
Magenta	5
Brown	6
White	7
Dark gray	8
Light blue	9
Light green	10
Light cyan	11
Light red	12
Light Magenta	13
Yellow	14
Bright White	15

The colors may be a short integer in the range of 0 through 31. The numbers from 16 to 31 have the same color sequence as the numbers 0 through 15 but will result in a blinking character.

To test these colors for yourself, set up a loop to run through the different numbers.

```
/*---------------------------------------------
      printing the colors
------------------------------------------*/
#include <graph.h>
```

```
void main( )
{
    int color;

    _clearscreen(_GCLEARSCREEN);
    for(color = 0; color < 15; color++)
    {
        _settextcolor(color);
        _outtext("color\n");
    }
}
```

If the background color function is called before a clear screen the entire screen will change. If the function is called just before a print statement (_outtext( ) is used with graphics) then only the background of the text printed will be in the color that was set.

```
/*----------------------------------------------
            entire screen in background color
------------------------------------------------*/
#include <graph.h>
#define CYAN 3
#define BROWN 6

void main( )
{
    _setbkcolor(CYAN);
    _clearscreen(_GCLEARSCREEN);
    _settextcolor(BROWN);
    _settextposition(12,40);
    _outtext("Hi");
}
```

The output will have the entire screen in cyan and the word "Hi" in brown.

```
/*----------------------------------------------
        only text with background color
----------------------------------------------*/
#include <graph.h>

#define CYAN 3
#define BROWN 6
```

```
void main( )
{
    _clearscreen(_GCLEARSCREEN);
    _setbkcolor(CYAN);
    _settextcolor(BROWN);
    _settextposition(12,40);
    _outtext("Hi");
}
```

In this situation, the overall background of the screen will remain black because the screen is cleared before a color is set for the background. The word "Hi" will appear in brown letters on cyan background.

Colors in Borland

The colors may be set in Borland C compilers by using the `setcolor( )` function prior to an `outtext( )` function. The color of the text will be the last color set using `setcolor( )`.

```
setcolor(color constant or number)
```

The color numbers are the same as Microsoft but the numbers have been assigned to symbolic constants in the graphics.h file, as follows:

Color Constants from Graphics

BLACK	0	BLUE	1
GREEN	2	CYAN	3
RED	4	MAGENTA	5
BROWN	6	LIGHTGRAY	7
DARKGRAY	8	LIGHTBLUE	9
LIGHTGREEN	10	LIGHTCYAN	11

Some modes will require palette colors which may be found in the `graphics.h` file.

textcolor( ) and textbackground( )

Two other functions available are `textcolor( )` and `textbackground( )`. These functions operate with the same color numbers and constants. However, they are used when printing characters in a text mode as opposed to a graphics mode. These functions are a part of the conio.h file and are used with the `cprintf( )` function. For an example, look at the section on windows in Borland.

SETTING TYPE FONTS

The type font used to print text on a graphics screen may use different fonts. The fonts available depend upon the compiler used. The fonts files must be available. In Microsoft, the fonts are in .FON files, while the .BGI files are needed for Borland.

Microsoft

To change the font used by an _outtext( ) requires the fonts to be registered with the registerfonts( ) function followed by a call to _setfont( ).

```
_registerfonts( "path for fonts" );
_setfont(option string)
```

The _setfont( ) function can take many different parameters called option strings. The easiest use is to just pass one of the predefined fonts. The fontname is enclosed in single quotes, preceded by a t.

Some of the fonts are:

Modern

Helv

Script

Modern

Times

The call for Helvetica would be

```
_setfont("t'Helv");
```

When the fonts are registered, it is a good idea to test if the function was successful. The function returns a negative number if there is a problem.

```
/*----------------------------------
          print in the Script font
--------------------------------*/
#include <graph.h>

void main( )
{
    _setvideomode(_VRES16COLOR);
    _clearscreen(_GCLEARSCREEN);
    _setcolor(2);
```

```
        if( _registerfonts( "a:*.FON" ) <= 0 )
        {
                _outtext( "Error: can't register fonts" );
                exit( 1 );
        }

    _setfont("t'Script'");
    _outgtext("A Font Demo");

  getche( );
}
```

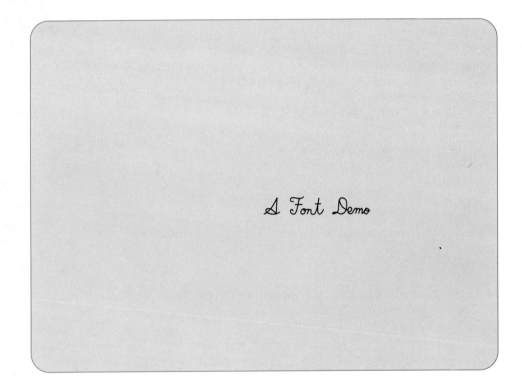

Borland Fonts

The function used to change the font is the settextstyle( ). It has three parameters:
the font name, the direction to print, and the point size of the characters.

```
settextstyle(font name, direction, point size);
```

The direction may be HORIZ_DIR or VERT_DIR. Some of the font names are:

```
TRIPLEX_FONT                          SCRIPT_FONT
SMALL_FONT                            SIMPLEX_FONT
SANS_SERIF_FONT                       COMPLEX_FONT
GOTHIC_FONT                           BOLD_FONT
settextstyle(GOTHIC_FONT, HORIZ_DIR, 10); /* sets font */
```

Summary of Text Graphics for Borland and Microsoft

	Microsoft	Borland
Header file	`graph.h`	`graphics.h`
Clear the screen	`_clearscreen(_GCLEARSCREEN)`	`clrscr( )`
Position cursor	`_settextposition(x,y)`	`gotoxy(x,y)`
Set text color	`_settextcolor(color#)`	`setcolor(#)`
Set fonts	`_setfont( )`	`settextstyle( )`

Self-Test

1. Code the statements to clear the screen and print "Programming in C", starting at column 30 on row 5.
2. Code the statements to print "Programming in C" in blue characters on a white background on a black screen.

Answers

1.
```
#include <graph.h>

void main( )
{
    _clearscreen(_GCLEARSCREEN);
    _settextposition(5,30);
    _outtext("Programming in C");
}

#include <conio.h>

void main( )
{
    clrscr( );
    gotoxy(5,30);
    puts("Programming in C");
}
```

2.
```
#include <graph.h>
#define BLUE 2
#define WHITE 7

void main( )
{
    _clearscreen(_GCLEARSCREEN);
    _setbkcolor(WHITE);
    _settextcolor(BLUE);
    _settextposition(5,30);
    _outtext("Programming in C");
}
```

TEXT SCREEN VS. GRAPHICS SCREENS

When working with text, we have been using a screen that holds 25 rows and 80 columns. Each position within this screen may contain 1 character. When working with graphics, pixels are used instead of characters. A **pixel** is a picture element—one dot which makes up the picture. The clarity or **resolution** of a picture is determined by how many pixels are in the picture. Normally, the greater the resolution within a picture, the fewer colors available. Of course, the resolution and the color are dependent upon the type of monitor that is being used.

C has the capability of testing the hardware configuration to determine if the proper hardware is being used for the program. If the program is written for VGA it cannot be run on EGA or CGA hardware. However, something written for a lower resolution monitor such as CGA graphics may be run on anything higher, EGA or VGA (see Figure 13.1).

pixel A picture element or dot comprising the graphics screen—the greater the pixel count, the higher the resolution.
resolution The clarity of the picture in graphics—the higher the resolution the better the picture.

MICROSOFT GRAPHICS

After setting the graphics video mode, several functions are available for drawing dots, lines, boxes, or circles.

Setting Video Mode

The video mode needs to be specified prior to using any graphics functions. The statement to set the graphics mode is

```
_setvideomode( mode   );
```

where mode can be as follows:

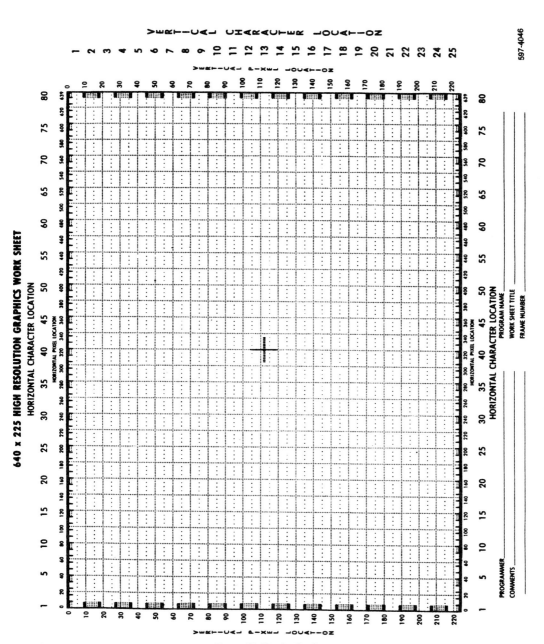

640 x 225 HIGH RESOLUTION GRAPHICS WORK SHEET

FIGURE 13-1
Sample Graphics Screen Layout

Video Modes

Constant	Mono	Text	Color	Graphics	Size	Adapter	Colors
_DEFAULTMODE			depends on the hardware				
_TEXTBW40	x	x			25x40	CGA	16
_TEXTC40		x	x		25x40	CGA	16
_TEXTBW80	x	x			25x80	CGA	16
_TEXTC80		x	x		25x80	CGA	16
_MRES4COLOR			x	x	320x200	CGA	4
_MRESNOCOLOR	x			x	320x200	CGA	4
_HRESBW	x			x	640x400	CGA	2
_TEXTMONO	x	x			25x80	Mono	1
_MRES16COLOR			x	x	320x200	EGA	16
_HRES16COLOR			x	x	640x200	EGA	16
_ERESNOCOLOR	x	x			640x350	EGA	1
_ERESCOLOR			x	x	640x350	EGA	64
_VRES2COLOR			x	x	640x480	VGA	2
_VRES16COLOR			x	x	640x480	VGA	16
_MRES256COLOR			x	x	320x200	VGA	256

The setvideomode( ) function can be used to set the mode to the default setting for the hardware on which the program is running. If any other setting is used it is wise to test for an error condition in case the hardware is not compatible.

```
if(_setvideomode(_MRES4COLOR)==0)
    }
    printf("%s", errormsg);
    exit(0);
}
```

Setting Graphics Colors

The colors in the graphics commands are set in several ways depending on the function. The most common will be the _setcolor( ) function. The _setcolor( ) uses the same numbers for sixteen color that were used with the text color functions.

```
_setcolor(color#);
```

Painting a Pixel

An individual pixel may be printed on a graphics screen by using the _setpixel( ) function. The function requires the x and the y coordinates of the dot to be given.

```
_setpixel(x, y);
```

The _setpixel( ) function may be used by itself to produce a single dot, or it may be placed in a loop to create a shape such as a line.

```
_setpixel(320,200);
```

would place a dot in the center of a 640 X 400 screen.

The color of the dot will be determined by whatever color was last set. The following program generates random numbers to select an x coordinate, a y coordinate, and a color.

```
/*--------------------------------------------------
                    random colored pixels
---------------------------------------------------*/
#include <graph.h>
#include <stdlib.h>  /* for the random function */

void main( )
{
    int x,y;     /* coordinates for the pixel */
    int color;   /*  to pick a random color    */
    int i;       /*    loop control            */

    _setvideomode(_VRES16COLOR);
    for(i = 0; i < 1000; i++)
    {
        x = (rand( ) % 640);     /* pick an x between 0 and 639 */
        y = (rand( ) % 400);     /* pick a y between 0 and 399  */
        color = (rand( ) % 15); /* pick a color between 0 and 14 */
        _setcolor(color);
        _setpixel(x,y);
    }
    getche( );  /* a pause to avoid the system message on
                   the graphics */
}
```

13-7.c

Output

Drawing a line with _setpixel( )

```
/*--------------------------------------------
            drawing a line with pixels
---------------------------------------------*/
#include <graph.h>
#define WHITE 7
#define BLUE 1

void main( )
{
    int x,y;

    _setcolor(WHITE);
    _clearscreen(_GCLEARSCREEN);

    _setcolor(BLUE);
```

```
      for(x = 5, y = 5; x< 100, y< 100; x++,y++)
      {
       _setpixel(x,y);
      }
}
```

Output

Drawing a Line with _lineto( ) and _moveto( )

Instead of setting up a loop to create the line pixel by pixel, it is faster to use the
_lineto( ) function. The starting point of the line may be set with _move-
to( ) or _setpixel( ).

```
_moveto(x,y)   /* positions the cursor */
_lineto(x,y)   /* draws a line from last point */

 _moveto(160,120);
 _lineto(480,360);
 _lineto(320,400);
 _lineto(160,120);
```

Drawing a Rectangle with _rectangle( )

The _rectangle( ) function will create a rectangular shape from the coordinates of two opposite corners. The shape may then be filled in or just outlined.

       _GFILLINTERIOR   will fill the shape in
       _GBORDER   gives just an outline

The color of the fill or of the outline depends upon the last _setcolor( ) function that was executed.

The format of _rectangle( ) is

```
_rectangle(fill or border, x1,y1,x2,y2)
```

Thus,

```
_rectangle(_GBORDER, 0,0,100,100);
```

will produce the outline of a rectangle. The top corner will be at the top left of the screen and the bottom right corner of the rectangle will be at 100,100.

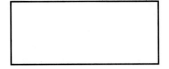

Drawing a Circle with _ellipse( )

The ellipse( ) function is very similar to _rectangle( ). With _ellipse( ), the opposite corners of a rectangle are specified to the function.

```
_ellipse(fill or border, x1,y1,x2,y2)
```

An elliptical shape will then be drawn within the rectangle, each side of the rectangle determining the size of the ellipse (see Figure 13.2). If the rectangle is square then the ellipse will be a circle. Otherwise, the aspect ratio of the ellipse will be determined by the shape of the rectangle.

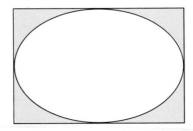

FIGURE 13-2
Circles Fit Within
Rectangle Coordinates

```
/*-----------------------------------------------
              drawing a circle
-----------------------------------------------*/
#include <graph.h>
#define BLUE 1
#define WHITE 7
#define RED 4

void main( )
{
  _setvideomode(_VRES16COLOR);
  _setcolor(WHITE);
  _clearscreen(_GCLEARSCREEN);
  _setcolor(BLUE);
  _ellipse(_GFILLINTERIOR,100,100,150,150);
  _setcolor(RED);
  _ellipse(_GBORDER,400,400,500,500);
  getche( );
}
```

Output

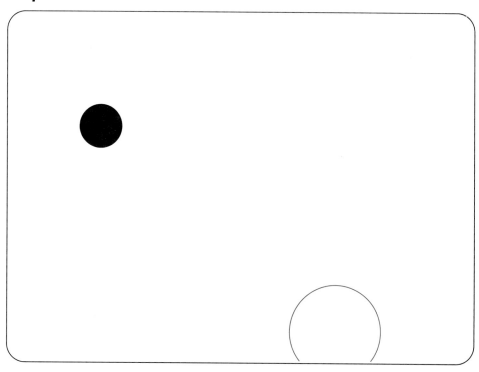

Drawing Partial Circles with _pie( ) and _arc( )

The pie ( ) function may be used to draw a partial circle, such as the classic Pacman. In addition to having the rectangle coordinates required by the ellipse ( ) function, the pie ( ) function has a second set of x and y coordinates to determine the arc of the pie that is to be "cut away."

```
_pie(fill or border,x1,y1,x2,y2,x3,y3,x4,y4)
```

Given the following pie ( ) function:

```
_pie(_GFILLINTERIOR,100,100,200,200,100,0,0,200)
```

The rectangle that borders the pie has

top left corner at	(100,100)
bottom right corner	(200,200)

The lines that determine the cutaway are the intersections from the center of the rectangle to (100,0) and from the center to ((0,200).

(150,150) to (100,0)
(150,150) to (0,200)

The _arc ( ) function is used to print just the arc of an ellipse using the same parameters as the _pie ( ) function without an option to fill or border.

_arc(x1,y1,x2,y2,x3,y3,x4,y4)

The arc function

_arc(100,100,200,200,150,0,0,200);

produces the arc:

1. Write the code to draw a line from the upper right-hand corner of the screen to the lower left-hand corner.
2. What is the difference between the _ellipse( ), the _pie( ), and the _arc( ) functions?
3. Code the statements to draw a happy face.

Answers

1.
```
_moveto(640,0);
_lineto(0,400);
```

2. The _pie( ) allows a filled in partial circle or a partial circle border, while the _ellipse( ) must be the complete circular shape. The _arc( ) also allows a partial circle but can only be the arc or partial perimeter of the circle.
3. The following program will produce a happy face using the _ellipse( ) and _arc( ) functions.

```
/*-----------------------------------------------
          happy face
-----------------------------------------------*/
#include <graph.h>
#define MAGENTA 5
#define WHITE 7

void main( )
{
 _setvideomode(_VRES16COLOR);
 _setcolor(WHITE);
 _floodfill(160,200,WHITE);

 _setcolor(MAGENTA);
 _ellipse(_GBORDER,160,100,480,400);   /*  FACE     */
 _ellipse(_GBORDER,260,180,290,210);   /*  LEFT EYE */
 _ellipse(_GBORDER,350,180,380,210);   /*  RIGHT EYE */
 _arc(240,250,410,340,0,300,640,300);  /*  SMILE    */
 getche( );
}
```

13-10.c

Filling in an Odd Shape or the Background

If _lineto( ) is used to create a polygon shape there is a way to color in the shape. The floodfill( ) function may also be used to color background areas. When filling in an area it must be bordered completely by a single color or the color will "leak" over the entire screen.

_floodfill(x,y,border)

where

    x, y   coordinates within area to be colored
    border   the color up to which the painting will occur

If a polygon is to be colored in with a _floodfill( ) function all of the lines of the shape must be the same color to provide a boundary at which the painting with _floodfill( ) will stop. The color used by _floodfill( ) is the last one used in a _setcolor( ) function.

The next program will create a triangle with white lines and then fill in around the rectangle in magenta.

```
/*--------------------------------------------------
                floodfill
---------------------------------------------------
*/
#include <graph.h>
#define MAGENTA 5
#define WHITE 7

void main( )
{
 _setvideomode(_VRES16COLOR);
 _setcolor(WHITE);
 _floodfill(160,200,WHITE);

 _setcolor(MAGENTA);
 _moveto(160,120);
 _lineto(480,360);
 _lineto(320,400);
 _lineto(160,120);
 _setcolor(MAGENTA);
 _floodfill(280,150,MAGENTA);
 getche( );
}
```

Setting up Windows

Windows can be set up to be a portion of the entire screen by using _settext window( ) or _setviewport( ). The text window will define where text information is to be printed, while the view port is used for graphics. Text within the window will scroll when the window is full. If an entire graphic does not fit within the view port it will show only the part that fits the port.

The opposite corners of a text window are given in row and column size while the view port is given in pixel size.

```
_settextwindow(row1,column1,row2,column2)
_setviewport(x1,y1,x2,y2)
```

```
/*------------------------------------------------------    13-12.c
              A text window
---------------------------------------------------------*/
#include <graph.h>
#include <math.h>

void main( )
{
    int i;
    _setbkcolor(2);
    _clearscreen(_GCLEARSCREEN);   /* clear entire screen */
    _settextcolor(1);
    _settextposition(5,30);
    _outtext("A Text Window Demo"); /* title outside window */

    _settextwindow(10,20,20,60);    /* create the window   */
    _setbkcolor(1);
    for(i=0; i < 300; i++)
    {
        _settextcolor(rand( )%15);
        _outtext("A Text Window\n");   /* print in the window */
    }


    _outtext("Press Any Key to clear window");
    getche( );
    _clearscreen(_GWINDOW);          /* clear window only */
    getche( );
}
```

This program will create a text window. A print statement is executed 300 times in random colors. The number of lines causes the text to scroll within the window. After the loop is complete, the window will be cleared (following a pause).

BORLAND GRAPHICS

After initializing a graphics mode, a variety of functions are available for drawing dots, lines, boxes, or circles.

Initializing a Graphics Mode

In Borland, it is necessary to initialize the graphics mode by setting a graphics driver and a mode before using the graphics functions. The graphics driver may be set to a default determined by the hardware by using the constant DETECT or a specific mode may be specified. The format for the function and the parameters is:

```
initgraph(graphdriver, graphmode, path of .BGI driver file)
```

The graphdrivers available are:

```
DETECT      0    /* determined by hardware present */
CGA         1
MCGA        2
EGA         3
EGA64       4
EGAMONO     5
IBM8514     6
HERCMONO    7
ATT400      8
VGA         9
PC3270      10
```

The graphmodes depend upon the driver:

Constant	Value	Pixel Size	Colors
CGAC0	0	320x200	
CGAC1	1	320x200	
CGAC2	2	320x200	
CGAC3	3	320x200	
CGAHI	4	640x200	
MCGAC0	0	320x200	
MCGAC1	1	320x200	

Constant	Value	Pixel Size	Colors
MCGAC2	2	320x200	
MCGAC3	3	320x200	
MCGAMED	4	640x200	
MCGAHI	5	640x480	
EGALO	0	640x200	16
EGAHI	1	640x350	16
EGA64LO	0	640x200	16
EGA64HI	1	640x350	4
EGAMONOHI	0	640x350	
HERCMONOHI	0	720x348	
ATT400C0	0	320x200	
ATT400C1	1	320x200	
ATT400C2	2	320x200	
ATT400C3	3	320x200	
ATT400MED	4	640x200	
ATT400HI	5	640x400	
VGALO	0	640x200	16
VGAMED	1	640x350	16
VGAHI	2	640x480	16
PC3270HI	0	720x350	
IBM8514LO	0	640x480	256
IBM8514HI	1	1024x768	256

The final parameter of the initgraph( ) function calls for the path to the graphics drivers, usually in the BGI subdirectory. The path may be specified or the quotes may be left empty, in which case the current directory will be searched.

The driver may be set and then tested for possible error codes to provide a graceful way out in the case of a problem with the graphics adapter.

```
/*-------------------------------------------------
        Initializing graphics mode in Turbo C++
-------------------------------------------------*/
#include <graphics.h>

void main( )
{
  int graphdriver, graphmode,errcode;
  graphdriver = DETECT;     /* find graphics mode */

  initgraph(&graphdriver, &graphmode, "c:\tc\bgi\egavga.bgi");

  errcode = graphresult( );
```

13-13.c

```
        if(errcode != grOk)
        {
           printf("Graphics Error %s\n", grapherrormsg(errcode));
           exit( );
        }
   }
```

The previous example uses the default mode. The mode could be specified as:

```
int graphdriver = VGA, graphmode = VGAHI;
initgraph(&graphdriver,&graphmode,"");
```

Setting Graphics Colors

The function used to set colors for graphics is the setcolor( ). It is the same function as for text because outtext( ) is considered a graphics function. This function only requires one parameter. The parameter may be an integer value referring to the color or one of the colors defined as constants in the graphics.h header file.

```
setcolor(color);
```

Drawing a Pixel

A single pixel may be drawn using the `putpixel( )` function. The function has three parameters: the x coordinate, the y coordinate, and the color number.

```
putpixel(x,y,color);
```

The following program prints random pixels with random colors using the `putpixel( )` function.

🄳🄾-🄳🄲.🄲

```
/*--------------------------------------------------
     Random pixels   Turbo C++
-----------------------------------------------*/
#include <graphics.h>
#include <stdlib.h>

void main( )
{
   int i, x,y,color;
```

```
   int graphdriver = VGA, graphmode = VGAHI;
   initgraph(&graphdriver, &graphmode, "c:\tc\bgi\egavga.bgi");

   for(i = 0; i < 1000; i++)
   {
     x = random(640);
     y = random(640);
     color = random(31);
     putpixel(x,y,color);
   }
}
```

Drawing a Line Using the putpixel( )

The putpixel( ) function may be used to create shapes by using a loop with the function. Any shape may be drawn just by placing the appropriate dots on the screen, a very tedious job.

The following program will draw a line using the putpixel( ) function.

`1 3 - 1 5 . c`

```
/*-------------------------------------------------
        Drawing a line with pixels in Turbo C++
-------------------------------------------------*/
#include <graphics.h>
#include <stdlib.h>

void main( )
{
  int x,y;
  int graphdriver = VGA, graphmode = VGAHI;
  initgraph(&graphdriver, &graphmode, "c:\tc\bgi\egavga.bgi");

  for(x = 0, y=0; x < 40; x++, y++)
  {
    putpixel(x,y, WHITE  );
  }
}
```

Drawing a Line with line( )

A line can be drawn faster and easier using the line( ) function. This function requires the x and y coordinates for the beginning and end of the line.

```
line(x1,y1,x2,y2)
```

The line in the program with pixels could have been created with one command rather than a loop.

```
line(0,0,40,40);
```

The line will go from point 0,0 to point 40,40.

Drawing a Rectangle

The function for creating a rectangle is `rectangle( )` with parameters for the coordinates for two opposite corners of the rectangle.

```
rectangle(x1,y1,x2,y2)
```

Thus,

```
rectangle(0,0,100,100);
```

will produce the outline of a rectangle. The top corner will be at the top left of the screen and the bottom right corner of the rectangle will be at 100,100.

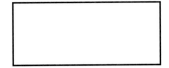

Drawing a Circle

Borland provides three functions for doing circular outlines: `arc( )`, `ellipse( )`, and `circle( )`. In addition, the `pieslice( )` function provides the ability to create a filled-in shape. With the other functions, the shapes may be filled in after being drawn.

circle( )

The `circle( )` function will always produce a complete circle and requires the parameters for the center of the circle and the radius.

```
circle(x,y,radius);
```

where x,y are the coordinates for the center of the circle.

```
/*------------------------------------------------------------
        Drawing circles with circle( ), ellipse( ), and arc( )
------------------------------------------------------------*/
#include <graphics.h>
#include <conio.h>

void main( )
{
  int x,y;
  int graphdriver = VGA, graphmode = VGAHI;
  initgraph(&graphdriver, &graphmode, "c:\tc\bgi\egavga.bgi");

  setcolor(WHITE);
  clrscr( );
  circle(125,125,25);
  setcolor(BLUE);
  ellipse(150,150,0,360,50,50);
  arc(300,300,0,360,50);
}
```

arc( )

The arc( ) draws a partial circle based on a start angle and an end angle. It still requires a radius and the coordinates of the center point.

```
arc(x,y,start angle, end angle, radius)
```

The start and end angles are based upon a circle in which the 0 point begins at the three o'clock position and continues around 360° to three o'clock (see Figure 13.3).

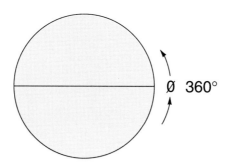

FIGURE 13-3
Start and End Angles of arc( )

FIGURE 13-4
Half Circle from 0° to 180°

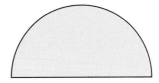

To draw a half circle, the function call would be as follows (see Figure 13.4):

```
arc(320,200,0,180,100);
```

320, 200	mark the coordinates of the center
0, 180	the start and end of the arc in degrees
100	radius in pixels

ellipse( )

The `ellipse( )` function can be used to draw elliptical shapes that may not be circular. The aspect ratio (how oblong the circle is) is determined by giving both an x radius and a y radius. Similar to `arc( )`, `ellipse( )` can draw a complete circular shape or an arc. To draw a complete circle, the start angle would be 0 and the end angle would be 360.

```
ellipse(x,y, start angle, end angle, x radius,
y radius)
```

pieslice( )

The `pieslice( )` function uses the same parameters as the `arc( )` function to create a partial circle drawn in the current `setcolor( )` and filled in with the current fill style. The fill style will be discussed in a while. The format for the `pieslice( )` function is

```
pieslice(x,y,start angle, end angle, radius)
```

where the start angle and end angle are based on the same system used with the `arc( )` and `ellipse( )` functions.

FIGURE 13-5
Pie Slice

1. Write the code to draw a line from the upper right-hand corner of the screen to the lower left-hand corner.
2. What is the difference between the circle( ), the ellipse( ), the pieslice( ), and the arc( ) functions?
3. Code the statements to draw a happy face.

Answers

1. `line(0,0,640,400);`
2. The circle( ) will always be a complete circle, while the ellipse and the arc may be partial circular shapes. The ellipse allows a nonsymmetrical shape. Only the pieslice provides the ability to fill in as part of the function.
3.

```
/*------------------------------------------------------------
                    a happy face
----------------------------------------------------------*/
#include <graphics.h>
#include <conio.h>

void main( )
{
  int x,y;
  int graphdriver = VGA, graphmode = VGAHI;
  initgraph(&graphdriver, &graphmode, "c:\tc\bgi\egavga.bgi");

  setcolor(WHITE);
  clrscr( );
  circle(320,240,160);        /*  outline of face */
  circle(260,150,30);        /*  left eye      */
  circle(380,150,30);        /*  right eye     */
  arc(320,240,180,360,80);    /*  smile        */
}
```

Setting Fill Colors and Fill Styles

Colors can be "painted" into an existing figure using the `floodfill( )` function. The `floodfill( )` requires a point on the screen to paint and a border color up to which the painting will occur.

```
floodfill(x,y,border color);
```

If a circle has been drawn in white it may be filled in by giving a point within the boundaries of the circle and then specifying white as the border color. The fill-in color may be the same as the border or may be different as determined by `setfillstyle( )`.

The `setfillstyle( )` function provides the ability to determine the color and the pattern to be used for filling in a figure. It is possible to use predefined styles or to create your own. These styles are convenient when trying to distinguish different figures on a black and white printer through the use of different patterns. This would be important, for example, in creating a bar or pie chart.

The format for `setfillstyle( )` is:

```
setfillstyle(pattern, color);
```

The patterns may be a constant from the following:

EMPTY_FILL	background color
SOLID_FILL	solid fill color
LINE_FILL	fill with ——
LTSLASH_FILL	fill with ////
SLASH_FILL	fill with thick slashes
BKSLASH_FILL	fill with thick backslashes
LTBKSLASH_FILL	fill with \\\\
HATCH_FILL	light cross hatch
XHATCH_FILL,	heavy cross hatch
INTERLEAVE_FILL,	interleaving line fill
WIDE_DOT_FILL,	widely spaced dot fill
CLOSE_DOT_FILL,	closely spaced dot fill
USER_FILL	defined by the user

The colors may be any that have been used before.

13-18.c

```
/*-------------------------------------------------------
            floodfill
----------------------------------------------------*/
#include <graphics.h>
#include <conio.h>

void main( )
{
   int x,y;
```

```
      int graphdriver = VGA, graphmode = VGAHI;
      initgraph(&graphdriver, &graphmode, "c:\tc\bgi\egavga.bgi");

      setcolor(WHITE);
      clrscr( );

      setcolor(MAGENTA);
      line(160,120,480,360);
      line(480,360,320,400);
      line(320,400,160,120);
      setfillstyle(SOLID_FILL,MAGENTA);
      floodfill(0,0,MAGENTA);    /* color around the triangle */
}
```

window( )

The window( ) function in Borland is not a part of the graphics functions. It is contained in the conio.h header file along with the textcolor( ) and textbackground( ) functions. The format uses the coordinates of a text window to give the top left and bottom right corners as integers.

```
window(top,left, bottom, right);
```

The following example demonstrates these functions.

```
/*---------------------------------------------------
          Borland text window
-------------------------------------------------*/
#include <stdlib.h>
#include <conio.h>

void main( )
{
   int i;

   textbackground(CYAN);
   clrscr( );
   gotoxy(30,5);
   cprintf("A Text Window Demo");

  window(10,10,60,20);
  textbackground(BLUE);
```

`13-19.c`

```
            clrscr( );
            for(i=0; i < 300; i++)
            {
                textcolor(rand( )%15);
                cprintf("A Text Window\n\r");
            }

            textcolor(BLACK);
            cprintf("\nPress Any Key to clear window");
            getche( );
            clrscr( );
            getche( );
        }
```

setviewport( )

The setviewport( ) function is a part of the graphics library routines. The
size of the graphics area is determined by giving the coordinates of the top left
and the bottom right in terms of pixels according to the graphics modes. In addition, it is necessary to specify whether the graphics should be truncated or clipped
to the edge of the viewport.

Try the following program.

```
/*-------------------------------------------------------
          Borland viewport
----------------------------------------------------*/
#include <graphics.h>
#include <stdlib.h>
#include <conio.h>

void main( )
{
    int i;
    int graphdriver = VGA, graphmode = VGAHI;
    initgraph(&graphdriver, &graphmode, "c:\tc\bgi\egavga.bgi");

    setcolor(CYAN);
    clrscr( );
    outtextxy(300,5,"A Text Window Demo");
```

```
    setviewport(100,50,540,300,1);
    setcolor(BLUE);
    clrscr( );
    for(i=0; i < 300; i++)
    {
        setcolor(rand( )%15);
        outtextxy(0,i,"A Text Window\n\r");
    }

    setcolor(BLACK);
    outtext("\nPress Any Key to clear window");
    getche( );
    clrscr( );
    getche( );
}
```

USES OF GRAPHICS IN BUSINESS PROGRAMMING

Business graphics frequently present information in bar chart or pie chart form. Data values can be used to create proper proportions in the charts.

Creating a Bar Chart

The functions for drawing a rectangle can be used to depict data in a bar graph form. The first y coordinate for each bar will be the same but the second y coordinate will depend on the value being represented. The x coordinates will be sequential for the beginning and ending of each bar, keeping the bar width consistent.

The following example bases the height of each bar on the total per area. Notice that each total is divided by 5 to get a number in the appropriate pixel range for high resolution pixels of 640x480. The lower y coordinate of each bar is 400, so the second y coordinate must be smaller to go "up" the display.

```
/*--------------------------------------------------
            Bar Chart of Totals by Area Microsoft
---------------------------------------------------*/
#include <graph.h>
#define NUM 4
```

`13-20.c`

```c
void titles( );
void drawgraph(char(*area)[], int * total);

void main( )
{
    char area [NUM][6] = {"North","South","East","West"};
    int total[NUM] = {1712,1543,1901,1833};

    _setvideomode(_VRES16COLOR);

    titles( );
    drawgraph(area, total);
}


/*---------------------------------------------
    draw the barchart
------------------------------------------------*/
void drawgraph(char (*area)[6], int *total)
{
    int i;

    for(i = 0; i < NUM; i++)
    {
     int height, leftcorner, rightcorner, loweredge;
     /*   calculate coordinates of bar */
     height = 350-total[i]/10;
     leftcorner = i*100+100;
     rightcorner = leftcorner + 100;
     loweredge = 350;

     _setcolor(i+1);
     _rectangle(_GFILLINTERIOR,leftcorner, loweredge, rightcorner,
                        height);
     _floodfill(leftcorner+1,349,i+1);
     _settextcolor(i+1);
     _settextposition(22,leftcorner/8+5);
     _outtext((area+i));    /* pointer to array */
    }
    getche( );
}
```

```
/*-------------------------
        titles
-------------------------*/
void titles( )
{
    _setcolor(2);
    _settextposition(5,30);
    _outtext("A Bar Chart");
    _settextposition(11,8);
    _outtext("2000");
    _settextposition(14,8);
    _outtext("1500");
}
```

Notice that the colors are incremented, so that each bar is a different color.

Output

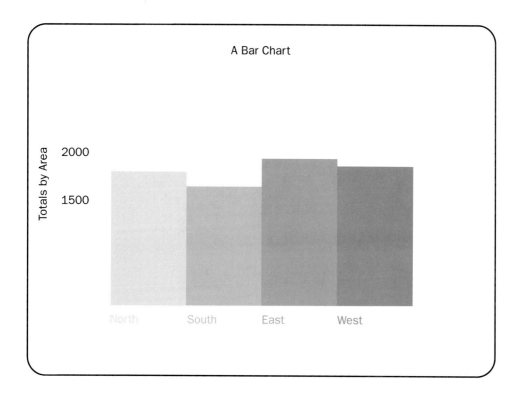

```
13-21.c
/*-------------------------------------------------
        Bar Chart of Totals by Area in Borland
----------------------------------------------------*/
#include <graphics.h>
#define NUM 4

void main( )
{
  char area[NUM][6] = {"North", "South", "East", "West"};
  int total[NUM] = {1712,1543,1901,1833};
  int i, graphdriver = VGA, graphmode = VGAHI;
  initgraph(&graphdriver, &graphmode, "c:\tc\bgi\egavga.bgi");

  setcolor(YELLOW);
  moveto(300,5);
  settextstyle(GOTHIC_FONT, HORIZ_DIR, 10); /* top title */
  outtext("A Bar Chart");

  moveto(25,150);
  settextstyle(GOTHIC_FONT,VERT_DIR,10); /* vertical title */
  outtext(" Totals by Area");
  settextstyle(GOTHIC_FONT,HORIZ_DIR,10);
  moveto(50,150);
  outtext("2000");
  moveto(50,200);
  outtext("1500");

  for(i = 0; i < NUM; i++)
  {
    int height, leftcorner, rightcorner, loweredge;

    /*    calculate coordinates of bar */
    height = 350 - total[i]/10;
    leftcorner = i*100+100;
    rightcorner= leftcorner + 100;
    loweredge = 350;

    setcolor(i+1);
    rectangle(leftcorner,350,rightcorner,height);
```

```
      setfillstyle(SOLID_FILL,i+1);
      floodfill(leftcorner+1,349, i+1);
      moveto(leftcorner,loweredge+10);
      setcolor(i+1);
      outtext(area[i]);
    }

}
```

Creating a Pie Chart

A pie chart is based upon percents of the whole. Each number being charted will be assigned a portion of the pie relating to the percent that number is to the total.

In Borland the percent may be used directly in the `pieslice( )` function. However, the nature of the graphics commands in Microsoft require more manipulation of the data. The start and stop angles and associated pie slices must be calculated.

When creating the chart, it is important to consider how the pie will be labeled to show what each portion represents. One method would be to produce a legend with a label for each part. A **legend** will display each color or pattern within the chart alongside the item name of what is being represented.

legend Descriptive title attached to a graphical chart.

```
/*---------------------------------------------------
      Pie Chart of Totals by Area Microsoft
-------------------------------------------------*/
#include <graph.h>
#define NUM 4
#define PI 3.1415927

void main( )
{
  char area[NUM][6] = {"North", "South", "East", "West"};
  int total[NUM] = {1000,2000,3000,4000};
  int i, row;
  int starty, startx, endx, endy;
  float grandtotal, subtotal, angle[NUM];
  _setvideomode(_VRES16COLOR);

  _setcolor(3);
  _settextposition(5,30);
  _outtext("A Pie Chart");
```

13-22.c

```c
for(i = 0; i < NUM; i++)   /* find total of pie */
{
   grandtotal += total[i];
}
for(i = 0, startx= 0,starty =0; i < NUM; i++)
  /* find parts of pie */
{

  /*     calculate pie slices degrees */
  angle[i] = (total[i]/grandtotal*2*PI);

  if(angle[i] > 2*PI || angle[i] < -2*PI)
     angle[i] -= ((int) angle[i] /2*PI) * 2 * PI;
  if(angle[i] <= 2*PI)
  {
     endx = 120 * cos(angle[i]);
     endy = 120 * sin(angle[i]);
  {
  else if(angle[i] <= PI)
     {
        endx = cos(PI-angle[i]) * 120;
        endy = sin(PI-angle[i]) * 120;
     }
  else if(angle[i] <= 3*PI/2)
     {
        endx = cos(angle[i] - PI) * 120;
        endy = sin(angle[i] - PI) * 120;
     }
  else
     {
        endx = cos(2*PI - angle[i]) *120;
        endy = sin(2*PI - angle[i]) * 120;
     }

  _setcolor(i+1);
   _pie(_GFILLINTERIOR,150,100,390,300,
        startx,starty,endx,endy);
  startx = endx;
  starty = endy;
}
```

```
  row = 200;                  /*  print legend */
  for (i =0, row = 10; i < NUM; i++, row ++)
  {
    _settextposition(row,5);
    _settextcolor(i+1);
    _outtext(area[i]);
  }
}



/*-------------------------------------------------
      Pie Chart of Totals by Area   Borland
-----------------------------------------------------*/
#include <graphics.h>
#define NUM 4

void main( )
{
  char area[NUM][6] = {"North", "South", "East", "West"};
  int total[NUM] = {1712,1543,1901,1833};
  int i, row, graphdriver = VGA, graphmode = VGAHI;
  float grandtotal, subtotal, percent[NUM];
  initgraph(&graphdriver, &graphmode, "c:\tc\bgi\egavga.bgi");

  setcolor(YELLOW);
  moveto(280,5);
  settextstyle(GOTHIC_FONT, HORIZ_DIR, 10); /* top title */
  outtext("A Pie Chart");

  for(i = 0; i < NUM; i++)  /* find total of pie */
  {
     grandtotal += total[i];
  }

  for(i = 0; i < NUM; i++)  /* find parts of pie */
  {
    /*     calculate pie slices */
    percent[i] = (total[i]/grandtotal*360);

    setfillstyle(SLASH_FILL,i+1);
    pieslice(320,200,subtotal, subtotal + percent[i], 100);
```

```
      subtotal += percent[i];
   }
   row = 200;/*  print legend */
   for (i =0; i < NUM; i++, row += 20)
   {
      moveto(50,row);
      settextstyle(GOTHIC_FONT, HORIZ_DIR, 10);
      setcolor(i+1);
      outtext(area[i]);
   }

}
```

Output

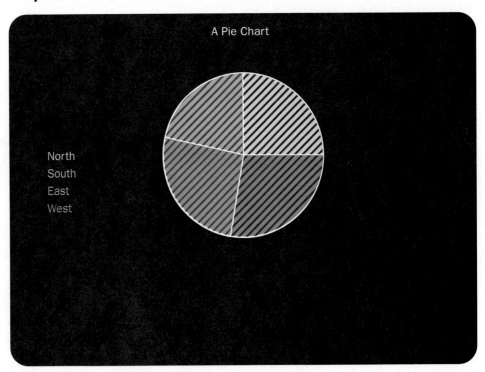

Using Graphics Functions for a Light Bar Menu

A menu program can be accessed through the use of the cursor keys as well as having the user enter an option. A menu using the cursor keys typically highlights the options as the cursor reaches that choice. The following code segments are for Microsoft but could be converted for Borland.

The cursor control can be determined by finding the position of the cursor on the screen and by testing for the characters representing the up and down arrows.

```
choice=(char) getch( );
do {
     switch(choice) {
          case 72:               /*  up arrow  */
               up_arrow( );
               break;
          case 80:               /*  down arrow  */
               down_arrow( );
               break;
          case '1':
               one( );
               break;
          case '2':
               two( );
               break;
          case '3':
               three( );
               break;
          case '4':
               four( );
               break;
          case '5':
               _settextwindow(1, 1, 23, 79);
               _settextposition(23, 1);
               exit(0);          /*  terminate  */
          case 13:               /*  return key  */
               option( );
               break;
          default:
               if(choice)
               printf("\a");     /*  beep  */
     }
     choice=(char) getch( );
} while(choice !=5);
```

A character is input from the keyboard using the getch( ) function. The character is tested using the *switch* statement. A case of 72 tests for the up arrow, 80 is the down arrow, and 13 is an enter key. The user may select by typing the actual number for the choice or by using the arrow keys and the enter key. A define could be used to represent the 72 and the 80 for improved readability.

Assume that the menu options are stored in an array:

```c
char *options[]= {
    "1. Option #1",
    "2. Report to Screen",
    "3. Report to Printer",
    "4. Dir/p a:",
    "5. Leave menu System"
};
```

Each time a down arrow is pressed the selection will increase to the next position in the array while an up arrow will cause the option position to decrease.

```c
void up_arrow(void)
{
    _settextcolor(ORANGE);
    _settextposition(x, 30);        /* change previous */
    _outtext(options[sel]);         /* selection */
    sel-, x-=2;
    if(x<9) {x=17; sel=4;}
    _settextcolor(YELLOW);
    _settextposition(x, 30);            /* print new */
    _outtext(options[sel]);             /* selection */
}
```

This function changes the highlight color of the old option back to normal and then highlights the new selection, which is one less than the previous (sel—).

13-24.c

```c
/*
    *
        *   Program:        Anita-6.c Menu System
        *   Programmer:     George Gumler
        *   Date:           November 1991
        *   Class:          Beginning C   */




#include <stdlib.h>/*  These two are for the  */
#include <process.h>/*  system function   */
#include <graph.h>
#include <stdio.h>
```

```
#define BLACK   0
#define BLUE    1
#define LBLUE   3
#define ORANGE 6
#define WHITE   7
#define YELLOW 14

char *options[]= {
    "1. Option #1",
    "2. Report to Screen",
    "3. Report to Printer",
    "4. Dir/p a:",
    "5. Leave menu System"
};

int x=9, sel=0;

/*             function prototypes        */
void main(void), option(void), print_menu(void), up_arrow(void);
void down_arrow(void), one(void), two(void), three(void), four(void);
void heading(int topx, int topy, int botx, int boty);
void draw_border(int top, int left, int bottom, int right);
void draw_shadow(void), print_screen( ), list_file( );
void e_linc(void), output_screen(void), output_printer(void);
void title(void), title_p(void);
int getch(void);

void main(void)
{
    char choice;

    _setvideomode(_TEXTC80);
    print_menu( );
    choice=(char) getch( );
    do {
        switch(choice) {
            case 72:              /*  up arrow   */
                up_arrow( );
                break;
            case 80:              /*  down arrow   */
```

```
                    down_arrow( );
                    break;
            case '1':
                    one( );
                    break;
            case '2':
                    two( );
                    break;
            case '3':
                    three( );
                    break;
            case '4':
                    four( );
                    break;
            case '5':
                    _settextwindow(1, 1, 23, 79);
                    _settextposition(23, 1);
                    exit(0);          /* terminate */
            case 13:                  /* return key */
                    option( );
                    break;
            default:
                    if(choice)
                    printf("\a");     /* beep */
        }
        choice=(char) getch( );
    } while(choice !=5);
}



void option(void)
{
    switch(sel) {
        case 0:
                one( );
                break;
        case 1:
                two( );
                break;
        case 2:
```

```
                three( );
                break;
            case 3:
                four( );
                break;
            case 4:
                _settextposition(23, 1);
                exit(0);              /* terminate */
        }
}


void print_menu(void)
{
    int xpos, opt=0;

    _setbkcolor(LBLUE);
    _clearscreen(_GCLEARSCREEN);
    heading(3, 13, 5, 65);
    draw_shadow( );
    draw_border(7, 23, 19, 57);
    _settextcolor(ORANGE);
    _setbkcolor(BLUE);
    for(xpos=9; xpos<18; xpos+=2) {          /* print menu */
        _settextposition(xpos, 30);
        _outtext(options[opt]);
        opt++;
}
    _setbkcolor(BLUE);
    _settextcolor(YELLOW);
    _settextposition(x, 30);          /* highlight */
    _outtext(options[sel]);          /* first choice */
}


void up_arrow(void)
{
    _settextcolor(ORANGE);
    _settextposition(x, 30);            /* change previous */
    _outtext(options[sel]);            /* selection */
    sel—, x-=2;
```

```
        if(x<9) {x=17; sel=4;}
        _settextcolor(YELLOW);
        _settextposition(x, 30);            /* print new */
        _outtext(options[sel]);             /* selection */
}



void down_arrow(void)
{
        _settextcolor(ORANGE);
        _settextposition(x, 30);
        _outtext(options[sel]);             /* change previous */
        sel++, x+=2;                        /* selection */
        if(x>17){ x=9; sel=0; }
        _settextcolor(YELLOW);
        _settextposition(x, 30);             /* print new */
        _outtext(options[sel]);             /* selection */
}



void one(void)
{


  print_menu( );
}



void two(void)
{
        output_screen( );
        print_menu( );
}



/* Prompt user before printing */
```

```
void three(void)
{
     char ch;

     _setbkcolor(BLUE);
     _clearscreen(_GCLEARSCREEN);
     _settextposition(10, 15);
     _outtext("Type \'Y\' when printer is ready, any other key to abort");
     ch=getch( );
     if(toupper(ch)=='Y') output_printer( );
     print_menu( );
}




void four(void)
{
     _setbkcolor(BLACK);
     _clearscreen(_GCLEARSCREEN);
     system("dir/p a:");
     getch( );
     print_menu( );
}




/* Print heading and its shadow */

void heading(int topx, int topy, int botx, int boty)
{
     _settextwindow(topx, topy, botx, boty);
     _setbkcolor(BLACK);
     _clearscreen(_GWINDOW);
     _settextwindow(topx-1, topy+1, botx-1, boty+1);
     draw_border(topx-1, topy+1, botx-1, boty+1);
     _settextposition(3, 24);
     _outtext("M E N U   S Y S T E M");
     _settextcolor(BLUE);
}
```

```
/* shadow for the body of the menu */

void draw_shadow(void)
{
    _settextwindow(8, 22, 20, 56);
    _setbkcolor(BLACK);
    _clearscreen(_GWINDOW);
}




/* Draw line around the body of the menu */

void draw_border(int top, int left, int bottom, int right)
{
    int i;
    char stuff[1];

    _setbkcolor(BLUE);
    _settextwindow(top, left, bottom, right);
    _clearscreen(_GWINDOW);
    _settextwindow(1, 1, 23, 79);
    _settextcolor(YELLOW);
    stuff[1]='\0';
    stuff[0]=(char) 196;
     for(i=left;i<right;i++) {
        _settextposition(top,i);
        _outtext(stuff);
        _settextposition(bottom,i);
        _outtext(stuff);
    }

    stuff[0]=(char) 179;
    for(i=top;i<bottom;i++) {
        _settextposition(i,left);
        _outtext(stuff);
        _settextposition(i,right);
        _outtext(stuff);
    }
    stuff[0]=(char) 218;
    _settextposition(top,left);
```

```
        _outtext(stuff);
        stuff[0]=(char)191;
        _settextposition(top,right);
        _outtext(stuff);
        stuff[0]=(char) 192;
        _settextposition(bottom,left);
        _outtext(stuff);
        stuff[0]=(char) 217;
        _settextposition(bottom,right);
        _outtext(stuff);
        _settextwindow(1, 1, 23, 79);
}
```

PROGRAMMING/DEBUGGING TIP

Many other features are available for making graphics more efficient. This section covers finding the sizes of the graphics mode and setting a program list.

Working with Various Graphics Modes

Functions are available that will find out the maximum pixel positions depending on the graphics mode used. These functions would be necessary when using the default modes for the hardware. These functions include getmaxx( ) and getmaxy( ). These functions could then be used to find a certain portion size of the screen.

```
getmaxx( );   /*returns the largest x coordinate available */
getmaxy( );   /*returns the largest y coordinate available */
```

The middle of the screen could be determined by dividing these functions.

```
/* find coordinates for the center of the screen */
center_x = getmaxx( )/2;
center_y = getmaxy( )/2;
```

Setting a Program List

If the version of Quick C being used is an earlier version (1.5 or earlier) it will be necessary to set a program list in order to do graphics. In the newer versions the graphics library has been included as part of the editing environment. With the earlier versions, an

```
unresolved external
```

error message will be generated. If the message refers to a function or constant that is defined in the `graph.h` file, then a program list must be made as well as doing an include of the header file.

KEY TERMS

bar chart	**light bar menu**	**pixel**
legend	**pie chart**	**resolution**

CHAPTER SUMMARY

Although graphics functions are not standard in the C language, they do play an important role in business programming. Once the file is compiled to an EXE file, it can be transported from one system to another. The problem with nonstandard functions is that the source code is not portable from one compiler to another.

Graphics functions are available for handling text on the screen. Other functions are available after setting a graphic video mode. These additional functions may be used to draw lines, boxes, or circular shapes.

The graphics functions may be utilized in business applications for charting and for screen design. This chapter demonstrates the use of graphics for bar graphs, pie charts, and for light bar menus.

REVIEW QUESTIONS

1. What is the difference between a text and a graphics mode?
2. What is the disadvantage of using the graphics libraries when creating programs that may be used on multiple systems?
3. If an executable file is being created and used, is the portability affected by the use of graphics commands?

EXERCISES

1. Draw a picture of a house. Use a structured approach, for example the roof will be created with a function called roof( ). Document carefully with comments on the graphics lines.
2. Create a bar chart for the sales data from the following departments.

Shoes	17,546
Dresses	31,899
Menswear	25,762

3. Use the data from Exercise 2 and present each department as a percent of the whole, using a pie chart. Use appropriate titles and legends.

4. Create a flyer advertising a computer consulting firm. Use your name and phone number and include a list of at least three software related services.

5. A weekend course in Microcomputer Applications featuring a series of products will be offered starting the first weekend in April through the end of May. Create a flyer with an appropriate graphic.

6. Create a letterhead including a company name, address, and company logo. (You may design the logo.)

HAYLEY OFFICE SUPPLIES

Create a bar chart to compare the sales for the past three years.
For sample data use sales of:
   225,000
   274,000
   245,000
Hint: *Plot the graph in thousands, and label appropriately.*

CHAPTER

14

CHAPTER OBJECTIVES

By the end of this chapter, you should be able to:

- Introduce the concepts of encapsulation, inheritance, and polymorphism as they relate to object-oriented programming.

- Explain the relationship between the ANSI C language and the C++ language.

- Use the standard input/output functions available in iostream.h.

- Create an object and use it in a program

- Examine the use of constructor and destructor functions.

A Look at C++ and Object-Oriented Programming

This chapter is intended to give a short introduction to the world of object-oriented programming related to the C language. The terminology of C++ will be introduced along with the relationship between C and C++.

Some example programs will be used to demonstrate the new features that supplement C and to create objects that may be used in further programming.

C++ also provides many tools for use by programmers. Some of the containers that are provided will be discussed.

OBJECT-ORIENTED PROGRAMMING

object-oriented programming
Method of programming in which
data and functions are handled as
a unit called an object.

C++ is an extension to the C language that provides the capability for **object-oriented programming (OOP)**, which refers to the analysis of data into abstract classifications or classes.

To break down programming into classes is an attempt to model the way in which items in general are broken down into classifications within the real world. For example, a general class of objects is automobiles. Automobiles have many different features or attributes that resemble each other. The term automobile may then be used without referring to any specific details about a specific type of car.

An extension to the analogy of an automobile is that the car is really a class within the class of vehicles. Vehicles is a class within modes of transportation. Each one of these classes has specific traits that become more general as the class becomes more general.

With an object-oriented programming language, the primary goal is to generate reusable code. This results in greater control over the structure of the program. In addition new operators provide greater security for data.

CHARACTERISTICS OF AN OOP LANGUAGE

encapsulation Hiding of data
within an object.

class An object.

inheritance The ability to have
an object be derived from a base
class and carry over the data types
and functions of the parent class.
derived class A class that
inherits characteristics from another
class.
base class An object-oriented
programming referring to an object
from which other objects are
derived; an example of
inheritance.
hierarchy A chart depicting the
relationship of user-created
functions.
polymorphism Ability of an
object to work with more than one
data type using virtual functions—
the object's type is not known until
run time.
virtual function More than one
function is defined to handle
multiple types of data; the function
to be executed is determined at run
time, according to the actual data
type used.

The three characteristics of an OOP language are encapsulation, inheritance, and polymorphism. **Encapsulation** combines data structures with the actions that are used to manipulate the type of data. In C++ encapsulation is denoted with a structure that contains both data and functions, called a **class.**

Inheritance is a feature of object oriented models that allows one class (or object) to be derived from another class. The **derived** class has similar features and actions but requires greater specificity than the **base** class with which it is associated. The automobile would be a derived class from vehicle base class. The concept of inheritance leads to a relationship of classes known as **hierarchy** of classes.

The ability to have many versions of the same function and to select the appropriate version at run time is called **polymorphism.** This allows functions to be written for various data types and the compiler will select the proper function to be used in a particular execution of the program. The functions are known as **virtual functions** because they may change throughout a class hierarchy.

CHARACTERISTICS OF C++

The C language is actually a subset of the C++ compiler. It is possible to run C programs using Turbo C++ or Borland C++ as well as the other C compilers on the market. However, the C++ compilers have many features beyond ANSI C. At this time there is no ANSI standard for C++.

Comments

C++ provides the ability to use single line comments within a program. The symbol for these comments is two slashes //.

// this is a single line comment in C++, no close needed
// second line would need new set of slashes

A problem with using these comments is the lack of portability back to a C compiler.

A First Program in C++

The first code we will examine in C++ uses two functions from the iostream.h file. The iostream.h replaces the stdio.h for most standard input and output functions. The *cin* function performs input from the standard input device while *cout* handles standard output. There is no need for format specifiers because the functions will handle all standard data types correctly.

A new operator used with the functions is "put to" which sends data to a stream. The operator << or >> is differentiated from the bitwise operator by the context within which it is used. This is an example of operator overloading.

```
// A comment in C++ only needs the // mark at beginning
// of line
// the stdio.h is replaced by iostream.h
#include <iostream.h>

void main( )
{
    char word[20];
    int number;

    // cout and cin do automatic flushing
    // and process all std data types
    cout << "This will print on the screen";
    cout << "Input a word";
    cin > word;
    cout << "Enter an integer number";
    cin > number;
```

```
        cout << "The number is " << number << " The word
is " << word;
}
```

Output

```
This will print on the screen
Input a word Object
Enter an integer number 5
The number is 5 The word is Object
```

Self-Test

1. Code the statements to prompt for and input a first name, a last name, and a float amount.

   ```
   char lastname[12], firstname[10];
   float amount;
   ```

2. Assuming the appropriate data was entered, print the following:

   ```
   John Smith    $57.89
   ```

3. Write 2 comment lines with your name and course title.

Answers

1. ```
   cout << "Last Name: ";
   cin  > lastname;
   cout << "First Name: ";
   cin  > firstname;
   cout << "Amount:       ";
   cin  > amount;
   ```

2. ```
   cout << lastname << " " << firstname <<
        "$" << amount;
   ```

public A function within an object can be accessed by any function within the scope of the class definition.
protected A function within an object can be accessed by member functions of the same class or derived classes only.
private A function within an object that is visible only to that object.

3. ```
   //     my name
   //     Programming in C
   ```

Security of Data and Functions

In C++ the access to a structure or class may be specified to be **public, protected,** or **private**. The **public** items are available to any member function within the
   ```

scope, the **protected** items provide limited access, while the **private** items allow access to only those members granted specific access. This is used for increased control over access to both code and data.

In C, all data is public as determined by the scope of the variable when it is declared. A struct is public by default while a class defaults to private. A union in C++, just as in C, is always public. In traditional C, the data is somewhat incidental to a program comprised of functions. In C++ the data and the functions are treated as a unit of equal importance.

The functions that are declared within a class are known as **member functions** unless they are specified as a friend. When a derived class is created the member functions of the base class are not available to the derived class unless the derived class is declared as a friend in the base class. A **friend** declaration provides access to private member functions.

Creating an Object

In C++ the concept of a structure is extended to contain data types as well as functions. This type of structure is called a class. The name of a class typically begins with a capital letter to distinguish it. In using an object there are frequently three parts:

1. A header file that declares the object.
2. A source for the function definitions which are then compiled and linked.
3. The C++ program which accesses the object (this is what the function definitions are linked to).

The Declaration of the Object   The following header file creates a class for property listings for a real estate office. Each listing may have up to 10 different features associated with it. The functions associated with a class will be private by default. Note that these are made public explicitly. Also note that one of the functions is declared within the property structure definition. This approach to declaring short functions is called an **inline** function.

```
// creating an object
// each object will be a parcel of real property
#include <string.h>

const int Maxfeatures = 10;

class Property
{
  char *address;
  char *features[Maxfeatures];
  int numfeatures;
```

```
                  public:                    // default is private
                     void enter_listing(char *a);
                     char *get_listing(char *f)
                      {
                         return strcpy(f, address);
                      };    //inline
                     void add_feature(char *);
                     char *get_feature(int, char *);
               };
```

Note that the functions are specified as public functions. If the word public had been omitted, the functions would have been private to this particular class only.

Definition of the Object Functions   The functions associated with the class are usually placed in a separate file. The functions are defined below and will then be compiled to an object file.

Two new features here are the scope resolution operator and the function new( ). The :: operator, referred to as the **scope resolution operator,** is used to specify which class the function is associated with. The keyword new replaces the familiar malloc( ) while delete replaces free( ).

scope resolution operator
Relates object function definitions
to the appropriate class definition.

14-2a.cpp

```
// Property functions
#include <string.h>
#include "ch14-2.h"


void Property::enter_listing(char *a)
{
  address = new char [strlen(a) + 1];    // allocates storage
  strcpy(address, a);                    // copies string
  numfeatures = 0;
}


void Property::add_feature(char *f)
{
  if (numfeatures < Maxfeatures)
    {
       features[numfeatures] = new char[strlen(f) + 1];
       strcpy(features[numfeatures++],f);
```

```
        }
}

char *Property::get_feature(int num, char *f)
{
    if (num >= 0  && num <= numfeatures)
      return strcpy(f, features[num]);
    else
      return 0;
}
```

Self-Test

1. What modification would be necessary to the class declaration if an additional function called delete_feature were to be added?
2. Write the delete_feature function which would be included in the file containing the coding of the functions. The delete_feature function will reduce the number in numfeatures by 1, no other actions will be necessary.

Answers

```
1. void delete_feature( );
2. void Property::delete_feature( )
   {
     if(numfeatures > 0)
        numfeatures--;
   }
```

Accessing the Object A program that uses the object called property will include the previous header file and will have the object code of the function declarations linked to it. The object file can be linked to the C++ program by using a project file. The integrated development environment provides an option for project files that can be used to link items together. This can also be accomplished from the command line.

```
// using the object class Property
#include <iostream.h>
#include "ch14-2.h"

main( )
void{
  Property property;
  char buffer[50];
```

```
property.enter_listing("111 Main Street");
property.add_feature("3 bedrooms");
property.add_feature("2 baths");
property.add_feature("1540 square feet");

cout << property.get_listing(buffer)<< "\n";
for(int i = 0; property.get_feature(i,buffer) !=0; ++i)
cout << i+1 << ". " << buffer << "\n";
}
```

Output

```
111 Main Street
3 bedrooms
2 baths
1540 square feet
```

Declaring Variables as Needed

In ANSI C all variables must be declared prior to the code that accesses the variable. This is not true in C++. A variable may be declared "on the fly" in the statement or expression that accesses the variable.

```
for(int i = 0; property.get_feature(i,buffer) !=0; ++i)
```

In this statement from the last program, the variable i is not declared until it is used.

Overloading

Overloading in C++ can apply to functions or operators.

overloading Using the same operator or function to perform differently under differing circumstances.

Functions   C++ provides the ability to have different functions with the same name, a feature known as **overloading.** This would allow functions to be defined depending upon the type of data that is to be processed. In C, a function is specified as to the type of data that it can handle. C++ may have several functions and will select the appropriate one according to the type of data being processed.
   Traditional C

```
float float_average(float num, float num2)
/* works for float data */
int_average(int num, int num2)
/* a function to average two integer numbers */
```

   C++

```
int average(int num, int num2)
float average(float num, float num2)
// appropriate function will be selected when average( )
// is called
```

Operators   It is also possible to overload operators allowing them to work differently in different situations. Earlier we used >> and << operators which are used for different purposes, "put to" and "get from" as well as bitwise operations.

Traditional C also overloads some operators as a part of the language. Even though the addition of float numbers differs from the addition of integer numbers in relationship to the way they are handled according to memory size, the same + operator is used for both data types.

The programmer can also overload operators as desired using the keyword operator. The operator word allows an existing operator to be defined in a different way. Many languages use the + operator for addition of numeric fields as well as concatenation of string fields. This can be done in C++.

Constructors and Destructors

Two special functions that are associated with a class are the constructor and the destructor. The constructor and destructor, if coded, are included with the functions that comprise the class declaration. The constructor has the same name as the class while the destructor is the class name preceded by a tilde.

```
Property{....}
~Property{....}
```

When objects are created by a copy or by the use of the operator new, some initialization action is usually necessary. These actions are known in C++ as **constructors.** A constructor may be defined by the programmer or set to a default by the compiler. A constructor includes memory allocation, initialization, assignment of values, and/or conversion from one data type to another.

constructor A function that is performed when an object is created.

When an object is destroyed, the actions that are required are known as a **destructor.** The destructor function may be called explicitly with the operator delete or will take place automatically when the object is out of scope. Once again, if a destructor is not defined by the user, one will be generated by default.

destructor A function that is executed when an object is deleted or moves out of scope.

CONTAINER LIBRARIES

The 3.0 version of C++ provides two container libraries in CLASSLIB: the object container library and the Borland International Data Structure (BIDS) library. The object container library contains a hierarchy of classes. The BIDS container provides a template approach for dealing with data structures.

The object container library contains classes (objects) which have already been created and may be used or modified by the programmer. The classes are of two types: abstract classes and instance classes. This class hierarchy uses both inheritance and polymorphism.

An **abstract class** cannot have any objects declared to be of its type but merely serves as an umbrella of associated classes. The abstract class has few data members and purely virtual functions as member functions. The abstract class may serve as a base class for either another abstract class or for an instance class.

If a derived class contains no virtual functions it is referred to as an **instance class.** Objects may be declared to be of the instance class type. The containers include objects for things such as linked lists, hashing, and sorted arrays (see Figure 14.1).

The Container and Association classes have **multiple inheritance** because they are derived from two base classes: object and TShouldDelete.

abstract class An object that acts as a base class for other objects, contains virtual functions, and does not have any objects of its type.

instance class An object defined in the container library that contains no virtual functions and may have objects of its class type.

multiple inheritance An object that is derived from more than one base class.

Categories of Classes

The classes can be divided into three different groups:

1. Noncontainer classes (cannot store objects).
2. Container classes (can store objects).
3. Utility and helper (not derived from object class).

Basically the classes that are listed on the hierarchy as instance classes are the container classes while the others are the noncontainer classes.

Utility and Helper Classes

In addition to the classes that are related to the object class there are helper and utility classes that can perform functions, such as traversing the objects within a container. The primary group of this type are the iterator classes.

ContainerIterator

HashTableiterator
Listiterator
DoubleListiterator
Btreeiterator
Arrayiterator

In addition, there are two instance classes: Memblocks and Memstack.

BIDS

BIDS allows more flexibility to the programmer by providing the templates for the classes that may be modified with very little coding. Each container has an abstract

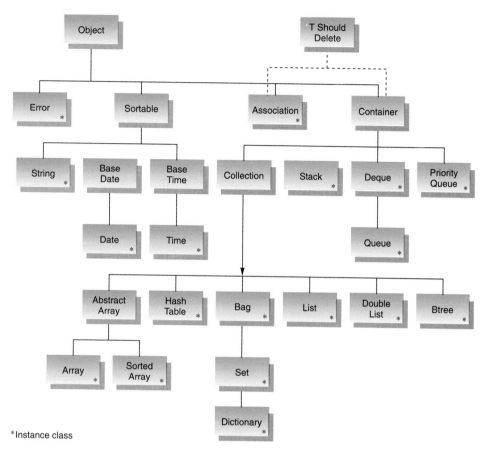

FIGURE 14-1
Class Hierarchies

*Instance class

data type (ADT) and an independent fundamental data structure (FDS). The structures and data types may be combined as needed.

The FDSs are vector, list, and double list. The ADTs provided are stacks, queues, deques, bags, sets, and arrays. Each of the FDSs and the ADTs are contained in separate header files.

KEY TERMS

abstract class	hierarchy	overloading
base class	inheritance	polymorphism
class	instance class	private
constructor	multiple inheritance	protected
container	object-oriented	public
derived class	programming	scope resolution
destructor	OOP	operator
encapsulation		virtual function

CHAPTER SUMMARY

A knowledge of C makes the transition to C++ easier but the change will require modification to the planning and structure of a program. The entire approach to designing the functions and defining the data takes on a new flavor. The terminology and concepts have been presented but a switch to C++ would take more than one chapter of differences.

Object-oriented programming provides structures that contain both data and functions known as classes. The object may have the properties of inheritance, encapsulation, and polymorphism. Encapsulation is the hiding of the data. Polymorphism allows a function to operate on more than one type of data, a feature which is created through the use of virtual functions. Classes that are derived from the base class demonstrate inheritance.

A tool provided with C++ is the library of container classes. These objects and templates allow the programmer to avoid having to write data structure routines.

REVIEW QUESTIONS

1. Define the following:
   a. Class.
   b. Encapsulation.
   c. Inheritance.
   d. Polymorphism.
   e. Object-oriented programming.
2. What is meant by operator overload?
3. Differentiate between public, private, and protected structures.
4. What is meant by the phrase "declaring a variable on the fly"?
5. Give an example of an inline function.
6. The header file iostream.h contains functions similar to what header file in C?
7. Relate the concept of constructors and destructors to traditional structured programming.
8. Of what benefit are containers to a programmer?
9. Differentiate between an instance class and an abstract class.
10. Give an example of an abstract class that has derivation classes of both instance and abstract types.

EXERCISES

1. Write a program to calculate simple interest, using cin and cout to create the interactive program. The input fields should be principle, rate, and time. The output should be the amount of interest and the compound amount.
2. Create an object for a Boy Scout troop. The object will contain the troop number and an array of member's names. Allow for up to 36 members. The object must also contain declarations for a function to add member names, and to list members.

3. Write the functions to add member names and to list member names.

4. Create and execute a program using the troop object. Add the following names, then list the names. Include a summary line that includes the number of members listed.

Al Garcia	Oscar Garcia
Mike Powell	John Curtis
Eric Fleming	Gary Songer
Travis Fleming	Rene Garcia
Eric Mills	

5. Add a function to the troop object that allows a member name to be deleted from the list. Execute a program that adds names, lists the names, deletes a name, and then reprints the list.

HAYLEY OFFICE SUPPLIES

A. Rewrite the letterhead program using the cin and cout functions.

B. Create an object for maintaining a list of inventory items. The object will contain declarations for the following:

Data: Number of items and an array of product descriptions.
Functions:
- Add an item
- Delete an item
- List the items

APPENDIX A
ANSI C RESERVED WORDS

auto Storage class for temporary variables, local variables are auto by default.

break Used to exit from a loop or switch; can be used on for, do, and while but only leaves the innermost block.

case Specify alternative possible values for a switch statement.

char Data type character.

const Specifies that a variable cannot be altered by the program (remains constant).

continue Continues with the next iteration of the loop without processing the statements following it in the current iteration.

default Specifies the statements that will be executed if none of the cases in a switch were true.

do A loop with the condition at the end, will always be executed at least one time.

double Data type, double precision of a floating point.

else Used with if to specify statements to be executed when the if condition is false.

enum An integer data type that allows constant names to be assigned to identify possible values of the variable.

extern External storage class, specifies that the actual declaration of a variable is outside of the current function or file.

float Data type for single precision floating point.

for Type of loop that allows for initialization, a condition, and an action expression to change values during execution.

goto Transfers control to a labeled statement. The label is followed by a colon (:).

if Decision statement.

int Data type for integer numbers.

long Data type for a large integer number.

register Storage class to process local integers as fast as possible.

return Terminate execution of a function and to optionally return a value.

short Data type for short integer numbers.

signed Default int data type for int or char.

sizeof Finds the number of bytes in a data item.

static Storage class for local variables to retain the value when the function is terminated, also used to "hide" functions.

struct Assign a name to a group of related variables.

switch Decision statement based on the value of a single variable.

typedef Assign a new name to an existing data type.

union Data type that declares a list of variables that share a storage address.

unsigned Integer data type that stores nonnegative values only, doubling the largest value that could be stored in a signed integer.

void Data type that specifies no return value from a function. When void * is applied to a pointer it may point to any type of data.

volatile A variable that may not be modified by the program but is altered by external factors such as the clock.

while Creates a loop with an entry condition.

Function Name	Library	Purpose
asctime( )	time.h	Converts from a tm structure to a string.
atexit( )	stdlib.h	Places a function on a Last-in First-out stack of routines that will be executed when the program terminates normally.
atof( )	math.h	Converts a string (alphanumeric) into a value of type double.
atoi( )	stdlib.h	Converts a string (alphanumeric) into a value of type integer.
ctime( )	time.h	Converts a time_t variable to a value of type char string.
difftime( )	time.h	Finds the difference in seconds of two variables of type time_t.
exit( )	stdlib.h	Terminates a program normally by flushing file buffers, closing all files, performing atexit( ) functions; can use arguments of EXIT_SUCCESS for normal exit and EXIT_FAILURE if errors.
fclose( )	stdio.h	Closes the file and empties the buffer (writes any data in buffer to the file).
fgets( )	stdio.h	Reads a line from a file until a newline or EOF is encountered.
fopen( )	stdio.h	Opens a file in a specified mode, assigning the physical file name to a pointer of structure type FILE; returns a NULL if the open operation is unsuccessful.
fprintf( )	stdio.h	Writes formatted output to a specified device.
fread( )	stdio.h	Reads a specified number of data items from the current position in the input stream.
free( )	stdlib.h	Returns to available memory space that had earlier been reserved with a calloc( ) or malloc( ).
fscanf( )	stdio.h	Reads formatted data from a specified device.
gets( )	stdio.h	Inputs string data from the keyboard.
isalpha( )	ctype.h	Returns a nonzero value if a character is a letter, if not a 0 is returned.
isdigit( )	ctype.h	Checks if a character is a decimal digit.
islower( )	ctype.h	Checks if a character is lowercase.
isspace( )	ctype.h	Checks if a character is a whitespace character such as a tab, newline, formfeed, or a blank space.
isupper( )	ctype.h	Checks if a character is uppercase.
localtime( )	time.h	Breaks down the time into minute, hour, day, month, year, etc. that are stored in a structure tm.
malloc( )	stdlib.h	Reserves a specified number of bytes of memory.
mktime( )	time.h	Converts localtime( ) to a long integer value (type time_t).
pow( )	math.h	Raises a number to a specified power.
printf( )	stdio.h	Outputs formatted data to the screen.
puts( )	stdio.h	Outputs a string to the screen.

Function Name	Library	Purpose
scanf( )	stdio.h	Inputs data from the keyboard according to the type specified in the format string.
sqrt( )	math.h	Finds the square root of a nonnegative variable of type double.
strcat( )	string.h	Concatenates two strings.
strcmp( )	string.h	Compares the value of two strings.
strcpy( )	string.h	Moves the value of a string into a string variable.
strlen( )	string.h	Finds the length of a string.
strncat( )	string.h	Concatenates a specified number of characters from one string into another.
strncmp( )	string.h	Compares a specified number of characters from two strings.
strncpy( )	string.h	Copies a specified number of characters from one string to another.
strstr( )	string.h	Locates one string within another.
system( )	stdlib.h	Executes an operating system command.
time( )	time.h	Returns the calendar time in a long integer form (implementation varies).
tolower( )	ctype.h	Converts a character to lowercase.
toupper( )	ctype.h	Converts a character to uppercase.

APPENDIX C
PRECEDENCE OF OPERATORS

Operator	Associativity
( ) [ ] . -> ++ — size of * / %	Left to right*
+ -	Left to right
< > <= >=	Left to right
== !=	Left to right
&&	Left to right
| |	Left to right
?:	Right to left
= *= += /= %= -=	Right to left

*Except unary operators which are right to left.

All operators on the same line have equal precedence and will be evaluated according to the appropriate associativity.

APPENDIX D
USING THE EDITORS

THE EDIT ENVIRONMENTS

Both the Borland and Microsoft QuickC packages contain very similar editing environments that are easy to work with. The Borland editor is referred to as an integrated development environment or IDE, while QuickC simply calls it the editing environment. This appendix will cover some of the major features to the editors and define the terms used for the debugging tools.

PARTS OF THE EDITING SCREEN

The editing environment screens are divided into menus, windows, and dialog boxes. Each of the parts have specific uses and are accessed differently.

A **menu** is a "pull-down" list of options across the top of the screen. Any menu item can be accessed or pulled down by using the ALT key and the desired option letter.

The word area of the screen may be divided into parts. Each part is called a **window.** The basic windows are for the program(s), error messages, and for program screen output. Switching from one window to another is accomplished with the F6 key for Microsoft and with the WINDOW menu for Borland.

Messages from the editor program are displayed to the programmer in a **dialog box.** A dialog box will appear when loading and saving programs, as well as in other situations when information is being requested from the programmer. When a dialog box is divided into several parts, the cursor may be moved from one option to the next with the TAB key.

With mouse access, the menus, windows, and dialog boxes can be used by clicking in the appropriate location. Without a mouse, many short cuts are available through the use of hot keys. A **hot key** is any key combination that can be used for performing actions as an alternate to accessing the menu. The hot keys will be shown in parentheses following the matching menu option.

ENTERING A PROGRAM

Typing a program into the computer using an editor is basically the same as typing a document into a wordprocessor. In fact, some people use a wordprocessor as a program editor.

A program is entered into the editor by typing each statement and pressing the Enter key at the end of the statement. The editor provides for an insert or a typeover mode that are set back and forth with the insert key. When the editor is in insert mode, any data typed in the middle of a line will be inserted at the cursor position. If the inter key is pressed in the middle of a line, the remainder of the statement will be sent to the next line. If the enter is entered inadvertently, the line may be reconnected by pressing the backspace key.

Marking a Block

A block of code may be marked using the SHIFT and cursor keys. The highlighted text may be copied, cleared, or printed. It is best to save the program before using the blocking features. It is possible to lose information if keys are not used in the proper sequence.

The EDIT Menu

The EDIT menu may be accessed with Alt-E. After a block of code is highlighted, it may be altered through the use of the CUT or COPY and PASTE or the CLEAR on the EDIT menu. Changes can be undone with the UNDO or RESTORE LINE options.

The CUT is used for statements that are to be moved to another location within the program. The COPY is used to make a duplicated set of statements, either in the current program or in another. To delete the highlighted code use the CLEAR option on the EDIT menu.

Both packages provide the ability to undo the last change, this is called UNDO in QuickC and RESTORE LINE in Borland's products. These features will restore the line to the way it appeared prior to the previous changes.

The SEARCH Menu

A specific word within the code can be located with FIND option on either of the SEARCH menus. To repeat the search, use the SEARCH AGAIN or the REPEAT LAST FIND(F3). Besides just locating a word, the editor can search and replace a word using REPLACE or CHANGE.

Saving the Program to Disk

In saving a program, three options are available: SAVE, SAVE AS, and SAVE ALL. The SAVE will replace the existing program if one exists with the same name. The SAVE AS allows the programmer to enter a name for the program, thus providing the opportunity to use a different name to avoid replacing the current program on disk. The SAVE ALL is used to save all files that have been changed.

Printing the Source Code Listing

A copy of the source code listing can be made using the PRINT option of the FILE menu. With Microsoft, a portion of the listing may be made by highlighting the desired code before invoking the PRINT option.

COMPILING AND RUNNING A PROGRAM

The current program in the editor can be complied and linked with a single command on the RUN menu or with the hot keys—(ALT-F9) for Borland and (SHIFT-F5) for Microsoft.

With the mouse or menu access use the RUN or the GO option. A dialog box will appear as the program complies and links. A count of the warnings and errors are listed in the error window.

Loading a Program from Disk

The OPEN option of the FILE menu is used to load a program from disk into the editor. This option provides a dialog box of the programs with a .C extension, by default. The extension may be changed, if desired.

Within the dialog box, the name of the program can be typed on the appropriate line or a TAB will bring the cursor into a list of programs that can then be selected using cursor keys (press ENTER when the desired program name is highlighted). Options within the dialog box also provide for a directory change.

Viewing Errors

A line of code that contains an error will be highlighted within the program window, along with the message in the error window. After a correction is made, the next error can be viewed. The next or previous error is located from the SEARCH menu or with hot keys.

DEBUGGING TOOLS

In addition to the editing portion of the environment, both companies have built-in debugger tools. These tools for isolating logic errors include trace, breakpoint, and watch.

A **trace** provides the capability of following the sequence of execution of the program line by line. Visually, this provides a method of "walking through" the program. With a trace, the program functions may be traced through or traced around (called a step over). A trace through is used to see each line of the function also execute while a step over shows the result of a function and then continues the trace with the next line.

Setting a **breakpoint** specifies a point in the program where execution will be stopped temporarily so that you may examine the status of various elements within the program. At that point in the program it is possible to find out the values of the variables or expressions with a watch expression.

A **watchpoint** makes it possible to observe the changing value of an expression or variable as the program executes. The value of the watch expression will be visible on the screen as the program executes. With a trace, the execution is slow enough to watch the value change. To know what the value is at a specific point, a breakpoint could be set.

GLOSSARY OF TERMS

abstract class An object than acts as a base class for other objects, contains virtual functions, does not have any objects of its type.

address A location in memory where data or a a function is stored.

address operator &, used to refer to an address in memory.

aggregate data types A data type that contains the declaration of more than one item; includes structures, unions, and enum.

analyze To break down a problem into parts.

argument A value being received by a function; enclosed in parentheses in the function header.

arithmetic conversion A predefined set of rules for converting data types during execution of a calculation involving multiple data types.

array A data item that contains multiple values.

assignment operator The = used to store a value in a specific memory location or named data item.

auto Storage type for local variables.

bar chart A graphical representation of a series of numbers using rectangles.

base class An object-oriented programming referring to an object from which other objects are derived; an example of inheritance.

binary operator A calculation operator that requires two operands.

binary search A table lookup of sorted data that begins the search in the middle of the data.

bind The order in which operands are combined according to the precedence of operators.

block A unit of code enclosed within braces { }.

braces { } Used to enclose a block of code.

break Reserved word to exit an *if* or *switch*.

buffer Temporary storage.

case Reserved word to specify a possible value for a variable and the appropriate actions to be taken.

chart A diagram of the user-defined functions in a program and the relationship between the functions.

class An object.

code To write a program in a computer language; refers to source code.

cohesion The relationship of statements within a function.

collision Two values resulting in the same key using a hashing algorithm.

compiler A program that translates a programmer's source code into object code.

compound condition Combines more than one condition using and/or.

concatenation Combining two string values.

conditional operator A ternary operator that can replace an *if* statement.

constant A value that does not change during execution of the program.

constructor A function that is performed when an object is created.

container An object defined within a precoded library.

control break   Causes a function to be performed when the value of a control variable changes.

coupling   The relationship between functions.

data type   The type of information that can be stored in a variable such as *int* and *float*.

date function   A function used to manipulate the system date.

debug   To eliminate errors in a program.

declaration   A statement that specifies an identifier to be used as a variable name and associates it with a data type.

decrement   Decrease the value of a variable by 1.

default   Automatic action to be taken if not specified otherwise.

dereference   Find a value associated with an address thereby reducing the level of indirection.

derived class   A class that inherits characteristics from another class.

destructor   A function that is executed when an object is deleted or moves out of scope.

detail   The main body of a report; processing for an individual transaction.

double   A floating point number with greater precision; more decimal positions.

double linked   A list that can be traversed to the next record or to the prior record.

element   A single value within an array.

encapsulation   Hiding of data within an object.

entry condition   A condition at the beginning of a loop that determines when the loop will be terminated, possibly will never be executed.

enum   An integer data type that allows a word to be used to represent a numerical value.

enumerated variable   A variable of type *enum*.

escape sequence   Value beginning with backslash usually used to control peripheral devices.

exit condition   A condition at the end of a loop that determines when the loop will be terminated; the loop will always be executed at least once.

expression   A part of a statement.

extern   Storage type for global variables or data items declared in another program.

float   A data type for real numbers.

form fccd   Advances the paper on the printer.

format specifier   A string that determines how the values of variables will appear when being displayed or printed.

function   A block of named code that may be called from within the code; values may be passed to a function and a single value returned; default data type is int for the returned value.

global variable   A variable that is visible to all functions after the point where the variable is declared.

hash addressing   An algorithm used to determine an address key for a random file.

hashing algorithm   The calculation used to determine the address key in a random file.

head element   The first element in a linked list.

hierarchy   A chart depicting the relationship of user-created functions.

identifier   A name given to a variable or a function.

increment   Increase the value of a variable by 1.

indirect value   The value stored at the address stored in a pointer variable.

indirection operator   The * used as a unary operator to denote a pointer at time of declaration or to dereference a pointer value.

inheritance   The ability to have an object be derived from a base class and carry over the data types and functions of the parent class.

instance class   An object defined in the container library that contains no virtual functions and may have objects of its class type.

integer   A type of variable or constant that represents a whole number.

key field   The data item used in performing a search or sort operation.

legend   Descriptive title attached to a graphical chart.

light bar menu   The current item selected on a menu is represented in a highlight color; normally uses the up and down arrow keys.

linked list   A method of storing multiple values by allocating memory as it is needed; each element contains the address of the next element in the list.

local variable   Only visible to the block in which the variable is declared.

loop   Code which may be executed repeatedly as necessary.

lvalue   The left side of an assignment statement; must represent a memory location.

macro   Statement defined at preprocessor time that will be substituted directly into the code before compilation.

main( ) function   A required function in C that contains the beginning and ending statements for the execution of the program.

menu   A list of options.

modulus   An operator which stores the remainder from a division calculation.

multidimension array   An array with multiple subscripts.

multiple inheritance   An object that is derived from more than one base class.

nested if   An *if* statement embedded within the block of another *if*.

node   An element in a linked list.

object code   The compiled version of the program that will be linked into the executable code.

object-oriented programming   Method of programming in which data and functions are handled as a unit called an object.

OOP   Object-oriented programming.

operand   One of the fields used in a calculating statement.

operator   A symbol representing an action to be performed on data.

overloading   Using the same operator or function to perform differently under differing circumstances.

parallel arrays   Multiple arrays in which the elements of one array are related to the elements in the same position within another array.

parameter   A value being sent when calling a function.

pie chart   Depicts a percentage of a circle for each of the parts being represented.

pixel   A picture element or dot comprising the graphics screen—the greater the pixel count the higher the resolution.

pointer   A variable that contains an address of a variable, a function, or another pointer.

polymorphism   Ability of an object to work with more than one data type using virtual functions—the object's type is not known until run time.

postfix   Increment or decrement action is taken after the expression is evaluated.

precedence   The sequence on which operations will be performed based on a predetermined hierarchy of operators.

prefix   Increment or decrement action is taken before the expression is evaluated.

priming input   The first input typically placed before the detail processing loop.

private   A function within an object that is visible only to that object.

prompt   A message on the screen directing the program user to input information.

protected   A function within an object can be accessed by member functions of the same class or derived classes only.

public   A function within an object can be accessed by any function within the scope of the class definition.

recursion   A declaration that includes a reference to its own data type.

register   A storage type for local integer variables used to increase speed of execution.

relational operator   An operator used in comparisons such as greater than, less than, or equal to (>, <, ==).

resolution   The clarity of the picture in graphics—the higher the resolution the better the picture.

root element   Head or first element in a linked list.

rvalue   The value on the right-hand side of an assignment statement; may be the value or a memory location.

scope   Visibility of a variable or function.

scope resolution operator   Relates object function definitions to the appropriate class definition.

search   Look up a value within an array or file.

serial search   A lookup that begins with the first element in the array and compares each item until a match is found.

single linked   A linked list that can only be traversed in a forward direction—each structure contains only a pointer to the next element in the list.

sort   To arrange a series of data into alphabetic or numeric order according to a key field.

source code   Programming instructions written in a programming language prior to compilation.

static   A storage classification allowing a local variable to retain its value and same memory location from one execution of a function to the next execution.

stdout   Stream name referring to the monitor; used with output functions.

stdprn   Stream name referring to the printer; used with output functions.

string length   Number of characters in a string.

string literal   A constant value enclosed in quotes that is stored as an array of characters.

structure   An aggregate data type consisting of a group of fields.

subscript   Position of an element within an array, starting with the first position at 0.

switch   A variable that may contain one of two values, such as "yes" or "no."

symbolic constant   An identifier specified in a preprocessor definition for which a value will be replaced prior to compilation.

tail element   The last element in a linked list—pointer to next will contain a NULL.

text editor   Used for entering the source code for a program; usually allows for editing features such as search and replace, cut and copy.

typedef Reserved word allowing a new name to be given to an existing data type or for a complex data type to be created.

unary operator An operator requiring only one operand, such as increment and decrement.

union An aggregate data type in which the data may be one of multiple specified types.

variable Value may change during execution of the program; an identifier is used in association with a memory location.

virtual function More than one function is defined to handle multiple types of data; the function to be executed is determined at run time, according to the actual data type used.

Index

address 33, 168, 183, 184, 194, 248, 249, 250–254, 257–259, 260–266, 268, 270–275, 277–280, 311

address operator 259, 293, 474

aggregate data types 226, 228, 251, 474

analyze 7, 19, 366, 474

ANSI 4, 5, 8, 13, 26–28, 44, 45, 51, 85, 103, 153, 157, 172, 188, 215, 252, 301, 402, 404, 405, 454, 457, 462, 468

arguments 8, 9, 15, 160, 167, 168, 172, 177, public, 215, 278, 282, 304, 314, 338, 370, 404, 405, 469

arithmetic conversion 102, 123, 474

array 29–31, 191–201, 204, 205, 206–215, 217

asctime() 243, 245, 469

assignment operator 5, 63, 94, 99, 120, 123, 474

atexit() 469

atof() 289, 293, 469

atoi() 289, 291, 293

auto 162, 164, 468

base class 456, 459, 464–466, 474, 476

binary operator 94, 97, 123, 474

binary search 189, 205, 206, 209, 210, 218, 219, 225, 474

bind 109, 118, 123, 270, 285, 474

block 8, 9, 28, 29, 52, 67, 68, 86, 93, 104, 105, 162, 163, 166, 338, 368–370, 372, 468, 474–476

braces{} 8, 9, 19, 104, 474

break 132

buffer 44, 45, 69, 145, 179, 243, 244, 286–289, 292–294, 311, 314, 338, 462, 469

case 63, 132, 133, 135–140, 143, 145, 146, 148, 151, 152, 176, 328–331, 349, 356, 392, 393, 443, 446, 468

char 24, 28, 190

chart 19

class 444, 456, 458–461, 463–466, 468, 474–477

code 2, 7

cohesion 161, 181, 182, 184, 474

comment 14, 20, 457, 458

compiler 4–6, 8

compound condition 86, 157, 474

concatenation 64, 86, 463, 474

condition 59–64

conditional operator 56, 110, 111, 123, 474

const 468

constant 24–27

constructor 454, 463, 465, 474

control break 342, 343, 351, 357–359, 363, 475

coupling 161, 181–184, 475

data type 24, 32, 33, 102, 168, 172, 174, 476–478

data validation 286–288

date function 251

debug 2, 7, 19, 475

declaration 29, 31, 32, 163, 174, 459, 461, 474–477

decrement 74, 96–99, 101, 123, 475–478

default 181

derived class 456, 459, 464, 465, 475
destructor 454, 463, 465, 475
detail 77–79
difftime() 469
do loop 66, 70
documentation 2, 14
double 24, 35, 468
double-linked list 366, 390, 399, 400, 475

element 183, 190–193
else 106–110
encapsulation 454, 456, 465, 466, 475
entry condition 66, 70, 86, 87, 475
enum 239
enumerated variable 238, 251, 475
escape sequence 11, 13, 24, 26, 51, 154, 155, 345, 404, 405, 475
exit condition 66, 70, 86, 87, 475
exit() 391, 426, 469
expression 58, 59, 61
extern 162–165, 183, 468, 475

fclose() 304, 338, 469
fgets() 469
float 24, 25, 28
fopen() 300, 302, 310, 311, 338, 469
for loop 72–76
format specifier 34, 52, 303, 307, 475
fprintf() 9, 12, 13
fread() 298, 314, 316, 317, 338, 469
free() 366, 368, 370, 372, 399, 460, 469
fscanf() 299, 300, 307, 308, 310, 335, 336, 338, 469
fwrite() 311
functions 4, 8, 15–17 456–464

gets() 22, 43–46, 52, 54, 69, 70, 168, 173, 469
global variable 29, 52, 163, 165, 475

head 375, 376, 382, 384, 390, 399, 475, 477
header file 9, 12, 50–52, 155, 209, 227, 241, 242, 252, 300, 307, 404, 405, 411, 426, 433, 452, 459, 461, 466
hierarchy 7, 17

identifier 26, 52, 167, 232, 241, 260, 475, 477, 478
if 104–107
include 12, 13
increment 96–99, 119–124, 266, 475
indirection operator 259, 263, 293, 476
inheritance 454, 456, 464–466, 474, 476
inputting data
    fscanf() 299, 300, 307, 308, 310, 335, 336, 338, 469
    gets() 22, 43–46
    scanf() 43, 44
int 35, 468
integer 24–26, 30–32, 35
isalpha() 469
isdigit() 469
islower() 469
isspace() 470
isupper() 470

key field 205–207, 209, 211, 218, 322, 323, 333, 334, 374, 375, 379, 400, 476, 477

library 4, 9, 12, 15, 167, 220, 338, 404, 434, 451, 463, 464, 466, 469, 474, 476
linked list 366, 367, 373–375, 379, 382, 384–386, 389–393, 398–400, 475–477
local variable 52, 163, 165–169, 173, 174, 184, 191, 278, 295, 296, 476, 477
localtime() 243, 245, 470
logic error 8
long 24, 28, 470
loops 56, 57, 66–72, 74–79
    do 66, 70
    for loop 72–76
    while loop 63–69

macro 26, 27, 45, 52, 85, 147, 157, 286, 476
main() function 2, 4, 8, 9, 12, 18–20, 29, 30, 50, 51, 140, 157, 172, 173, 476
malloc() 366, 368–371, 399, 400, 460, 469, 470
menu 70, 139–154, 156–159,
modulus 94–96, 99, 121, 123, 124, 334, 335, 476

multidimension array 218, 476
multipage output 344, 346

nested if 108, 123, 124, 476
node 375, 399

object code 6, 12, 19, 26, 461, 474, 476
object-oriented programming 454–456, 465, 476
OOP 456, 465, 476
operand 58, 94, 102, 260, 476, 478
operators 4, 5
    arithmetic operator 94
    binary operator 94, 97, 123, 474
    logical operator 61, 62
    relational operator 60, 86, 120, 477
    unary operator 94, 120, 123, 476, 478
output 2, 7, 9–15, 300, 303, 305, 308, 309, 311,
    314, 329, 335
    fprintf() 9, 12, 13
    fwrite() 311
    puts() 47, 48
overloading 457, 462, 465, 476

parallel arrays 206, 218, 222, 225, 476
pointer 258–266, 269–279, 282, 284, 285, 287,
    291, 293, 294, 296,
polymorphism 454, 456, 464–466, 476
postfix 97, 98, 122–124, 270, 476
pow() 103, 470
precedence 5, 61, 92, 94–96, 98, 101, 109,
    118–121, 123, 124, 184, 266, 271, 275, 470,
    471, 474, 477
prefix 97, 98, 122, 123, 254, 477
preprocessor 12, 18, 26, 27, 44, 45, 50, 51, 124,
    155, 308, 344, 476, 477
priming input 68, 80, 86, 477
printing data 384
private 294, 306, 313, 321, 346, 458–460, 465,
    466, 477
prompt 44, 48, 51–54, 64, 78–80, 83, 88–90, 126,
    153, 178, 179, 184, 204, 207, 220, 222, 224,
    232, 290, 296, 340, 387, 400, 448, 458, 477

protected 458, 459, 465, 466, 477
public 458–460, 465, 466, 477
puts() 47, 48

recursion 367, 375, 399, 477
register 164
relational operator 60, 86, 120, 477
reserved word 9, 86, 172, 229, 240, 474
return 25, 59, 130, 154, 168, 216, 282, 288, 292,
    325, 468

scanf() 43, 44
search 18, 188, 189, 205–211, 213, 218, 219, 222,
    225, 314, 316, 322, 324, 326, 336, 379, 391,
    392, 396, 400, 474, 476, 477
serial search 188, 189, 205, 206, 218, 219, 222,
    477
short 28, 468
signed 24, 28, 468
single-linked list 399, 477
sizeof 118, 470
sort 21, 188, 213–215, 217, 218, 220, 225, 314,
    382, 476, 477
source code 6, 9, 12, 19, 26, 165, 404, 452, 474, 477
sqrt() 470
static 162–165, 181, 183, 184, 191, 197, 273, 274,
    280, 295, 296, 331, 348, 360, 468, 477
stdout 13, 15–19
stdprn 13, 15, 17–19
strcat() 64
strcmp() 62, 63, 216, 282, 470
strcpy() 33, 34, 65, 470
stream 13, 14, 19, 40, 44, 45, 85, 299–301, 303,
    304, 307, 311, 314, 337, 338, 457, 469, 477
string length 63, 86, 477
string literal 25, 26, 29, 31, 47, 52, 477
strlen() 63, 64, 103, 470
strncat() 65, 470
strncmp() 63, 225, 470
strncpy() 33, 470
strstr() 470
struct 229–235, 248, 290, 326, 360, 379, 380, 393,
    468

structure 228–237
subscript 191–193, 198, 204–207, 209–212, 218–220, 232, 272, 273, 275, 477
switch 132, 138, 139, 143, 145, 146, 151, 152, 156, 176, 320, 330, 349, 356, 468
symbolic constant 26, 52, 191, 477
syntax error 8, 75, 106
system() 153, 157, 470

tag 228, 229, 233, 234, 238, 240, 242, 251, 252
tail 375, 376, 378, 382, 385, 390, 399, 477
text editor 5, 6, 19, 20, 51, 477
time() 243, 245, 470
tolower() 470
toupper() 470
typedef 240

unary operator 94, 120, 123, 476, 478
union 226–228, 235–238, 248, 251, 252, 459, 468, 478
unsigned 24, 28, 216, 282, 468

variable 24, 26, 28–36
virtual function 465, 478
void 468
volatile 468

while loop 63–69